Table of Contents

Acknowledgements

Compiling the information for this collector's guide would have been impossible without the aid and encouragement from the groups and individuals listed below:

All the collectors I have met in the last twenty-five years who helped in the search for "white treasure." I added to earlier lists these contributors of information: Dale Abrams, Adys, Allers, Jack Anspaugh, Armbrusters, Bedfords, Ted Brockey, Arene Burgess, Carlsons, Casavants, Geoffrey Godden, Frances Hills, Hurts, Kerrs, Knorrs, Lautenschlagers, Harry Lowe, Ann Miller, Morelands, Nobles, Jill O'Hara, Dan Overmeyer, Julie Rich, Ed Rigoulot, Sally Scrimgeour, Upchurches, Walkers, Washburns, Judy Young and many others, each of whom added to our bank of knowledge concerning white ironstone.

My daughter Linda who scouted for pieces, carried, sorted, and constantly encouraged me to complete this task and to her husband Karl who did much of the computer work and freely offered practical advice.

The readers of my former books who wrote appreciatively, asked pertinent questions, enclosed facts, and urged me to keep compiling.

My patient, accurate typists - Laura, Janice, Julia, and Kristi who cheerfully types and retyped.

My editor, Kyle Husfleon, and his competent staff who were interested in accurately recording facts about the white granite potted during the 19th century. We all hope this will be a commendable, useful tool for ironstone collectors. Thanks, Kyle.

The many photographers who worked and worked to "catch" the shapes in black and white, the excellent pictures that make the following pages speak.

Dale Abrams	Diane Dorman	Howard Noble
Chester Ady	Fleischman	Dan Overmeyer
John Anderson	Groff	Julie Rich
Adele Armbruster	Horner	Dorthy Riley
Ann Bedford	Patty Hurt	Ed Rigoulot
Bill Beyer	Richmond Jones	Ray Secrist
John Black	Jim Kerr	Nancy Upchurch
Clair Blair	Arnold Kowalsky	James Walker
Arene Burgess	John Ladd	E. Washburn
Tom Chadwick	Harry Lowe	Diane Weber
Graf Diemer	Ann Miller	Win Wetherbee
Jane Diemer	Tom Moreland	P.D. White
Bev Dieringer	Bill Neuhauser	
Susan Dollard	Rick Nielsen	

Other collectors who sent drawings and photos that I could not use in this book but which added to our collective knowledge.

Clarke Blair who rescued photos that had been used in the "Look" books.

My special thanks goes to Ernie Dieringer for careful retouching of some of the photographs and to his wife Beverley who traveled and donated time and materials in order to take photos that you readers just needed to see.

And finally, sincere thanks to Bee Andrews of Landmark Specialty Publications who worked with Kyle Husfleon and me to make this new and expanded guide to "white treasure" a reality.

ON THE COVER: A grouping of President Shape ironstone by John Edwards and an open compote in Panelled Columbia shape by Pinder, Bourne & Hope. From the Dalenberg Collection. Photo by Diane Weber.

Foreword

Information concerning English White Ironstone, called "white granite" by English ceramics historians, must necessarily be gathered in an unorthodox manner. A wave of popularity for the white-embossed dishes raged in the United States and Canada, from the mid-1850s through the 1870s gradually subsiding into a demand for plain graceful white sets, widely purchased for every day use throughout the rest of the century.

Very little of this "white granite" was purchased in England itself, the continents of Europe, South America, Australia, or in other parts of the British Empire. Today, collectors gather the surviving pieces, record the marks on the underside, verify years that each manufacturer worked, catalog dated shapes, sketch or photograph each item, and study shards found at digs all from relics found in the United States and Canada. A compilation of all of these facts are gathered in this book. It is my hope that other researchers will add to this white ironstone record.

The most helpful references I have used are *Encyclopaedia of British Pottery and Porcelain Marks* and *Mason's China and the Ironstone Wares* by Geoffrey Godden, Jewitt's *Ceramic History of Great Britain* (written at the same time that white granite was being manufactured), and Miller's *Classification and Economic Scaling of 19th Century Ceramics* (based on shards found at American sites). Miller also quotes from Staffordshire price lists, old invoices, bills of lading, etc. located in England. Collectors have found some old advertisements that add information about sets potted in the 1870 to 1890 period. All these sources helped me to modify some of my generalizations recorded in former books.

The greatest gap in my information relates to the creative period from 1840 to 1870 when hundreds of different embossed treatments were used to make white ironstone attractive. It is these patterns that are most collectible today. There were rather definite shifts in desired patterns through those years. I have loosely gathered these shapes into groups: sometimes chronologically, and sometimes by similar treatments or styles. Many patterns could have fit into several different categories: for example *Ceres Shape* could have been included in chapters 9, 11, or 14.

Obviously, I could not have gathered and recorded the lines of the many shapes or noted the variety of pieces without the help of avid collectors. Their curiosity, persistence, encouragement, photos, sketches, facsimiles of marks, and phone calls kept me compiling.

Here are the generalizations on which we agree at present:

1. Early in the 1840s, some daring Staffordshire potters first offered all-white ironstone sets of dishes to American consumers.

2. The attraction of these sets had to depend on newer lines, more exact detailing, new contours in handles and finials, and potting that could not be masked by color transfer-printing.

3. It was probably the offerings of T. & R. Boote, with their Boote's *1851 Octagon Shape* and their 1853 *Sydenham Shape,* that triggered the surge of popularity for white ironstone in America.

4. According to the pricing lists published by Staffordshire potters in the mid-1850s these all-white wares were sold for about the same prices as were the one-colored transfer-decorated patterns on ironstone bodies.

5. About 1850 some shapes of white ironstone were first trimmed with copper lustre band and a few years later, a copper lustre motif centered pieces of many sets.

6. During the affluent years of white ironstone sales in the United States, manufacture of transfer-decorated stonewares dropped to 70% of its 1830 to 1850 production.

7. After about 1870, less creative round and square shapes with plainer bodies were mass-produced, priced so low that most American homemakers could afford a set.

8. By 1900, the age of white ironstone popularity had passed except for use of sanitary wares for hotel and restaurant services.

Here, like a patchwork quilt, facts have been gathered, fitted and arranged to make a coherent picture, a story from our past.

To the 19th century Englishmen of the Staffordshire potteries who pleased Americans with serviceable, attractive tablewares that fitted our way of life. Their creations still delight us today.

Working in earth makes me easy-minded.
- Staffordshire men

Six quart punchbowl by Barrow & Co. in *Adriatic Shape* was potted in the early 1850s. The Lautenschlagers enjoy this prize. Photo: Richmond Jones

Reflecting on White Ironstone

The feeling of early American rural life is recaptured in a row of large octagonal ironstone plates across a hutch, in the smooth lines of a white pitcher filled with black-eyed Susans, or in a giant soup tureen overflowing with zinnias. This white stone china is at home near a roaring fire on the grate, mellow pumpkin pine furniture, an old polished churn, and braided rugs.

White ironstone *needs* to be used. Men and women, old and young, now collect pieces to use as everyday dishes or for entertaining with a flair. Some collect only one pattern, others group related motifs. A few search for the unusual: others may choose only sugar bowls, pitchers, or toddy cups. The typical fan buys what appeals to him and then narrows his field as the stoneware crowds him out of the house. With well over four hundred shapes from which to choose, white ironstone collectors keep active.

The graceful lines of the nineteenth-century white ironstone often are featured on the pages of country decorating magazines where homemakers admire the startling simple accent of white.

Always eager to learn more about these hardy nineteenth-century dishes, collectors have joined me in looking into the past. The following pages reflect what we've learned about white ironstone.

To find the "roots" of ironstone, we searched the English history of ceramics. *Ceramics* can be defined as all ware made of clay or fusible stone.

American collectors became curious about the marks on the bottom of their favorite dishes. The search was on. They found that books on English pottery marks such as *Godden's Encyclopaedia of British Pottery and Porcelain Marks* usually revealed the years that potters worked. However, the actual marks from the years 1840 to 1870 were often missing. Jewitt's *The Ceramic Art of Great Britain* gave information on the manufacture of white granite made in the 1870s and 1880s. Since most of the detailed white ironstone made during the prolific years was shipped to the United States or

Fig. 1-1 Here eight different hot toddy or punch cups are arranged together. Do you recognize *Hyacinth, Full-Ribbed, Bootes' 1851 Octagon* and *Curved Gothic* on the top shelf and *President, Fig, Sydenham* and *Arbor Vine* on the bottom?

Canada, it is from those locations that a white ironstone study had to originate. What shapes were made from 1840 to 1870?

Jewitt did include helpful information concerning the excellent skills, wise methods and creativity of James Edwards, a Staffordshire potter of the 1840s, who initiated many new shapes and lines on his all-white china. (See Chapter 7)

However, Jewitt made little mention of the contributions of T. & R. Boote and no mention is made of Elsmore & Forster who executed the most detailed embossed decorations on white granite. This ceramic historian did mention a few patterns made by E. & C. Challinor and made a specific reference to *Dover Shape* made by Adams. (See p. 131)

Jewitt described other wares being made by the same potters who were producing and shipping white ironstone to American markets. Probably, he thought that most white granite sets were similar to those plainer offerings made in the 1870s and 1880s during the years when Jewitt did his excellent research.

1

Fig. 1-2 Treasuring white ironstone pieces with one function is fun. Above, the Morelands erect a pyramid with six pewter-lidded syrup servers. Pancakes, anyone?

Fortunately, some of the shapes potted from 1840 to 1870 were registered, including some drawings or photographs, and are still available for research! Slowly we compile our own descriptions, drawings and pictures to make a more complete white ironstone record.

Toward the close of the eighteenth century, Josiah Wedgwood, best-known of the Staffordshire potters, wrote about the general exporting of china: "Our consumption is very trifling in comparison to what is sent abroad . . . to the continent and the islands of North America. To the continent, meaning Europe, we send an amazing quantity of white stoneware and some of the finer kinds, but for the islands, meaning America, we cannot make anything too rich or costly."

The American markets were very important to the Staffordshire potters who had been supplying cream wares, sponged wares and transfer-printed colorful china to those consumers. A great wave of popularity for all-white ironstone occurred in the United States and Canada about the middle of the nineteenth century. During the following years, the Staffordshire companies near the port of Liverpool were very competitive with each other and were always alert to the protection of their large colonial market.

The production of the white ironstone wares was mostly of interest in England as part of the story of capable potters who created a good product that grew in demand across an ocean. However, the American story of those bluish-white dishes is a part of our heritage. Beautiful in its simplicity and well adapted to the American way of life, the use of these white wares has been absorbed along with the culture and language of England.

Fig. 1-3: An open bathroom cupboard in the Dieringer household contains a gathering of 19th century, white granite shaving mugs. Introductions move from left to right.

Top row: *Scalloped Decagon, Jumbo, James Edward's Classic Gothic, T. J. & J. Mayer's Classic Gothic*

Second row: *Hyacinth, Athens Shape, Corn n' Oats, Shaw's Chinese*

Third row: *Sharon Arch, Wheat Harvest, Potomic Shape, Sydenham Shape*

Fourth row: *Nut with Bud, Huron Shape, For-Get-Me-Not, Morning Glory*

Bottom row: *Washington Shape, President Shape, Vintage Shape, Moss Rose*

Fig. 1-4   The Allers choose a corner cupboard to display one shape, *Bootes' 1851 Octagon*. The graceful white shapes are emphasized by a dark background.

Fig. 1-5   Collecting all available pieces of one shape is fascinating as shown by Jack Anspaugh's dining room arrangements. *President Shape* is his choice.

We perceive that this plain ware had little cultural or historical significance to English ceramic records. In America, this white granite china was important to daily life. The early colonists were so busy wresting a living from the land and clearing their acres that, except for the wealthy gentry, there was little time to be concerned with elegant table services. They used wooden trenchers, pewter dishes if they could be secured, and rough redware that was not dissimilar to our common flowerpots. The few potters labored diligently, making bricks and tiles for construction and shaping crude housewares such as pots, jugs, milk pans and crocks which were clumsy to import.

Wedgwood had noted that America was rich in all the resources necessary for making dishes. Especially during the periods when England and the colonies were waging wars, abortive attempts were made to produce simple tableware, but the American potteries did not flourish until the 1870s and 1880s. Perhaps the average citizen of this new and untried land was so concerned with the hills and valleys that stretched beyond the western horizon that he had no time to examine or shape the clay at his feet.

Therefore, when the potters from the Staffordshire area of England began to offer less expensive wares, the American housewife was a hun-gry customer. Many of the blue-and-white dishes, simply labeled Staffordshire wares today, were imported and eagerly purchased during the first half of the nineteenth century. By the early 1840s, those who worked with English clay had perfected another inexpensive, durable, and plentiful type of earthenware dish. Even the poorest of rural families gladly put away their wooden trenchers and redware to set their tables in spotless white.

Undoubtedly, it was in the hearts of many of these homes that the restless urge to go West originated. The earthenware could be packed easily and was tough enough to survive trail life. One of our ancestors writes that, from his home on the bank of the Mohawk River, the greatest break in the Appalachian Chain that stretches from Canada to Georgia, he could watch the covered wagons going up the valley "like ships under full sail." Loaded with water jugs, the "bread loaf" trunks, the homespun blankets, and the churn, there must have been sturdy white ironstone.

In the pioneer homes that were built along the way, some homemakers urged their frugal husbands to use a little of their year's profit to buy a set of dishes. Today, by looking in the homes of the descendants of those pioneers, we can piece together a picture of that first treasured set.

Prior to Ironstone

Let's go back in history to set the stage for the advent of English white ironstone in the first half of the 19th century.

As the use of China tea became popular, especially in the British Isles, tea-drinkers thought the beverage tasted better when sipped from porcelain ware. Thus grew the name "china" for the fine translucent tableware imported from the Far East. Tea bowls or cups were both desirable and fairly expensive. Soon whole sets of porcelain tablewares were being imported by England as well as by her neighbors on the continent of Europe.

Some fine wares were shipped to English ports from Germany. German manufacturers, as well as other European potters, were trying to perfect a hard porcelain similar to the Oriental products. Near London, the English began to offer a version of Dutch Delft, an earthenware covered with a tin glaze. Its manufacture spread to Bristol, Liverpool, Lambeth and other pottery centers. These bodies, with a gray white finish that chipped easily, were a rather poor attempt at copying the whiteness and decorations of the fine Oriental pieces.

By 1700, England was making stoneware that rivaled that of the Germans. It was made of special clays mixed with sand and fired at such a high temperature that the body became partly vitrified or waterproof.

A great period of creativity began in the Staffordshire area with the work of the Elers brothers who made fine redware. They glazed their earthenware by casting salt into hot kilns, creating an "orange peel" appearance on the surface. Eight of their fellow potters were enraged at the resulting clouds of smoke that blanketed their potbanks.

Slipware decoration was made by trailing slip (liquified clay) over the outside of clay bodies. This practice dated back to medieval times.

The Elers brothers introduced many improvements and, so the story goes, worked under great secrecy, only employing workmen who appeared to be dull-witted. Two young men, John Astbury and Josiah

Twyferd, worked "under cover" in the pottery for two years, trying to learn the Elers' skills and methods.

In 1720, still trying to imitate Chinese porcelain, John Astbury produced a hard, strong, white body by adding calcined flint to light-colored clay. He, too, used a **salt** glaze, plunging the pottery settlement into partial darkness in the resulting smoke.

A new method of forming dishes was mastered as potters introduced molds, usually made of two or more pieces that were notched together and were easily removed after the clay body dried.

William Cookworthy had discovered the Cornish stone called "growan" about 1754 or 1755. This growan stone and growan clay were found to be remarkable raw materials for potters, better than any other native earths.

Added to these discoveries, other potting practices during the last half of the 18th century caused the industry to flourish. Among the changes were these:

(1) the accepted use of calcined flint
(2) the decoration by transfer-printing
(3) the digging of canals to move raw materials and finished products in and out of the pottery settlements
(4) the introduction of steam power to mix clay and run machines
(5) favorable trade treaties with other European countries
(6) wise marketing of creamwares
(7) and by the 1790s, tariffs to discourage the importation of porcelain from China

The Nankin imports of porcelain had been underselling native English porcelain. In 1777 and 78 alone, the English East India Company imported 348 tons of Chinese porcelain packed as ballast under millions of pounds of tea loaded in China. English potters struggled on, endeavoring to manufacture an acceptable, durable, inexpensive type of chinaware that would be able to compete with Oriental wares. The tariff of the 1790s encouraged English potters to experiment. By the close of the eighteenth century, the better practices made England dominant in the production of tablewares on a worldwide basis.

Geoffrey Godden, in his *Godden's Guide to Mason's China and the Ironstone Wares*, advances a more logical explanation for the end of the importation of Chinese porcelain by the English East India Company. Tons of these porcelain dishes had been used in ships as "vital cargo, being both water resistant and heavy to make the vessels sailworthy." On top of this porcelain ballast, eighteen to twenty million pounds of tea each year traveled safely to England in the late eighteenth century.

The crates of inexpensive china were to be sold at bulk auctions to the English "chinamen." Godden quotes old records to prove that, in 1791, the directors of the East India Company decided to cease their bulk importations of Chinese porcelains; because the china dealers were conspiring to cheat the importers.

The conspiracy was a familiar one–the practice of forming a pool or "ring" of buyers who agreed before an auction not to bid against each other, thus wrongfully lowering the sale price. Then the dealers would privately divide their items. The company was convinced in the 1790s that the chinamen had been systematically "fleecing" them for years. The china dealers were understandably concerned and objected vehemently, but the English East India Company had no more patience with the wily purchasers.

The great Josiah Wedgwood, who headquartered his pottery in Staffordshire, did not make the durable ware we know as white ironstone, but he certainly influenced its later production. He was interested in many fields other than the business of pottery and was aware of the forces at work in the countries and continents of the world. Wedgwood followed avidly the news that came back to England from her colonies across the wide Atlantic. Although he supported the causes of the American Revolution, he was still businessman enough to become concerned that his firm might lose its colonial market.

Wedgwood made his popular cream-colored earthenware called **Queen's Ware** in the 1760s and marketed it on the continent of Europe as well as other world markets. As that craze lessened, he introduced his new body, **Pearl White.** These two bodies were inexpensive precursors of white granite, which was to become one of the main exports of the Staffordshire potteries from the 1840s through the second half of the nineteenth century.

Eight or nine years before the War for Independence began, Wedgwood sent a Mr. Griffith to South Carolina to collect white clay, a fine white earth

Fig. 2-1 This tureen with its Foo dog finials and boar's head handles is marked "Masons Patent Ironstone China." The mark includes a crown with a drapery in blue. This Chinese-influenced decor was used on this early all-white ironstone dish before white graniteware became popular. Collection of Janet and Jack Allers.

called "Ayoree" by the natives. The Cherokee Indians there had been making excellent pipes from the clay for years. Mr. Griffith brought back five tons of this clay which was found to be of fairly good quality. However, the Cornish clays were superior and could be had more simply and cheaply.

Wedgwood continued to voice his fear that able English potters would go to America and be lost to the English industry, but the Revolution kept the colonists so busy that no serious potteries were established. The white clays of the Cherokee lands were daubed with the blood of the battling colonists and the invading English. Meanwhile, the American housewives gladly drank their "liberty tea" from rough, molded redware cups. In reality, Wedgwood had little to fear, as the American Revolution destroyed all competition.

Surprisingly, the war was scarcely over when trade with England flourished again. The English merchants were eager to supply the American markets, and the new country had a hankering for goods that were too time-consuming to manufacture themselves. Also, the Americans had few of the potting skills that characterized the English craftsmen.

Backing up a bit, remember that William Cookworthy had discovered the Cornish 'growan' and received a patent in 1768 that gave him the right to the sole use of that **china clay** and **china stone.** This patent-right was purchased from Cookworthy by Richard Champion in 1774, causing a group of Staffordshire potters to angrily protest. As spokesman, Wedgwood objected to one person having a monopoly on the

Cornish materials, especially one who had not discovered them himself. Champion then offered to allow the materials to be used for the production of earthenware but not for porcelain.

"How do you define the difference between earthenware and porcelain?" asked the potters. Of course, Champion did not want to impart the secret of his porcelain formula to the public. Reluctantly, he defined the difference and was granted the use of the Cornish earths to manufacture transparent ware only. This opened a whole new field, for after this, any potter had the right to experiment with Cornish materials in the potting of opaque china.

In 1784 Richard Champion left England for South Carolina where he unsuccessfully worked with the Cherokee clays. Attracted to the stretching acres, he settled on a plantation nearby, became a planter and eventually filled several public offices. In this case, Wedgwood's fears of American rivalry in the pottery business again proved groundless.

Meanwhile, china buyers looked elsewhere for new bodies to satisfy market demands. The production of new durable stone chinas just as the new century dawned solved both of these problems.

In January of 1800, William and John Turner patented and marketed an inexpensive, durable type of earthenware that attracted buyers. It was composed of "New Rock" Cornish stone and prepared flint. The decorations were an imitation of the Chinese. The Turner's firm went bankrupt in 1806.

Josiah Spode II, from Spoke-on-Trent, manufactured a similar china. It was opaque, with a far finer texture than previous earthenware. It emitted a clear ring when lightly tapped, and its dense body was so fine that it resembled porcelain. The body of Spode's original version of felspathic ware had a delicate blue-gray tint. Spode called this ware "Stone China" at first; later, it was marked "New Stone."

Other potters, such as Davenport and Hicks & Meigh, marketed sets of china with a hard opaque body also decorated to imitate the Chinese imports. There was a vast world market begging for these useful stonewares.

Working with his sons, Miles Mason of Lane Delph mastered a similar process. In 1813, his son, Charles James Mason, made public his "Patent Ironstone China." Although the product was not much different from that of his competitors, the name appealed to the buyers. Mason was a good huckster, and soon housewives on the Continent and in America clamored for "ironstone china," a term which soon became a permanent addition to the ceramics vocabulary.

The abstract of Mason's July 1813 patent read as follows:

"A process for the improvement of the manufacture of English porcelain, this consists of using

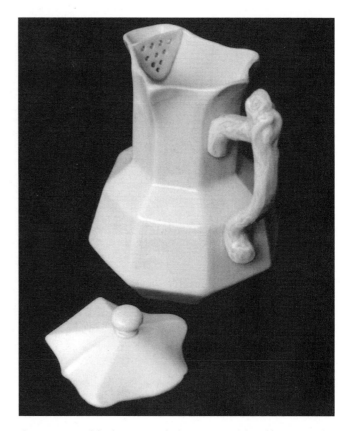

Fig. 2-2 One of the few pieces of white granite marketed by Mason. This 1830s hot beverage pitcher in *Hydra* shape has an early mark. Owned by Howard and Dorothy Noble.

the scoria or slag of Ironstone pounded and ground in water with certain proportions, with flint, Cornwell stone and clay, and blue oxide of cobalt."

Mason's patent was granted for a period of fourteen years and was not renewed, probably because the other major potters had perfected their own ironstone body recipes by 1827.

In his *Encyclopaedia of British Pottery and Porcelain Marks*, Geoffrey Godden lists the following potters of "Mason's Ironstone":

C. M. & C. J. Mason	ca. 1813 - 1829
Charles James Mason & Co.	ca. 1829 - 1845
Charles James Mason and 1851 - 1854	ca. 1845 - 1848
Francis Morley (& Co.)	ca. 1848 - 1862
G. L. Ashworth & Bros.	ca. 1862 -

These early stone chinas or ironstone wares were decorated with many colors over the durable white bodies. Such wares were popular at the native English marketplaces as well as at the export markets. **Ironstone** had come to stay. ▨

Advent of White Ironstone

Nearly all of the English dishes we call ironstone were produced in the Staffordshire area of England, where materials were available and the port of Liverpool was a convenient distance to the north and west. Here, in the settlements of Tunstall, Longport, Burslem, Cobridge, Hanley, Stoke, Fenton, Lane End, and Longton, lived colonies of proud, capable potters. Other areas of England undoubtedly produced similar wares, but we seldom come across them in the United States.

Wedgwood, in 1779, while discussing his pearl-ware mentioned that it was "not transparent, and consequently not china, for transparency will be the general test of china." Ceramic historians have generally accepted his definition. However, the Staffordshire potters themselves ignored his words as they labelled early ironstone sets as 'china.' With apology, I will also use the term when I refer to the white granite earthenware. The list of bodies on pages 17 and 18 reveal the faulty term 'china' again and again.

The ironstone-type stoneware of the early nineteenth century was decorated as colorfully as had been the Chinese porcelains. Our American ancestors loved to buy the ironstone covered with blue underglaze transfer printing. This "Historic Staffordshire" china attempted to picture places and events dear to the hearts of both growing America and Mother England. It has been said that the sale of these cobalt blue designs applied to white ironstone did more to heal the wounds caused by the War of 1812 than all the words of the great British and American leaders. In the twenty-five years following the conflict, dish-hungry America was flooded with mass-produced ironstone china decorated with cobalt blue. Wealthy citizens still preferred porcelain, but the blue-and-white earthenware was purchased eagerly by merchants and professionals. Soon these dark blue dishes lowered in price so that more households were able to own a set. With the over-production, though, some shoddy, poor-quality pottery was produced.

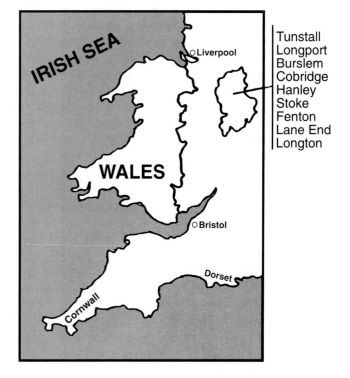

Map of western Britain highlighting the Staffordshire district.

Many of the cobalt blue pieces were not marked but can be attributed to certain potters by their border designs—a sort of prideful trademark. You may find marked plates from two different firms with the same center scene or design. The shrewd potters blatantly borrowed scenes from each other but left the borders to their originator. W. Adams circled his plates with baskets of roses and medallions; Wood used shells in his borders; Stubbs mixed eagles, scrolls, and flowers on the edges of his earthenware.

The old blue dishes were decorated by transfer methods. Designs were kept uniform by using a die that was coated with color. A thin paper was pressed on the coated design, removed, and then placed on the area to be decorated. About sixty-five known artists

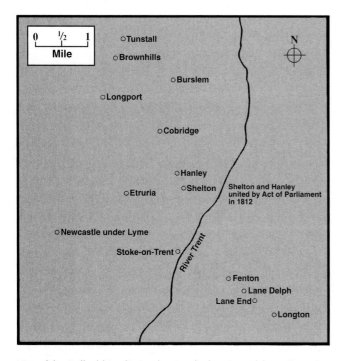

Map of the Staffordshire district showing the locations of the main potting towns.

to flow. Today both of those colors on transfer-decorated stone china are very desirable.

Some English porcelain (real china) was being shipped to America during this period. It was more expensive and better made, purchased by more affluent families. We can probably conclude that persons decorating porcelain had higher levels of skill.

Then one-color transfer-printed sets of dishes were offered to American markets. Non-flowing colors were light blue, brown, deep red, green and black. The potting years for these products began in the late 1830s and overlapped the early years when the all-white dinnerware was growing popular.

Miller in his Classification and Economic Scaling of 19th Century Ceramics throws light on the comparative values of all these ironstone products. According to his account, "Robert Heron's 1855 price list has flowing colors at almost 60% above the price of simple-transfer printed patterns."

He continues to conclude that in the 1850s, white ironstone (white granite) came into market at a status level comparable to transfer-printed wares.

Bills studied from 1857 to 1860 have white ironstone and transfer-printed wares at the same price. From the 1850s on into the 1880s, white ironstone was very common in bills examined while the numbers of transfer-printed pieces declined steadily. Miller states that these last vessels dropped almost 70% in wholesale prices from 1796 to 1855.

depicted more than seven hundred subjects. The rich, dark-blue color is the most collectible today.

The Staffordshire firms used a blue that was purposely allowed to bleed a little into the white background. A mulberry colored transfer was also allowed

Fig 3-1 Almost every potter of the late 1840s and early 1850s manufactured sets of white granite Gothic-type shapes. These three pieces were made by James Edwards, Dalehall. In the center is a Full-Panelled Gothic hot beverage server flanked by a Pedestalled Gothic creamer and sugar bowl.

By the mid-1850s, price lists and bills began listing large quantities of undecorated (by color, that is) white ironstone or "white granite."

It was during the 1840s that white ironstone was really introduced. Probably, it was the creative, energetic work of James Edwards who alerted buyers to the beauty of new shapes and new treatments using white alone. A few other potters such as the Mayer Brothers, John Ridgway & Co., and J. Wedgwood offered attractive all-white shapes in the 1840s. At least a dozen hexa-gon shapes were used and there were other echoes copied from some of the transfer-decorated wares.

According to Jewitt, some Staffordshire potters dealt only with the white granite wares for export but most continued to supply wares suitable for home markets in England and Europe as well as producing ironstone for the lucrative overseas trade.

Some white ironstone shapes described in this book were first used under flow blue or mulberry colors: many hexagon shapes, *Classic Gothic, Grape*

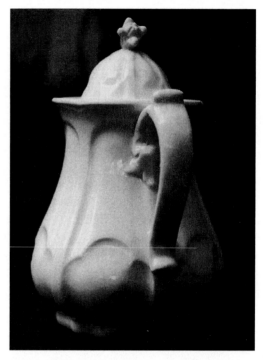

Fig 3-2 From 1851 to 1854, the T. & R. Boote company sold octagonal sets with added ogee arches on their *Boote 1851 Octagon* and *Sydenham Shape*. Other potters copied the design with small variations. Famous places were stamped as names of shapes throughout the 1850s. The above soapbox, for example, is clearly impressed as *Atlantic Shape*.

Fig 3-3 Many unnamed patterns of the `50s included arched vertical divisions: quarters, sixths, eighths, loops or panels. Above is an *Elaborate Six-Panelled Trumpet* teapot with added trefoil indentations.

Fig 3-4 Fluted shapes (concaved ribs) were introduced between 1845 and 1850 by John Wedge Wood. A few other potters used similar treatments on white ironstone bodies.

Fig 3-5 In 1856, Elsmore & Forster registered their *Tulip* shape which included a quartered body. A light blue and cobalt trim was added to the photographed pieces over the little scrolls and tulip finial.

Octagon, Panelled Grape, Grand Loop, Gothic Cameo, Prize Bloom, Primary, and others.

We see some similarities to the earlier wares in handles, finials, and other lines. We see again handleless cups, tureens with stands and ladles, a few mugs, leaf-shaped servers, nests of open servers and platters, octagon-shaped plates—all first having been offered under one-color transfer-printed tablewares and toilet sets.

From the 1850s to approximately 1870, Staffordshire potters continued to produce sharply angled or detailed molded shapes that attracted the American buyers. In the `70s, the shapes grew simpler, emphasizing plainer round and square shapes. Jewitt's writings during the 1870s and `80s reveal that some English potters were producing mainly "white granite" wares that were exported to Canada and the United States. The more affluent Americans sometimes referred to these later offerings as "farmer's or thresher's china." He makes almost no reference to the better potted shapes of the mid-1800s. Most shapes had not been registered but fortunately some of the shapes had been drawn or photographed and recorded in the English patent office. Hopefully, a researcher someday will verify those facts for collectors.

By the close of the century most white ironstone bodies were used as toilet wares or hotel china. The age of white ironstone popularity drew to a close. That gleaming whiteware had served us well. ▧

Fig 3-7 About the mid-1850s, designers started molding realistic grains, leaves, fruits and flowers over rounded bodies. This close-up of the lug on a *Fig* tureen details exactly veined foliage and fruit.

Fig 3-8 Note the copy of real fruit and leaves on this *Texas Furnival* teapot by J. F. who also used a pear-shaped round body.

Fig 3-6 A close-up shot of this *Fuchsia* jug reminds us of the Art Noveau style that was to become popular a half century later. Notice the rounded pear-shaped body.

Fig 3-9 The detail on this *Fig Cousin* jug is very exact, almost three dimensional in appearance. This careful representation of naturalistic fruits and foliage was reflected on most 1860's white granite shapes.

Fig 3-10 In 1859, Elsmore & Forster used naturalistic wheat and husks on their *Ceres Shape*, which was mimicked with slight variations by most working potters of the 1860s.

Fig 3-11 There was a sudden interest in ribbed body shapes during the late 1860s as revealed on this *Ribbed Bud* tureen by J.W. Pankhurst.

Fig 3-12 Elsmore & Forster combined ribs and a wreath in their *Laurel Wreath Shape* (sometimes marked *Victory Shape*)

Fig 3-13 Lilies-of-the-valley decorate this shaving mug with rounded body by James Edwards & Son. ←

Fig 3-14 Also in the late 1860's, some shapes adapted names taken from the classics such as *Victory, Athens, Greek Key, Olympic*, etc. To the right is a covered tureen marked *Athens Shape*. →

Fig 3-15   As the 1870s dawned, mass-production of white granite was attained. Quantities of plainer round and square shapes became available. By the following decade, these inexpensive sets were sometimes referred to as "farmer's china" or "thresher's china."

Fig 3-16   Very popular and useful were lady-finger ribbed servers that were round or square. The individual bowls are the hardest to find. Collectors like to collect them and use these 1880's dishes today!

Fig 3-17   During the last decade of the 1800s, a weak attempt was made to add some impressed decorations to white granite. Most designs were vague, poorly-made attempts to popularize white ironstone again, like the *Tracery* shape pieces shown.

Fig 3-18   Let's see, about when do you think each of these three sugar bowls was made? The first sided-bowl was fashioned by J. Alcock in the 1850s; the second plain round was shaped around 1880; the right hand sugar with its detailed wheat, vines, and grapes was potted in the 1860s.

Fig 3-19   Through all these years from 1840 to 1890, children's sets (22 pieces) were potted as exact mimics of adult sets. Here is a late plain children's set owned by D. Dorman.

On The Underside: Potters' Marks

Most of the facts and acceptable generalizations made by collectors and researchers have resulted from study of the weight, the color and the potter's information printed or impressed on the underside of pieces.

How old is it? Was it made in England or the United States? Is it an original or a reproduction? You can become quite knowledgeable by handling these old dishes, using a magnifying glass, studying books of marks and talking to other collectors.

Watch out for quick generalizations, however. The English potters were, first of all, businessmen who adapted methods to improve sales. They sometimes interchanged finials or reshaped a handle if the result was more expedient. Brush holders are often found in either a horizontal or vertical shape. The Bootes varied *Atlantic Shape* with three different patents. *Sydenham* pitchers underwent small changes during their production. *Virginia Shape* by Brougham & Mayer was made with two different plate borders. We find at least six shapes (totally unrelated) marked *Montpelier* by John Ridgway & Company during the 1840s. Perhaps this referred to a certain ironstone body recipe. Confusing, isn't it?

Those potters wanted to sell tableware; they had no concern about confusing collectors years and years later. Therefore, I've learned to avoid broad generalizations and practically banished "never" and "always" from my ironstone vocabulary.

You will soon be able to recognize an old white ironstone piece by its weight and bluish-white color. Many of the American wares, most 20th century reproductions, and a very few early patterns (mostly a few Alcock offerings) appear creamy when set next to the old English dishes.

Typical English Ironstone Markings

Godden's Encyclopaedia of British Pottery and Porcelain Marks lists some general rules for reading the marks on the bottom of dishes potted during the nineteenth century.

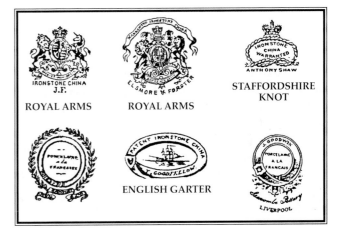

A variety of early English ironstone marks.

"Any printed mark incorporating the name of the pattern may be regarded as subsequent to 1810."

"Use of the word 'Royal' . . . suggests a date after the middle of the nineteenth century."

"Any printed mark incorporating the Royal Arms (or versions of the Arms) are 19th century or later."

"The quartered Arms without the central inescutcheon are subsequent to 1837."

"Many 19th century marks are based on stock designs—variations of Royal Arms, a garter-shaped mark (crowned or uncrowned) or the Staffordshire knot."

"The garter-shaped mark was used from 1840 onward. The Staffordshire knot may occur from about 1845 . . . much used in 1870s and 1880s . . . ." (It was not used extensively on white ironstone.)

Printed marks became popular after 1800 and were applied either before or after glazing. Impressed marks were made by applying a metal die to the dish before the first firing. This is generally referred to as "impressed under glaze." This type of mark usually is found on older pieces of china. However, many of the older pieces had only the black printed mark, while some had both impressed and printed marks. You may have to use your magnifying glass to search for impressed letters around the rim of the base of a gravy boat, vegetable dish, or open compote.

Applied marks were more rare. They were actually impressed marks placed on a raised pad. The potter formed them separately from the rest of the dish and, before firing, adhered the potter's identification on the base with a little slip. This type of mark was used by S. Bridgwood & Son and Richard Alcock. Elsmore & Forster used it on such patterns as *Ceres, Morning Glory,* and *Laurel Wreath.* Other examples undoubtedly can be found.

By American law, the word *England* had to be affixed to imported goods after 1891. Some potters, however, had proudly marked their wares *England* before the law was passed, so the collector will have to become acquainted with the few potters who did this. An example is the firm of J. & G. Meakin, who began labeling dishes with *Burslem, England* as early as 1869.

Made in England is a twentieth-century dating, used after 1921. *Limited, LD., Ltd.,* etc. indicate that a piece was made after the 1860s, but this word was not generally used before the 1880s. *Trade Mark* followed the Trade Mark Act of 1862. Usually it referred to a date after 1875.

A Special Note on Mason's Marks

Of special interest to white ironstone collectors are the rare pieces of early white granite marked by the Mason's with "Mason's Patent Ironstone China."

Below are illustrated two of the earlier blue printed Mason's marks. On the left is the crown mark used until around 1840. Note its rounded lobes. On the right is their crown mark used after 1840 when the sides of the crown became angular.

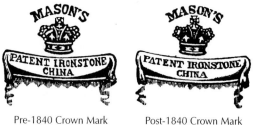

Pre-1840 Crown Mark   Post-1840 Crown Mark

Date Marks on English Wares

Much ceramic ware produced between 1842 and 1883 bore a diamond-shaped registry mark either printed or impressed on the bottom of a dish. Employed to prevent design piracy, this "bundle" contained the date the original design was filed at the English Patent Office. The date recorded indicated when the design was introduced and was not necessarily the date when the item was potted. The protection lasted for an initial period of three years, so the mark is a guide in dating. The marks generally related only to the shape and the impressed design. As a result, don't be surprised to find

a copper Tea Leaf or other colored decoration over a design that had already been potted in plain white. A chart of letters, numbers and their interpretation is illustrated on the facing page.

From 1884 on, designs were registered by numbers as listed below:

Rd. No. 1	-	Jan. 1884
19754	-	Jan. 1885
40480	-	Jan. 1886
64520	-	Jan. 1887
90483	-	Jan. 1888
116648	-	Jan. 1889
141273	-	Jan. 1890
163767	-	Jan. 1891
185713	-	Jan. 1892
205240	-	Jan. 1893
224720	-	Jan. 1894
246975	-	Jan. 1895
268392	-	Jan. 1896
291241	-	Jan. 1897
311658	-	Jan. 1898
331707	-	Jan. 1899

If the number is above 360,000 the date is after the year 1900.

The word *Warranted* nearly always designated American work, but, here again, the rule does not always prove true. For instance, the English potter John Edwards often marked his late-nineteenth-century dishes with the words *Warranted Ironstone China,* and Anthony Shaw marked his later pieces *Stone China Warranted.* Yet, I repeat, the addition of *Warranted* occurred most often in American ironstone marks. If you are in doubt, check to see if the potter's name is included in the lists of English potters of white ironstone found in this book. If not, you probably are holding an American-made dish. Occasionally, a dish is found that gives the name of an English potter and, underneath, is marked *Made for* with the name of an American retailer beneath.

T. J. & J. Mayer and its subsequent firms (Mayer Bros. & Elliot, Mayer & Elliot, and Liddle, Elliot and Son) sometimes included the mark *Berlin Ironstone,* which was a name for the ironstone body used. This has caused some people to think this is the name of a shape, but it was printed on many different shapes.

A few thoughtful manufacturers impressed the potting date into the body of the clay itself. Davenport marked the last two digits of the year on either side of his famous anchor. Such firms as Liddle, Elliot and Son impressed two numbers, one above the other, denoting the month and year of the potting. For example, [11]/63 means November 1863. A few of the later potters simply impressed the last two digits of the year in a spot separate from the more familiar mark.

Index to Year and Month Letters

Years

1842-67
Year Letter at Top

A	=	1845		N	=	1864
B	=	1858		O	=	1862
C	=	1844		P	=	1851
D	=	1852		Q	=	1866
E	=	1855		R	=	1861
F	=	1847		S	=	1849
G	=	1863		T	=	1867
H	=	1843		U	=	1848
I	=	1846		Z	=	1850
J	=	1854		W	=	1865
K	=	1857		X	=	1842
L	=	1856		Y	=	1853
M	=	1859		Z	=	1860

1868-83
Year Letter at Right

A	=	1871		L	=	1882
C	=	1870		P	=	1877
D	=	1878		S	=	1875
E	=	1881		U	=	1874
F	=	1873		V	=	1876
H	=	1869		W	=	Mar. 1-6
I	=	1872				1878
J	=	1880		X	=	1868
K	=	1883		Y	=	1879

Months
(Both Periods)

A = December
B = October
C or O = January
D = September
E = May
G = February
H = April
I = July

K = November (and December 1860)
M = June
R = August (and September 1st-19th. 1857)
W = March

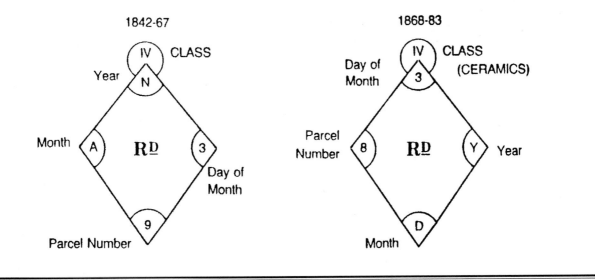

The "Wedgwood" Question

The well-known "prince of potters," Josiah Wedgwood, contributed much to the development of white ironstone, as had been discussed elsewhere in this book. His descendants produced a "Stone China" from about 1827 to 1861, with limited production, and marked it "Wedgwood's China" (a rare marking). However, the Josiah Wedgwood firm manufactured and usually labeled their excellent and beautiful wares simply 'Wedgwood."

Several makers of ironstone china used the name "Wedgwood" in their markings although they had no direct connection with the firm founded by Josiah. These marks were meant to mislead china buyers in the 19th century and they still confuse collectors today.

The following is a discussion of the "other" Wedgwoods.

Podmore, Walker, & Wedgwood of Tunstall marked their wares as illustrated below. Godden remarks that it was advantageous to use the name *Wedgwood* alone. From about 1860, this firm was retitled Wedgwood & Co. and it continued as Wedgwood & Co. Ltd., until 1965 when the name was changed to Enoch Wedgwood, Ltd. Some of the marks collectors can attribute to this company are shown below.

Several familiar patterns, such as *Scalloped Decagon, Fig, Corn and Oats*, and *Sharon Arch* are marked J. Wedgwood. These pieces have been assigned to John

Wedge Wood, since the Josiah Wedgwood potteries did not use marks with the initial "J." Sometimes the marks of John Wedge Wood have a slight gap or dot between "Wedg" and "Wood." A group of marks traced to John Wedge Wood are also shown.

These uses of the Wedgwood name undoubtedly were intended to influence consumers. This problem plagued the Josiah Wedgwood firm for generations. Misleading marks stamped on other types of pottery through the years have been "Wedgewood," "Vedgewood." and "Wedgwood Ware"—all wares inferior to the Wedgwood standards. If the renowned Wedgwoods ever produced the inexpensive white ironstone that influenced American life, I have never been able to find an example. White ironstone potters have contributed to the Wedgwood puzzles.

Nevertheless, I have heard antique dealers proudly proclaiming, "It was made by Wedgwood," and I have been as guilty as they in adding magic and value because of a name. I hope the poor Josiah's (there were five of them) have not been too bothered by the misuse of that great Wedgwood label.

A "Pearl of a Mark"

Beginning collectors often report that they have found a shape named *Pearl*. Once I did too. However, when I investigated, I found the word pearl included

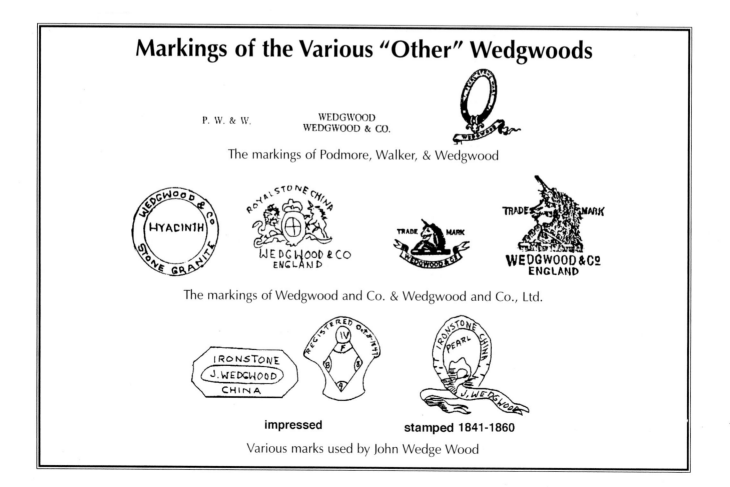

Markings of the Various "Other" Wedgwoods

P. W. & W.   WEDGWOOD
                    WEDGWOOD & CO.

The markings of Podmore, Walker, & Wedgwood

The markings of Wedgwood and Co. & Wedgwood and Co., Ltd.

impressed   stamped 1841-1860

Various marks used by John Wedge Wood

again and again in the marks of nineteenth-century potters. I have already mentioned that Josiah Wedgwood introduced his new china body in 1779 by calling it Pearl White. Other Staffordshire potters, following his lead, produced similar bodies called pearlware. These pearl white wares kept evolving and becoming something a little different. In fact, there were eight different formulas for the pearl body used in the Wedgwood factory from 1815 to 1846. Small changes continued through the following years.

Godden's Encyclopaedia of marks confirms our research under the heading:

"Pearl Ware or Pearl Stone Ware—a name for a special earthenware body used by many nineteenth century firms."

Miller reports that more than 15 English marks using the word "pearl" predate the McKinley Tariff Act of 1890. Among these labels were those applied by T. Walker; Cork & Edge; Podmore, Walker & Company; E. Challinor & Co.; J. & G. Meakin; J. Wedgwood; Wm. Baker & Co.; F. Jones & Co.; G. Phillips; Samuel Alcock; Wedgwood & Co.; and other white granite manufacturers.

During the late 1700s and the early 1800s most pearlware was decorated with colors using pseudo-Chinese motifs. By the middle of the nineteenth century, it was difficult to distinguish between pearlware bodies and white granite bodies.

According to Hughes, this borrowed term was thought to make white ironstone more attractive to buyers. He goes on to refer to "white granite as being the final phase of pearlware."

Other Names for Ironstone

The following names for white ironstone bodies have been taken from marks on the underside of various examples:

Various Early Marks That Include The Word "Pearl"

A la Perle
Berlin Ironstone
Dresden Opaque China
Felspar China
Felspar Opaque China
Fine Stone
Flint Ware
Genuine Ironstone China
Granite
Granite China
Granite Ware
Imperial French Porcelain
Imperial Granite
Imperial Ironstone China
Imperial Parisian Granite
Imperial Stone
Imperial White Granite
Improved Granite China
Improved Ironstone China
Improved Stone China
Indian Ironstone
Ironstone China
Ironstone Pearl China
New Stone
Opaque China
Opaque Granite China
Opaque Pearl
Opaque Porcelain
Opaque Stone China
Oriental Stone
Parisian Granite
Parisian Porcelaine
Paris White
Patent Opaque China
Patent Paris White Ironstone
Patent Ironstone China
Pearl China
Pearl Ironstone China
Pearl Stone Ware

Pearl White Granite
Pearl White Ironstone
Pearl White
Porcelaine a la Perle
Porcelaine a la Francais
Porcelaine Opaque
Quartz China
Real Ironstone China
Real Stone China
Rock Stone
Royal Granite
Royal Ironstone China
Royal Patent Ironstone
Royal Patent Ware
Royal Premium
Royal Premium Ironstone
Royal Stone China
Royal Vitreous
Special White Stone Ware
Staffordshire Ironstone China
Staffordshire Stone China
Staffordshire Stone Ware
Stone China
Stone Granite
Stone Ware
Superior Stone China
Superior White Granite
Warranted Best Ironstone China
White Granite
Warranted Ironstone China

Warranted Stone China
White Granite Ware

From around 1840 to 1850, the Staffordshire firms felt threatened by French potters who began exporting quantities of inexpensive hard, white porcelain to the United States and Canada. The English firms were afraid that housewives would prefer the glittering gray-white porcelains to the English transfer-colored earthenwares that had been so popular.

The crafty British potters took immediate steps to imitate the gray-white wares of the French, and the resulting tough, white granitewares with sharp, detailed potting and gleaming glazes seized the American market. White ironstone with descriptions such as *A la Perle, Parisian Granite, Paris White,* and *Porcelaine Opaque* are reminders of this international contest, but, nevertheless these were names printed on English white ironstone bodies.

According to Williams, several bills from a china wholesaler in Baltimore to retailers in Gettysburg, Pennsylvania mention sales of white granite, white china, and white French China during the second half of the 19th century. Yes, there really was rivalry between the French and English potters. However, today we can identify few examples of the "white French China." A most unusual name for a white stone china body was marked *Porcelaine a la Francaise* by John Ridgway, registered in 1844. It was neither porcelain nor was it French!

English Ironstone Potters

Potters whose marks have been found on White Ironstone made in England in the nineteenth century. As additional information becomes available through current research, updating of this listing will be possible.

Potter	Location	Dates of Location
Adams, Wm. & Sons	Tunstall, Stoke	1796 - present
Alcock, Henry & Co.	Cobridge	1861 - 1910
Alcock, John	Cobridge	1848 - 1861
Subsequently Henry Alcock & Co.		
Alcock, John & George	Cobridge	1839 - 1846
Alcock, John & Samuel	Cobridge	1848 - 1850
Alcock, Richard	Hanley	1870 - 1882
Alcock, Samuel & Co.	Cobridge	1828 - 1853
Ashworth, Geo. & Bros	Hanley	1862 - present
Baker, W. & Co.	Fenton	1839 - 1932
Baker & Chetwynd		
Barrow & Co.	Longton	1853 - 1856
Bates, Elliott & Co.	Longport	1870 - 1875
Beswick, Robert	Tunstall	1842 - 1860
Bishop & Stonier	Hanley	1891 - 1939
Bodley, Edward F. & C.	Burslem	1862 - 1898
Boote, T. & R.	Burslem	1842 - 1906
Bourne, Joseph	Denby	1833 - 1860
Bowers, George Frederick	Tunstall	1842 - 1868

Bridgwood, S. & Son	Longton	1805 -
Bridgwood & Clarke	Burslem, Tunstall	1857 - 1864
Subsequently Edw. Clarke & Co.		
Brougham & Mayer	Tunstall	1853 - 1855
Brownfield, Wm. & Sons	Cobridge	1850 - 1891
Burgess, Henry	Burslem	1864 - 1892
Burgess & Goddard	Longton	ca. 1870
Burgess & Leigh	Burslem	1867 - 1889
Challinor, C. & Co.	Fenton	1892 - 1896
Challinor, Edward	Tunstall	1842 - 1867
Challinor, E. & Co.	Fenton	1853 - 1862
Subsequently E. & C. Challinor		
Challinor, E. & C.	Fenton	1862 - 1891
Clarke, Edward (& Co.)	Tunstall	1865 - 1877
Clementson Bros.	Hanley	1865 - 1916
Clementson, Joseph	Hanley	1839 - 1864
Close & Co.	Stoke	1855 - 1864
Cockson & Chetwynd (& Co.)	Cobridge	1867 - 1875
Subsequently Cockson & Seddon		
Cockson & Seddon	Cobridge	1875 - 1877
Collinson, C. & Co.	Burslem	1851 - 1873
Cork & Edge	Burslem	1846 - 1860
Cork, Edge & Malkin	Burslem	1860 - 1871
Corn, Edward	Burslem	1840 - 1864
Corn, W. & E.	Burslem	1864 - 1891
	Longport	1864 - 1904
Davis, I. (John)	Hanley	1881 - 1891
Davenport	Longport	1793 - 1887
Edge, Malkin & Co.	Burslem	1871 - 1903
Edwards, James	Burslem	1842 - 1851
Edwards, James & Son	Burslem	1851 - 1882
Edwards, John (& Co.)	Longton	ca. 1847 - 53
	Fenton	ca. 1853 - 1900
Edwards, T.	Burslem	ca. 1840s
Elsmore & Forster	Tunstall	1853 - 1871
(Sometimes spelled "Foster")		
Elsmore, Thomas, & Son	Tunstall	1872 - 1887
Ford & Challinor	Tunstall	1865 - 1880
Forester & Hulme	Fenton	1887 - 1893
Freakly & Farrall	Hanley	ca. 1850s
Furnival, Jacob (& Co.)	Cobridge	1845 - 1870
Furnival, Thomas (& Sons)	Cobridge	1851 - 1890
Furnivals (Ltd.)	Cobridge	1890 - 1968
Gator, Thomas & Co.	Burslem	1885 - 1894
Gelson Bros.	Hanley	1868 - 1875
Goddard & Burgess	?	?
Goodfellow, Thomas	Tunstall	1828 - 1859
Goodwin, John	Longton	Prior to 1851
See Seacombe Pottery		
Goodwin, Joseph		
Grindley, W. H. & Co.	Tunstall	ca. 1880 - present
Hancock, Sampson (& Sons)	Tunstall	1858 - 1870
	Stoke	1858 - 1937
Hawthorne, John	Cobridge	1854 - 1869
Harvey, C. & W. K.	Longton	1835 - 1853
Heath, Joseph	Tunstall	1845 - 1853
Holland & Green	Longton	1853 - 1882
Hollinshead & Kirkham	Tunstall	1876 - 1890
Hope & Carter	Burslem	1862 - 1868

Hughes, Thomas	Burslem	1860 - 1894
Hulme, T.		c. 1855 -
Hulme & Booth	Burslem	1851 - 1854
Johnson Bros.	Hanley	1883 - present
Jones, Frederick & Sons	Longton	1865 - 1886
Jones, George	Burslem	ca. 1854
Jones, George & Sons	Longport	1861 - 1951
Liddle, Elliot & Son	Longport	1862 - 1870
Livesley & Davis	Hanley	?
Livesley, Powell & Co.	Hanley	1851 - 1866
Maddock, John	Burslem	1842 - 1855
Maddock, John & Sons	Burslem	1855 - present
Maddock & Gater	Burslem	1874 - 1875
Malkin, R.	Fenton	1863 - 1881
Mason, Charles James	Fenton	1845 - 1848
		1851 - 1854
Maudesley J. & Co.	Tunstall	1862 - 1864
Mayer, Thomas & John	Longport	1841 - 1843
Mayer, T. J. & J.	Burslem	1843 - 1855
Subsequently Mayer Bros. & Elliot		
Mayer Bros. & Elliot	Burslem	1856 - 1858
Subsequently Mayer & Elliot		
Mayer & Elliot	Longport	1858 - 1861
Subsequently Liddle, Elliott & Son		
Meakin, Alfred	Tunstall	1875 - present
Meakin, Charles	Hanley, Burslem	1883 - 1889
Meakin & Co.	Cobridge	1865 - 1882
(Meakin Bros.)		
Meakin, Henry	Cobridge	1873 - 1876
Meakin, J. & G.	Hanley	1851 - present
Meakin, Lewis	Shelton	1853 - 1855
Meigh, Charles	Hanley	1835 - 1849
Meigh, Charles & Son	Hanley	1851 - 1861
Meigh, Charles, Son & Pankhurst	Hanley	1849 - 1851
Meir, John & Son	Tunstall	1837 - 1897
Mellor, Taylor & Co.	Burslem	1880 - 1904
Mellor, Venables & Baines		1834 - 1851
Moore Bros.	Cobridge	1872 - 1905
Morley, Francis (& Co.)	Hanley	1845 - 1859
Old Hall Earthenware & Co.	Hanley	1861 - 1886
Oulsnam, W. E. (& Sons)	Tunstall	1867 - 1871
	Burslem	1872 - 1892
Pankhurst & Dimmock	Hanley ?	?
Pankhurst, J. W.	Hanley	1850 - 1851
Pankhurst, J. W. & Co.	Hanley	1852 - 1882
Pearson Edward	Burslem	1850 - 1854
	Cobridge	1853 - 1873
Penman, Brown & Co.	?	?
Phillips, George	Longport	1834 - 1848
Pinder, Bourne & Co.	Burslem	1862 - 1882
Pinder, Bourne & Hope	Burslem	1851 - 1862
Podmore, Walker & Co. (Podmore,	Tunstall	1834 - 1859
Walker & Wedgwood)		
Subsequently Wedgwood & Co.		
Powell & Bishop	Hanley	1876 - 1878
Powell, Bishop & Stonier	Hanley	1878 - 1891
Pratt & Simpson	Fenton	1878 - 1883
Proctor, John	Longton	1843 - 1846
Ridgway, Bates & Co.	Hanley	1856 - 1858
Ridgway, John & Co.	Hanley	1830 - 1855

Ridgway & Morley	Hanley	1842 - 1844
Ridgway, Wm. & Co.	Shelton	1830 - 1854
Ridgway, Wm., Son & Co.	Hanley	1838 - 1848
Rogers Bros		late
Seacombe Pottery	Seacombe	1851 - 1870
	(near Liverpool)	
Shaw, Anthony	Tunstall	ca. 1851-56
	Burslem	ca. 1860-1882
Shaw, Anthony & Son(s)	Burslem	ca. 1882 - 1898
Shaw, Anthony & Co.	Burslem	ca. 1898 - 1900
Taylor, W.	Hanley	
Taylor Bros.	?	?
Till, Thomas & Sons	Burslem	1850 - 1928
Tomkinson, Bros. & Co.	Tunstall	
Tunnicliff, Michael	Tunstall	1828 - 1841
Turner, Goddard & Co.	Tunstall	1867 - 1874
Turner, G. W. & Sons	Tunstall	1873 - 1894
Turner & Tomkinson	Tunstall	1860 - 1872
Venables & Baines	Burslem	1851 - 1853
Venables, John	Burslem	1853 - 1855
(Venables, Mann & Co.)		
Walley, Edward	Cobridge	1845 - 1856
Walker, Thomas	Tunstall	1845 - 1851
Wedgwood & Co.	Tunstall	1860 - present
Formerly Podmore, Walker & Co.		
Wedgwood, J. (See Wood)		
Wileman, J. & C.	Fenton	1864 - 1869
Wileman, James	Fenton	1869 - 1892
Wilkinson, Arthur J.	Burslem	1885 - 1964
Wilkinson & Hulme	Burslem	1883 - 1885
Subsequently Arthur J. Wilkinson		
Wood & Hawthorne		1882 - 1887
Wood & Hulme	Burslem	1882 - 1905
Wood, John Wedge	Burslem, Tunstall	1841 - 1860
Wood & Son(s)	Burslem	1865 - present
Wood, Son & Co.	Cobridge	1869 - 1879
Wood, Rathbone & Co.	Cobridge	ca. 1868
Wooliscroft, George	Tunstall	1851 - 1853
(sometimes Woolliscroft)	Tunstall	1860 - 1864
	Scottish Potters	
Bell, J. & M. R. & Co.	Glasgow	1842 - 1929
Cochran, Robert & Co.	Glasgow	1846 - 1918
Methven, David, & Sons	Fifeshire	First half of 19th c. to ca. 1930
	Irish Potters	
Belleek Pottery Ltd.	Belleek	1863 - present
	Welsh Potters	
South Wales Pottery	Llanelly	1838 - 1858
(Made a "Pearl White Ironstone")		

The English coat of arms found on many sets of white ironstone (both from Staffordshire and America) bore two mottoes. Sometimes both were included. Most often printed around the quartered shield were the words *Honi soit qui mal y pense*, meaning "Evil to him who evil thinks." Supposedly, this is based on a remark made by King Edward III when he put on a garter lost by a countess who had been dancing with him. Some historians discount this as an amusing tale.

Frequently found below the coat of arms with its royal lion and mythical unicorn was a draped ribbon inscribed with the saying, *Dieu et mon droit*, which means, "God and my right." Thus, the arms of Britain, with many minute variations, proclaimed that the manufacturers were English.

Shaped in White Granite

Look what I found! Collectors bring unusual pieces and we speculate together. What was it used for? Why the divider? A strainer for what use? How many pieces in a nest? So our terms ebb and flow. Experts and researchers don't always agree. The rest of this chapter records some findings and generalizations.

Mid-nineteenth century ironstone sets generally copied pieces made earlier. Below I list some pieces located in earlier sets and the italics are my thoughts.

Early Chinese Export porcelain dinner set:

2	soup tureens and stands
4	smaller tureens
8	salad plates
2	deep salad bowls
4	sauce boats and stands
18	flat dishes (*6 sizes, three sets ?*)
72	dinner plates
36	soup plates
24	side plates
24	water(?) plates (*hot water?*)

Another 1827 sale list of a dinner set

2	soup tureens with covers, stands
4	vegetable dishes with covers
19	dishes in various sizes (*platters ?*)
2	fish plates
60	table plates
18	soup plates
48	pie plates

where are the cups ?

Collard, in her writing, quoted from an 1855 ad that 'one sett' of white granite contained 280 pieces.

Miller lists sizes of plates from mid-nineteenth century pricing lists:

table plates - 10 to 11 inches
supper plates - 9 inches
twifflers - 8 inches
muffin plates - 7,6,5 and 4 inches

Late (after 1875) open stock list:

jugs in 5 sizes
bakers and scallops - 6,7,8 and 9 inches
comports - 7,8 and 9 inches
covered dishes - 7,8, and 9 inches
dishes - 7,8,9,10,11,12,14, and 18 inch
  (*platters*)
salads - 7,8, and 9 inches
butters covered
pickles (*relish dishes*)
sauce boats
sauce tureens (complete)
soup tureens (complete)
teapots
oyster bowls
dishes - 3 or 4 inches (*individual*)
fruit saucers - 4 inches
tea sets, 56 pieces
toilet sets, 10 pieces
dinner sets, 100 pieces, 125 pieces

Old records reveal that tea sets before about mid-century contained no individual plates and the tea cups had saucers but the coffee cups (cans) had no saucers. There are several biscuit trays (cake plates) included.

We see echoes of early dessert sets in the first white ironstone made. These include low and high tazzas, leaf-shaped dishes, individual plates and several shapes for serving sandwiches, scones, or biscuits.

Collectors today feel fortunate to locate these related pieces. Many of the surfaces are completely covered with impressed designs as shown in Chapter 20.

In most of the book, I will refer to white ironstone as being early (1840 to 1870) or late (1870 to 1900).

Tea sets included teapot, covered sugar and creamer, waste bowl, handleless cups and saucers, 8 or 9 inch plates, and sometimes biscuit trays.

Most coffee sets were made with a larger coffeepot, larger set of creamer and covered sugar, larger waste bowl and larger cups with saucers (usually handleless but occasionally found with handles).

In Godden's ironstone book, he copies a pricing list that mentions simply "a white tea set, 45 pieces." What do you think might have been included?

Toilet sets in early white ironstone include ewer, basin, soap dish, brush (or razor) box, shaving mug, small hot water jug, and covered chamber pot. Harder to locate are the tall covered waste containers and matching foot baths.

"Dishes" usually referred to platters and "plates" related to flatware used for individual servings.

It's rewarding to search for the relish dishes to partner early sets. Motifs surround the edges of mitten servers, boat-shaped pieces, and round or oval bodies. A few sets such as *Bootes' 1851 Octagon*, *Sydenham*, and *Fig* had relish dishes with impressed designs totally unrelated to the rest of the set.

Large soup tureens with covers, ladles and stands (undertrays) are sometimes found in more than one size. The accompanying soup plates were made in an

Fig 5-1 Seven pieces form an early *1851 Boote Octagon* set: punch cup, one of nest of six open servers, gravy boat, handled cup, one of nest of sided open servers, and table pitcher.

Fig 5-2 Four sauce or gravy boats: left to right, (top) *Panelled Columbia, Trent;* (bottom) *Atlantic, Bordered Hyacinth.*

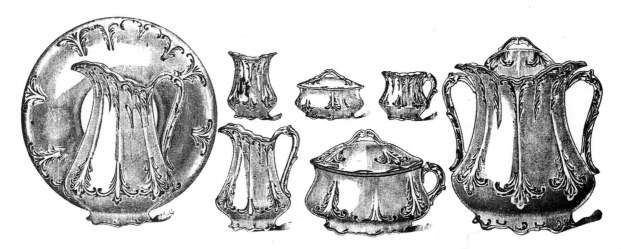

Early illustration of a typical turn-of-the-century ironstone toilet set.

Fig 5-3   A trio of soap boxes with inserts: (top) *Fig Cousin,* (bottom) *Baltic Shape* and *Sharon Arch.* From Moreland Collection.

Fig 5-4   Soap slabs were larger substitutes for soap boxes: (top) George Jones slab, (bottom left) T. & R. Boote plain piece, and the last was unmarked. Note raised sections used to keep the soap dry.

Three unusual mitten relish dishes. Left to right: Lined Glory, Sydenham, and Gothic Cameo.

Fig 5-5   This popular *Sydenham* soup tureen with ladle and cracker tray was made in several sizes by T. & R. Boote.

Fig 5-6   Ladles are always sought in the large soup size, the medium size for stew tureens or hot toddy bowls, and the smallest size for sauce tureens. Angles differed according to use. These rare octagon ladles are from the Ed Rigoulot and Ted Brockey Collection.

enormous 10 inch size, a common 9 inch size, and the more collectible 7$\frac{1}{2}$ inch size. Most sets had oval soup tureens and also large round tureens (I call them chowder tureens) with cracker trays and ladles. A large, low stew tureen was often included with no stand but equipped with a smaller ladle than the soup ladle. More tureens? Yes, there were usually three sizes of covered oval vegetable tureens as well as three round—all in the same decor. The small sauce tureens mimicked the soup tureens in miniature: same proportions in the body, cover, base and ladle. The bakers (don't bake in them!) were shaped in nests of six or more in a set. For instance, Bootes' *Sydenham* nests were sold in round, oval, and the rarer octagonal shape. The largest and smallest sizes are the hardest to locate. The largest has the same diameter as the toilet basins while the smallest can be clasped in your palm. Do not confuse these low nests with the later square and round ribbed nests of the 1870s and 1880s which can be easily found.

Fig 5-7 This cup population is arranged left to right (top) with a handleless punch cup, a shaving mug in *Edward's Lily-of-the Valley,* a cider mug in *Bordered Hyacinth,* an *Atlantic* coffee cup, a *Fig* punch cup; (bottom) handled *Sharon Arch* teacup, handleless *Sharon Arch* teacup, and a children's *Sharon Arch* set.

The most common white ironstone cup was a teacup made without handles and was similar to Oriental tea bowls. This style was cheaper to pot and more apt to survive ocean voyages intact. These handleless cups came in approximately two sizes: a 7 1/2 oz. teacup with a 6 inch saucer, and a 10 oz. coffee cup with a 6 1/2 inch saucer. Rarely, we locate the same cups with handles, so we must suppose that some cups were ordered with handles.

Other cups included shaving mugs, the unusual large cider mugs, handled and handleless demitasse cups, handled 4 inch punch or hot chocolate cups, the shorter handled hot toddy cups, and the popular miniature cups with saucers.

Fig 5-8 Handleless cups were easier to manufacture and ship. Some early cups are found with handles and we can suppose that some were ordered with handles. Posed (left to right) are a child's cup with saucer in *Sharon Arch,* a teacup in *Trent Shape,* and a *Plain* coffee set.

The jugs for the early sets ranged from the tiny child's pitcher, tea jug, coffee jug, three table pitchers, and 2 or 3 sizes of toilet ewers. That's about eight sizes. Can you complete a pitcher parade assembled from your favorite shape?

Can you spot the covered hot beverage servers depicted in this book? These jugs do not have a hole in the lid for ventilation as do teapots. The cover is rather pointed over the spout; there is definitely a resting rim for the cover.

Early sets had two extremes in their nests of platters: the tiny 8 or 9 inch one up to the 22+ inch turkey platter. Most desirable, but difficult to find, are the well and tree platters with perforated liners. Long, narrow

Fig 5-9　Well and tree platters, with or without perforated liners, are very collectible.

Fig 5-10　Heart-shaped ivy leaves help decorate this reticulated tray marked "Porcelain Opaque". This may have been a tray under a matching chestnut bowl. Owned by Ed Rigoulot and Ted Brockey.

platters were made to serve fish. There were several sizes of well and tree-type platters made in *President Shape;* the concave center is molded in a floral design.

Covered butter dishes are not easy to find. Many have been located that look brown, stained with an accumulation of butter fat. Usually, each had a perforated liner and some had an indentation for the lid to fit. These containers, if stained, usually can be cleaned professionally but will absorb the stain again if actually used. Although I urge collectors to use their ironstone, I make an exception with butter servers unless you can find a plastic liner to fit!

A few early butter tubs, with a round base and two vertical handles with holes for bales, have been discovered. Later sets of dishes often included a stack of individual butter chips.

All collectors treasure the pewter-lidded syrup pitchers about the size of creamers. I have seen a few pewter-lidded table pitchers in about a two-quart size. Hard to find!

Rarer still are the covered hotcake or muffin servers about 9 3/4 inches in diameter. Often the cover rests on the top of the plate surround which sometimes has no indentation for the lid. Some can be found with liners.

Experts have convinced me that children's sets were really made as toys. Some of the sets such as *Ceres, Bootes' 1851* and *Edward's Lily-of-the-Valley* are deeply impressed with fine detail. Each tea set is composed of 22 pieces: teapot, sugar, creamer, waste bowl, 6 cups, 6 saucers, and 6 plates. Most sugar bowls and waste bowls appear to be too large for the other pieces. Also, saucers are larger than the plates. It's alright, I collect them anyway. Not every pattern was made in miniature; some shape names will be listed in a later chapter.

Fig 5-11　This tall graceful fruit compote manufactured in the 1850s by James Edwards & Son is echoed by the tiny unmarked children's compote.

Few children's dinner sets were made in white ironstone. When found, pieces included are stacks of plates in several sizes, nests of platters and open servers, and covered tureens (even with ladles). Cups were not included. Pieces may number around one hundred. A set like this has not been discovered in an early 1840 to 1870 shape. Some collectors have acquired a covered tureen, a long octagonal server, or a miniature compote occasionally. We wonder if each might have been a part of an early set?

About half a dozen mustard pots with openings for a server have come to light. Also, some early shapes offered small egg cups: *Gothic, Full-Ribbed, Ceres,* and a larger one in *Shaw's Lily of the Valley* . These two kinds of pieces are among the rarest of white granite collectibles.

Toothbrush holders for toilet sets are formed in either of two shapes. The low horizontal covered box may have been replaced because the wet brushes needed air. We find a few with ventilation holes in the covers. The more sanitary vertical holders were made, some with drainage holes, resting on a small saucer-like stand. Later toilet sets included vertical brush holders with no drainage holes or supporting saucers. Some people fill the shelves of open bathroom cupboards with an assembly of brush holders.

Nineteen out of twenty ironstone collectors still search for a beverage bowl. Smaller handleless syllabub bowls hold 2$\frac{1}{2}$ to 3$\frac{1}{2}$ quarts; the covered and handled hot toddies are usually a little larger and often are bought and used without the cover. I've seen few of the large, 6- to 8- quart punch bowls. I still dream of the great scalloped edges on the beautiful proportions of the *Adriatic Shape* in the large punch bowl illustrated in Chapter 11. All of these offerings had accompanying ladles sized to fit each bowl.

I must discuss pedestalled servers, called compotes, comports, or comportiers. The high pedestalled fruit bowls are sought by most collectors. A few of them boast square plinths beneath the supporting columns and are sometimes reticulated. Low footed biscuit trays or donut stands (tazzas) with shallow centers are easier to locate. Both of the above were often included as parts of early dessert sets.

Let's see. Have I covered most of the pieces made in early shapes? No, I haven't mentioned early epergnes, bedside carafes, cheese bells, cheese cradles, or the 22 inch supper sets with center server surrounded by five separate servers. The details about high-relief jugs and reticulated pieces will be covered on later pages. Is your appetite increasing?

After 1870, English firms offered fewer pieces in their white ironstone services. By then, the plain white cups were seldom sold without handles. Saucers often had high walls. Butter chips, bone dishes, occasionally egg cups, and individual sauce dishes or little platters were added. Most sets contained one or two tureens plus open servers. Soup tureens became much smaller and almost disappeared from sets by 1890. Butter dishes with perforated liners above a space for ice were potted. Many of these were similar to the earlier round soap dishes that had been a part of the mid-century toilet sets. Cup plates and honey dishes were no longer parts of the dinner services. Sauce tureens were rarely made by that time, but the gravy boat remained popular. Nested round

Fig 5-12 Most collectors long to locate a large six-quart punch bowl like this one potted by Francis Morley about 1850.

or square bowls and the earlier waste bowl (with a new function) were freely used and can be picked up easily today. Some 16 oz. chowder cups without handles are occasionally found.

People interested in white ironstone have gathered the following unusually-shaped dishes and tools fashioned in white granite. Most of these were manufactured from 1870 to 1900:

barber's bowls	nests of compotes
cuspidors (spittoons)	egg stands
cheese molds	toast racks
pudding molds	invalid feeders
flasks	(bubby pots)
bed warmers	wall fountains
spoon warmers	scoops
mortars with pestles	spoons (wooden handles)
funnels	lemon squeezers
jar fillers	bar bowls
colanders	jardinieres
ice jugs	toast boards
scoops	sieve bowls
rests for corn cobs	cheese strainers
settling pans (milk pans)	

By the late 1800s, the more wealthy industrial class began to refer derogatively to the inexpensive, useful white wares. It is true that the rural folks gladly continued to use these plain, practical dishes long after the majority of Americans had purchased colored porcelains to set their tables.

This long list of names for pieces available somewhere out there should be a challenge. Bring that "white treasure" home in any shape you can find. ▓

Getting Down to Terms: Vocabulary

In order to describe ceramic decorations and body shapes we need a common white ironstone language. Let's talk terms

Acanthus – spiny leaves used as part of architectural ornament as in capitals of Corinthian columns

Age lines – small crazing lines that often appear in the glaze after years of use

Arcaded – decorated with a series of arches

Arches – construction for spanning an opening

Applied mark – potter's mark impressed onto a separate pad which is then added with the use of slip to the base of a ceramic piece

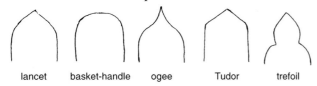

lancet   basket-handle   ogee   Tudor   trefoil

Baroque – style characterized by detailed natural foliage, cherubs, graybeards, sometimes grotesque ornamentation

Barber's bowl – round bowl with a section of the surround removed so that the bowl will fit under the chin

Base – molded piece that supports a serving jug, pot or tureen

Basin – the large toilet bowl that has a matching jug or ewer

Biscuit – condition of ceramic ware after first firing, before being dipped in glaze

Biscuit oven – the first kiln used in potting

Biscuit tray – an English term for a cookie or sandwich plate

Body parts – names for ceramic parts of a piece

Borders – a repetitive edging around a plate or the body of serving vessels

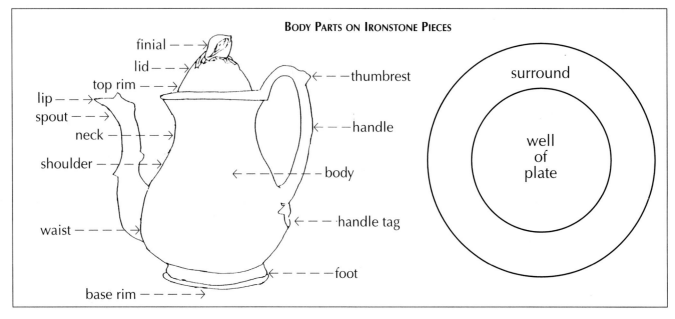

BODY PARTS ON IRONSTONE PIECES

VARIOUS BORDERS ON IRONSTONE PIECES

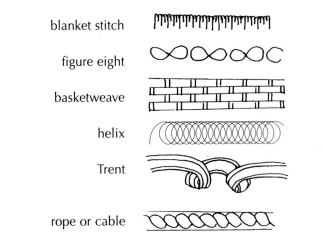

blanket stitch

figure eight

basketweave

helix

Trent

rope or cable

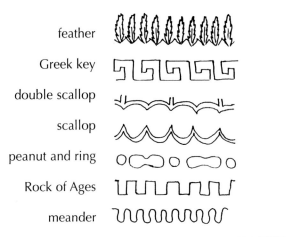

feather

Greek key

double scallop

scallop

peanut and ring

Rock of Ages

meander

Bottle kiln – early pottery oven with a tall narrow opening for escaping smoke

Broth bowl – caudle bowl, a two-handled cup often with a cover and under plate

Bubby-pot – see infant or invalid feeder, pap boat

Bull's eye – irreversible dark spot with a ring around it, caused by a break in the glaze which allowed stain to invade the clay body

bubby pot

Bun feet – little round knobs that support a server

Bun finial – little round knobs that serve as a handle on a teapot cover

Butter chip or pat – tiny dish to hold individual squares of butter, used in the late 19th century

Butter tub – open dish with two raised tabs equipped with holes for a wire bail, usually includes a perforated liner

Calcined – process of heating and then grinding an ingredient to powder; for example, flint

Cake stand – tall pedestalled plate with a wide, flat surface; also pie stand

Cameo – a human mask decoration used as a finial or handle decoration

Canteen – a water bottle used by campers or soldiers

Carafe – a bottom-heavy jar with matching tumbler used by the bed-side

Cartouche – an ornate decoration transferred to the underside of ceramics, often including both the name of the potter and the pattern

Chamber pot – the large one-handled vessel to match a toilet set in the pre-bathroom era

Charcoal dust – light black dust that was trapped under the glaze in the kiln, a potting flaw

cartouche

Charger – large, round platter

Cheese bell – a tall cylindrical shape with a top handle that rested on a large plate, with or without a short pedestal; used to serve a large, round cheese

Cheese cradle – a footed ceramic rack equipped with a curved area that could support a wheel of cheese; often used in taverns

Cheese drainer – a ceramic bowl with perforations to drain the whey from cottage cheese

Chestnut basket – an oval or rectangular reticulated bowl, often accompanied by a low matching tray - both used to serve hot chestnuts

Children's tea set – twenty-two miniature pieces composed of teapot, sugar bowl, cream jugs, six cups with saucers, six plates with a low matching bowl for dregs of tea

Chinamen – the English wholesaler who bid for and sold Oriental wares imported from China

Church spittoon – small one-handled ladies' or hand spittoon, said to have been carried under a cloak

Cinquefoil – a design of groups of five leaves gathered around a center, an often-used decoration

Cobalt – a source of a clear blue color used in flow blue wares, also used to make white appear whiter

Cockspur – spur or stilt, little ceramic pieces used to separate pieces in the kiln, employed in threes each leaving a mark under the glaze - an aid to dating

Coffee can – early coffee cup with no saucer, similar to current mugs

Concave – curving inward as in a thumbprint

Convex – curving outward as in a gadroon border

Copper lustre – an added metallic trim used extensively on white granite

Cornish clay – growan, a very desirable clay discovered near Cornwall

Crabstock – a method of decoration to make handles or finials look like twisted twigs or branches

crabstock

Crazing – checked glaze caused by poor potting or due to years of use

Cream Wares – (cc wares) early, inexpensive undecorated white wares sent to the Americas in the late 18th and early in the 19th century

Cross-hatched – checked ground pattern

Cuspidor – a spittoon, depository for juice from chewing tobacco

Decagon – ten-sided shape

Diamond-shaped registry – English mark used from 1842 to 1883 to patent and date ceramic shapes (see p. 15)

Dishes – generally refer to plates and platters over twelve inches in length

Donut stand – tazza, low pedestalled server for cookies or desserts

Ears or Lugs – side handles on tureens or sugar bowls

Edgings – see borders

English Arms – an often-used English pottery mark that included a lion, a unicorn and a quartered shield which may or may not be crowned. It was meant to verify English workmanship but American potters often appropriated variations of the coveted symbol (see p. 13)

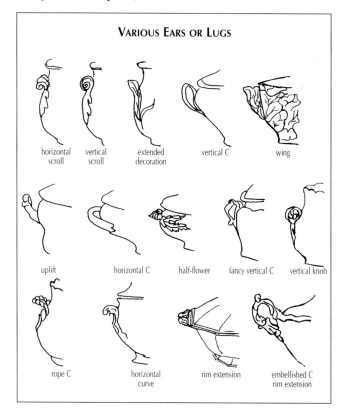

VARIOUS EARS OR LUGS

horizontal scroll, vertical scroll, extended decoration, vertical C, wing

uplift, horizontal C, half-flower, fancy vertical C, vertical knob

rope C, horizontal curve, rim extension, embellished C rim extension

Epergne – A pedestalled server with several plates, placed one above another and separated by vertical ceramic or metal pieces

Everted – turned outward as in the spout on a jug

Ewer – large jug, part of a toilet set

Felspar – a term sometimes included as part of a name for an ironstone body but, according to Godden, really refers to a fine porcelain body

VARIOUS FINIALS

spire, acorn, acorn, floral acorn, pagoda acorn

ring, rosebud, gooseberry, natural acorn, trumpet flower

split pod, split pod, knot, pine cone

gourd, ear of corn, fruit, fruit

eagle bar, dolphin bar, curved bar, bar

nut, nut, open flower, crabstock

Fictile – molded of earth, clay, or other soft material

Finial – top decoration or handle on a serving vessel

Flaw – a surface crack, stilt mark, little hole, or trapped charcoal dust that originated in the kiln, an irregularity due to the potting process

Fleur-de-lis – a stylized iris used in decorations

Flint – a massive hard quartz, calcined before being added to ceramic bodies

fleur-de-lis

Floral swag – flowers hanging in a curve between two points, festoon

Flow Blue – describes ceramic transfer wares decorated in cobalt blue ink, which has been caused to bleed or "flow" over the white granite body producing a blurred image after glazing

Fluting – vertical concave grooves as found on the outside of columns, the opposite of reeding

Foot bath – a large ceramic tub that sometimes was a part of a toilet set

Gadroon – opposite of a thumbprint, convex rather than concave

Garland – wreath or chaplet, a laurel headpiece awarded a victor

Glaze – the transparent, waterproof coating which is used to cover biscuit ware before the trip to the glost kiln

Glost kiln – the oven used to fire biscuit wares that have been dipped in glaze

Gravy or Sauceboat – a low, one-handled vessel with an open spout used to serve gravy or sauce; occasionally, can be fastened to a stand which would catch the drippings

Graybeard – a jug with a spout shaped like the bearded profile of an old man

Ground – an all-over repetitive design such as cross-hatching, brocade, seaweed, fishscale, or honeycomb

Growan – see Cornish clay

Handle tag – motif at lower terminal of a handle

Handles – handgrips on beverage servers

Hawthorn – a flowered woody branch often included in Oriental patterns

Hexagon – six-sided shape

Historic Staffordshire – cobalt blue transfer-decorated wares that depicted historic scenes from England or America, usually on ironstone bodies

---

VARIOUS HANDLES

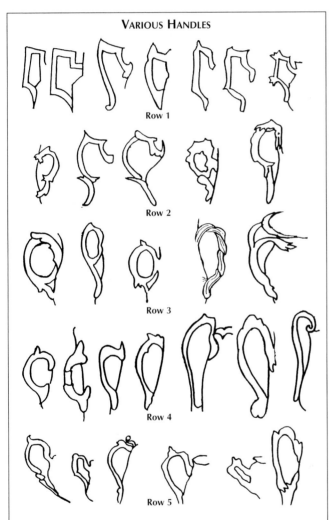

Row 1

Row 2

Row 3

Row 4

Row 5

Row 1:
Various bracket handles
from plain to embellished,
(left to right)

Row 2:
B handle
S handle
S handle
cockscomb
serpent or dragon
(left to right)

Row 3:
ring
ring
ring
crabstock
split handle

Row 4:
-various C handles from
 plain C to elongated C

Row 5:
-twisted C and various
 other C handles

Hot toddy bowl – a large, covered, round bowl with two side handles and a matching ladle used to serve hot beverages

Impressed mark – potter's mark made by pressing a metal die on the underside of clay shapes before firing

Incised mark – potter's mark scratched into the clay before the first firing, not a common practice on white ironstone

Intertwined – the winding together of two or more strands as with crabstock branches, ropes, or cables

Invalid feeder – see bubby-pot

Ironstone – name of a ceramic body made famous by Mason in 1813, a durable earthenware used widely in the 1800s

Japanized – Japonism, an influence on design during the 1870s and 1880s composed of prunus blossoms, bamboo and pine. Often included were round or small pictures of birds or boats, sashes of brocade, and Oriental touches. Nicknamed "Japanese Patchwork"

Jardiniere – tall, open vase for use in a wall niche or on a floor

Jug – Staffordshire name for a pitcher

Kiln – oven or furnace used in potting

Knob, Knop – finial, the terminal ornament on the top of a serving vessel

Married pieces – two pieces used together that were not originally sold together, such as covers with tureen bodies or cups with saucers

Lugs, Ears – side handles on a sugar bowl or tureen

Ladle – a deep-bowled, long-handled ceramic spoon used in soup tureens, stew tureens, sauce tureens, and punch or hot toddy bowls

Lobe – half-round ballooning protusion decorating the outside of a serving vessel

Mask jug – a pitcher whose pouring spout is shaped like the face of a person

Melon-ribbed – large ribs, small at the top and bottom, larger at the waist, used to form the outside of serving pieces

Mold – wooden or plaster of Paris form into which prepared clay is pressed to make a desired shape

Motif – usually a single design centered in copper lustre on plates and servers of white granite

Tea Leaf motif

Octagon – eight-sided shape

Ogee – pointed arch having on each side a reversed curve near the apex typical of the Sydenham shield

Overlay – a pattern added over a panelled or fluted background surface

Panelled – use of a flat, vertical surface

Pap boat – see bubby pot

Pearlware – name for a blue-white bodied earthenware, used by many firms in the 1800s

Pedestal – a wide foot with a narrow neck supporting a bowl or plate

Plateau Liner – underplate with a raised center surface that adds height to a tureen

Plate – usually refers to individual flat servers less than twelve inches in diameter

Plinth – a square block used as a pedestal base

Porcelain – a fine, hard, translucent ceramic ware; semi-porcelain is not transparent

Potting Flaws – ceramic irregularities that occur in the kiln; often do not effect value

Prunus – a re-occurring Japanese decoration of plum or peach blossoms

Printed Mark – a colored potter's mark applied under-glaze by a pottery firm

Pyriform – pear-shaped

Relish dishes – nappies, small servers in oval, round, or square shapes often with the appearance of shells or boats, used to serve pickles or preserves

Renaissance – a neo-movement in the 19th century that revived the classical influence

Reticulated – decorated with cut-out open areas on baskets or trays

Rim – top edge of a vessel

Rococo – style characterized by S and C scrolls, stylized foliage in scrollwork, fanciful curved spatial forms

Saggar, Sagger – a deep tray or box made of fire clay in which ceramic pieces are positioned for firing

Sauceboat – gravy boat

Sauce dish – individual, side dish used for serving fruit or dessert

Saucer – under plate for cup

Sauce tureen – four pieces comprised of a small tureen, underplate and ladle

Scoria – slag such as the refuse from reduction of ores

Seam Marks – traces visible where two parts of a mold were joined

Shards – relics of broken ceramic wares found by excavation at sites

Shaving mug – cup that is part of a toilet set

Shoulder – area between neck and waist of a pouring vessel

Slag – see scoria

Slip – clay moistened by water and used to fasten two parts of a molded piece

Slop bowl – waste bowl, round open bowl in a tea set, used to gather dregs of tea

Smalt – a deep blue pigment used as a ceramic color; fusing silica, potash, and oxide of cobalt and grinding to a powder

Soap box – a covered round, oval, or rectangular box usually equipped with a perforated basket-form liner

Soap slab – an open holder for soap, part of late 19th century toilet sets

Spittoon – see cuspidor

Spout – a long narrow pouring piece for tea- or coffeepots; an everted area on jugs allowing liquids to be poured

Staffordshire – area of famous English potteries located to the south and east of Liverpool

Stone China – a name often used for ironstone

Stylized – designed to conform to an art style rather than to nature

Supper set – a large round server that includes separate compartments for various foods

Surround – area between outer rim and well of a platter or plate

Sydenham shield – an 1850s design used by T. & R. Boote around edges of plates and bodies of servers, copied by many other potters

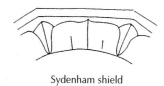
Sydenham shield

Tariff – a tax levied on imported goods to protect home industries

Tazza – low, footed compote often with handles

Tea sets – sets of ironstone that included teapot, covered sugar bowl, cream jug, slop bowl, six cups with saucers, six plates and sometimes handled biscuit or sandwich trays

Three friends – elements often used in Japonized designs: prunus, bamboo, and pine

Thresher's china – "farmer's china", a derogatory name sometimes used to describe white granite sets in the late 19th century

Thumbprints – series of concave areas used to decorate ironstone bodies

Transfer wares – ironstone bodies decorated by colored designs lifted by tissue paper from prepared copper plates and laid on biscuit ware before glazing

Tree trunk – surface of a body molded to resemble a tree trunk, usually in deep relief

Twiffler – an eight-inch plate

Unaker – Cherokee clay

Underplate – a stand or tray made to be used under a soup, sauce, or chowder tureen, occasionally under vertical brush-holders.

Vintage – relating to the vine, usually grape

Vitrify – make waterproof

Waist – largest diameter of a beverage server

Wall Fountain – an ironstone wall piece to hold water, often includes a half round basin at the bottom and shelves for toiletries

Waste Bowl – slop bowl from a tea set

Waste Pail or Jar – large, covered, handled vessel which is a part of a toilet set

Well – deep area inside the surround of a plate or platter

White Granite – English potters' term for white bodies shaped in ironstone

White Ironstone – collectors' term for white granite. I'm afraid it's here to stay. ✽

Pioneers in White

Nothing follows in history more surely after love of colour than colour weariness and a tendency to renunciation of colour.
- Hannover

The nineteenth century has been called the age of imitations and fads. Some students of design say that, during those years, some old styles found renewed attention. They identify a neo-classic trend with the use of fleur-de-lis, the acanthus decoration, fluted surfaces, garlands and classical borders. Neo-baroque treatment with excessive coverage as in tree trunk bodies, crabstock handles, cherubs, and graybeards is noted on jugs; neo-rococo decorations with much swirling scrollwork is found on white ironstone shapes such as *New York Shape, Napier Shape,* and *Hill Shape.* We too can see ogee lines, arcaded surfaces, Gothic arches—all lines used earlier in historical design.

Nevertheless, more potting improvements were made and more ceramic ideas were introduced in the first half of that 19th century than had ever occurred in the past. During the following years, the Staffordshire potters were desirous of preserving their American markets and were alert to any method, idea, or decoration that might help to sell their products. Borrowing ideas from the past as well as creating new forms ensured variety in the marketplace.

Thousands of sets of colored transfer ironstone dishes manufactured in English potteries and shipped across the Atlantic early in the century had appealed to American buyers. These wares were durable, attractive, and inexpensive—just what the local market desired.

When did the idea of all-white tableware originate? Why was the change made? Perhaps, the American housewives did become "color weary"; perhaps they were ready for a change.

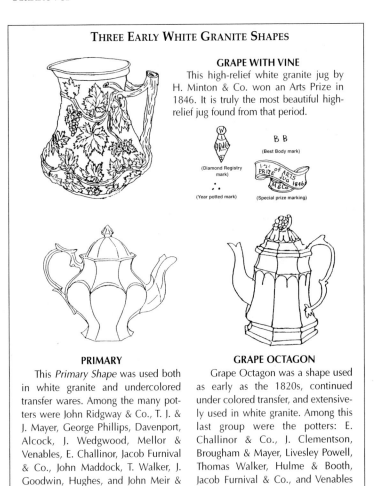

THREE EARLY WHITE GRANITE SHAPES

GRAPE WITH VINE
This high-relief white granite jug by H. Minton & Co. won an Arts Prize in 1846. It is truly the most beautiful high-relief jug found from that period.

(Diamond Registry mark)

(Year potted mark)

B B
(Best Body mark)

(Special prize marking)

PRIMARY
This *Primary Shape* was used both in white granite and undercolored transfer wares. Among the many potters were John Ridgway & Co., T. J. & J. Mayer, George Phillips, Davenport, Alcock, J. Wedgwood, Mellor & Venables, E. Challinor, Jacob Furnival & Co., John Maddock, T. Walker, J. Goodwin, Hughes, and John Meir & Sons.

GRAPE OCTAGON
Grape Octagon was a shape used as early as the 1820s, continued under colored transfer, and extensively used in white granite. Among this last group were the potters: E. Challinor & Co., J. Clementson, Brougham & Mayer, Livesley Powell, Thomas Walker, Hulme & Booth, Jacob Furnival & Co., and Venables Mann & Co. (also see page 103).

I have shown in Chapter 2 two unusual pieces of marked "Mason's Patent Ironstone China" produced in white. On the whole, however, very little white granite was manufactured by this firm. I do remember locating a stack of twelve dessert dishes with scalloped edges—marked with the early blue Mason mark.

Perhaps, the two examples illustrated portray some of the earliest white ironstone made in England.

WHITE IRONSTONE JUGS - IN HEXAGON SHAPES

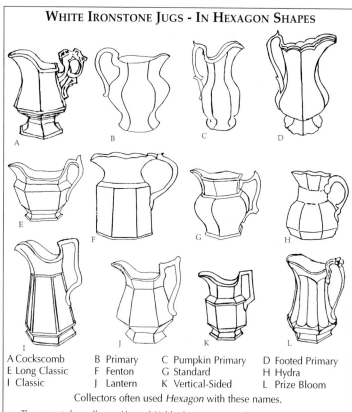

A Cockscomb	B Primary	C Pumpkin Primary	D Footed Primary
E Long Classic	F Fenton	G Standard	H Hydra
I Classic	J Lantern	K Vertical-Sided	L Prize Bloom

Collectors often used *Hexagon* with these names.

The present-day collector, Howard Noble, has spent many hours researching the early hexagonal shapes. He was able to gather many examples of those early six-sided jugs potted in the 1840s. His discoveries are shown above.

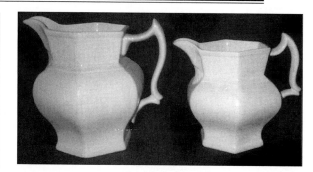

Fig. 7-1   Here are two examples of early 1840's hexagonal shapes represented by two jugs by John Ridgway & Co.

Fig 7-2   Two more hexagon shapes, *Framed Classic* by James Edwards to the left and *Footed Primary* by Frances Morley to the right, were posed by Howard Noble.

Fig. 7-3   These *Standard Hexagon* covered servers were each made by a different potter in the 1840s. Many potters of that era made similar non-covered jugs. Courtesy of Howard Noble.

Fig. 7-4   The added word "Montpelier" at the top of the Ridgway wreath mark prompts us to name this shape *Montpelier Hexagon*. Dan Overmeyer Collection.
←

Fig. 7-5   This *Pumpkin Primary Hexagon* ewer was located by Howard Noble.
→

EARLY IRONSTONE GOTHIC SHAPES

Almost every ironstone potter of the 1840s and early 1850s produced the shape we call *Classic Gothic*. Illustrated here are only a few of the Gothic variations of that era.

In the top row are a sugar bowl by Davenport, a teapot by Ridgway, and mitten-form relish in the *Classic Gothic* shape.

The center row has a *Full-Panelled Gothic* pitcher on the left, a *Gothic Rose* footed tureen, produced by C. Meigh & Son, is in the center, and a *Vertical-Sided Gothic* teapot on the right.

A *Curved Gothic* shape platter by J. Edwards is on the left in the bottom row.

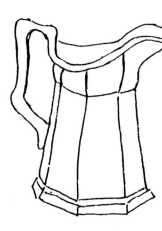

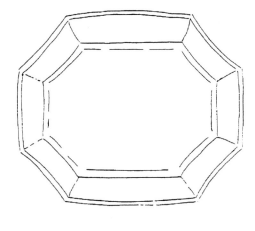

Gothic Design Details

Bordered Gothic was a shape used by T.Walker, John Alcock, Davenport, Samuel Alcock, and other potters. A border detail is shown on the left as well as the bar handle with parallel leaves used as a finial on Davenport's *Bordered Gothic*. The finial and lid on the right was used by Francis Morley on his *Classic Gothic*.

GOTHIC DESIGN TEAPOTS

Fig. 7-6 An unusually broad *Pedestalled Gothic* unmarked teapot has a pedestal base, a bracket handle, and an acorn finial. ⬅

Fig. 7-7 Closely related but shaped by two different potters: shorter teapot by Samuel Alcock and taller 12 1/2" coffeepot by C. & W. K. Harvey. Dan Overmeyer owns this *lassic Gothic* pair. ⬇

Fig. 7-8 A related shape, *Vertical-Sided Gothic* (above left), is another variation of the early *Classic Gothic* shape. Owned by the Nobles.

Fig. 7-9 This covered server (above right, center) has *Full-Panelled Gothic* lines with leaves added under the spout. The *Pedestalled Gothic* sugar and creamer balance each side. Note the same flowered acorn finial on both shapes. These are examples of shapes made by James Edwards.

Fig. 7-10 This 8¼" *Pinch-neck Gothic* teapot has full-panelled sloping sides. The collector is Dan Overmeyer. ➡

MORE INTERESTING GOTHIC SHAPES

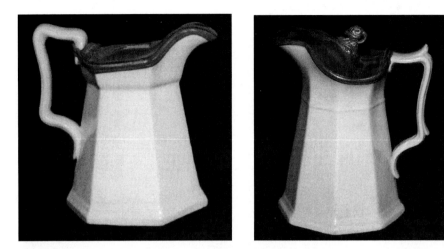

Fig. 7-11 Above at the left is a rare six-sided pewter-lidded *Full-Panelled Hexagon* syrup server. Compare this piece to the hard-to-find much larger 8¼" tall pewter-lidded table pitcher on the right. This *Full-Panelled Gothic* pitcher is unmarked. Owned by Dan Overmeyer.

Fig. 7-12 An unusually large finial leans on the cover of this hot beverage server in *Classic Gothic*, potted by C. & W.K. Harvey. Photo furnished by Dan Overmeyer.

Fig. 7-13 Jacob Furnival produced this *Gothic Grape* covered butter dish in the mid-19th century. Owned by Dan Overmeyer.
←

Fig. 7-14 Rarely we see pieces of *Boote's Gothic*. The plates are sided with little walls around the outer edge. The mark is an impressed rectangle with the words "Porcelain Opaque." This tall pitcher is owned by Ray Secrist.
→

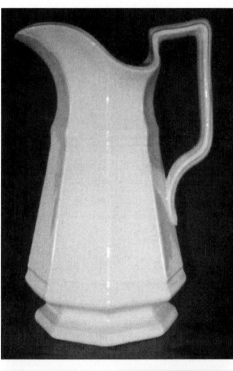

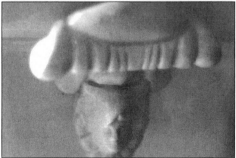

Fig. 7-15 Several potters made this shape, *Gothic Cameo:* J. Wedgwood, Davenport, John Alcock, and James Edwards. Note the cameo face detail above. This open compote is owned by the Nobles.

Fig. 7-16 This huge master waste jar in *Classic Gothic* was potted by Jacob Furnival and the horizontal toothbrush holder was shaped by James Edwards. Owned by the Dieringers.

Fig. 7-17 Davenport's *Bordered Gothic* chamber pot sits with the rare James Edwards' carafe in *Classic Gothic*. We'd all like to own both pieces. Collection of James and Doris Walker.

James Edwards - White Ironstone Pioneer

Let's pause to consider another pioneering potting family, the Edwards. Their potting story began when a Nova Scotian named Cunard contracted to provide a mail service from Liverpool to Halifax to Boston. Four ships regularly carried mail, crossing the Atlantic ocean in a little more than twelve days to Halifax, landing in Boston two days later. The first trip was completed in July of 1840, and citizens on both sides of the ocean became excited.

An alert pair of British brothers saw in this achievement an opportunity for ceramic enterprise. On Sept. 2, 1841, James and Thomas Edwards of the Kiln Croft Works, Burslem registered a new design to celebrate the event. The one-color transfer designs in light blue, lavender, or black showed medallions depicting the four Cunard ships around the border and included interior scenes inside the plate well. The sets were called "Boston Mails" or "Royal Mails" depending on the nationality of the speaker. There was much more white area than usual on each piece. Consumers eagerly bought the new pattern.

One of those brothers, James Edwards, was to become the pioneer for a new, ceramic style: all-white, carefully shaped, beautifully glazed tableware.

James Edwards had prepared himself well to become a master potter: he had been a thrower at the Dale Hall Pottery belonging to the Rogers' Brothers; he had used his managerial skills for both Phillips and

John Alcock; he had been a partner to John Maddock and later with his brother in Burslem. We would agree that he had done his "undergraduate" work well. In 1842, he launched out on his own, when he purchased the Dale Hall Pottery from the Rogers family.

Jewitt says of this potter, "James Edwards was an entirely self-made man, and was one of those bright examples of indomitable perseverance, unflinching rectitude, steadiness of purpose, and genuine benevolence, which crop up every now and then among our most successful manufacturers." He adds a remark that should be of great interest to collectors of white ironstone:

> *"To him (Edwards) his white granite ware which had become so important a feature in the Pottery district mainly owes its excellence, that made by him being considered to be all that could be desired by our transatlantic brethren, and to be the standard of perfection to which the aims of other houses were directed."*

Hughes contributes more information, telling us that James Edwards in 1842 installed modern appliances in his factory, thereby causing a sixfold increase of production without enlarging the premises.

We do locate a few creamy pieces of white granite with fluted shapes, marked by T. Edwards. On April 3, 1844, Thomas Edwards did register six shapes but we do not know if they were made of white granite. Still, it is the relics marked "J. Edwards, Dalehall" (not to be confused with J. Edwards who was John Edwards of Fenton) that tell us the story of early white ironstone production. He innovated with many new shapes and set the standard for sharp details of design, pleasing lines, and excellent bond between body and glaze that would not craze through years of use. On the following pages we will be illustrating a wide variety of collectible James Edwards ironstone body styles.

JAMES EDWARDS BODY SHAPES

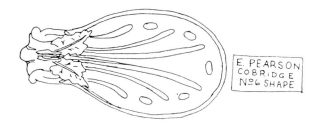

James Edwards (Dale Hall Pottery) designed the *Ball and Stick* shape in the 1840s. He produced the teapot on the left, but the E. Pearson relish (right) looks related.

Fig. 7-18 James Edwards used this *Crabstock Dozen* shape to fashion a dessert set with compotes, relish dishes, tea plates, etc., each having crabstock handles and a dozen divisions.

Fig. 7-19 This beautiful large tureen shaped by James Edwards is called *Fluted Gothic*. It includes sharp "cookie-cutter" corners. Owned by Howard and Dottie Noble.

Fig. 7-20 *Flowered Hexagon* (left), an Edwards creation, was patented the same day as *Twin Leaves Hexagon* (right), Aug. 29, 1851. Note the similarity. The *Flowered Hexagon* Sugar Bowl is owned by the Nobles. The *Twin Leaves Hexagon* teapot is owned by Nancy Upchurch. A heavy octagonal tureen with a crabstock bar finial has also been reported in this shape.

Fig. 7-21   This *Fluted Panels* piece, a punch bowl, is flanked by eight *Classic Gothic* punch cups.

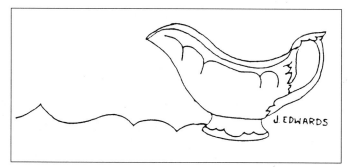

James Edwards and G. Wooliscroft both used this shape, *Line Trim*. The border motif and a sketch of a gravy boat by James Edwards are shown.

Fig. 7-22   We often find James Edwards' pieces in *Fluted Panels* as in the foot bath above. The three-piece soap box was made by John Edwards of Fenton in the *President Shape.*

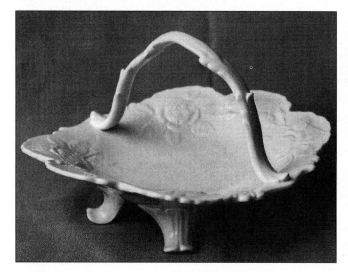

Fig. 7-23   Fortunate indeed are those collectors who treasure their *Open Roses* china basket by James Edwards.

Fig. 7-24   These two excellent James Edwards pieces are a *Rolling Star* platter joined by a *Sqaure Rosebud* gravy boat.

EDWARDS' SPLIT POD PATTERN

Fig. 7-25 Decorative foilage also adorns this graceful *Split Pod* sauce tureen with matching tray. The Nobles own this set.

Fig. 7-26 This ewer with alternate concave and convex panels, made by James Edwards, is part of a *Split Pod* toilet set. From Anne's Antiques.

EDWARDS' "SQUARE" PATTERNS

Fig. 7-27 This *Square Rosebud* soup tureen by James Edwards has a square shape with "chopped off" corners. It was registered on Dec. 16, 1848 and has a rosebud finial. Collection of the Dieringers.

Fig. 7-28 This *Square Open Flower* teapot is the same basic shape as *Square Rosebud* and was also registered by Edwards on Dec. 16, 1848. James used this finial on other shapes. Photo sent by Dan Overmeyer.

Fig. 7-29 The third least-known square shape, *Square Tumbling Petals* was also registered on Dec. 16, 1848. It has an acorn finial with an eight-petalled flower that is stylized. Those same petals seem to tumble under the side ears, also in a balanced stylized design. Finial and handle details are illustrated above.

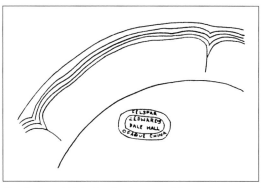

Fig. 7-30   *Triple Border*, impressed James Edwards of Dalehall, has the well known three-lined border around the rim and the foot of this large oval compote. The curled ears are formed by grape clusters. Collection of Ed Rigoulot and Ted Brockey.

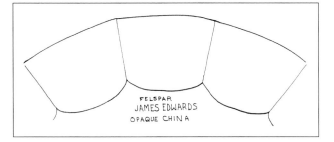

The lines used on *True Scallop* plates were employed by James Edwards, E. & C. Challinor, John Alcock and other potters. Here is a detail of a plate rim.

Fig. 7-31   The *Wild Rose Twig* shape was first used by James Edwards, later by C. Meigh and Son. Illustrated is a handsome covered tureen. ➡

Fig. 7-32   This surface of *Edwards Leaf* tazza is completely covered with veins and dappled background. Relish dishes and cookie plates have also been found in this shape. Several American potters copied this design.

Fig. 7-33   Another small pedestalled server with double border and ruffled edge is pictured above. Also by Edwards.

John Ridgway
Another White Ironstone Pioneer

John Ridgway & Co. marked many of their early white granite shapes "Porcelain a la Francaise" and sometimes added the word "Montpelier" within the top of the garter circle. Since this last term has been discovered on at least six or seven known shapes, can we assume that 'Montpelier' related somehow to the recipe for the clay body?

In September of 1844, Ridgway patented a *Hexagonal Primary* shape that boasts a crown finial and includes a scrolled arch across each panel. The horizontal ears cling to the waists of the tureens. The soup tureen rests on a plain hexagonal underplate.

Four years later, Ridgway & Co. registered another hexagonal shape in September of 1848. The word "Montpelier" was included in this mark so we nickname it *Montpelier Hexagon*. The final and side handles are both ring-handled trimmed with foliage and a ribbon nearby.

Featured here are photographs of two early Ridgway jugs that both include "Montpelier" in the mark. We call the one on the left *Montpelier Graybeard* and the one on the right *Montpelier Gothic*.

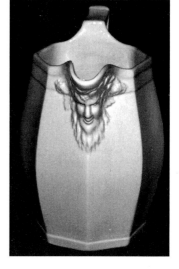

Fig. 7-34 These beautiful covered *Primary Hexagon* pieces are owned by the Morelands. In the upper right corner is a sketched detail of the ornate finial.

Fig. 7-35 This *Montpelier Graybeard* jug by John Ridgway & Co. belongs to Dan Overmeyer. It was probably not part of a dinner set.

Fig. 7-36 The Morelands also own these lovely *Montpelier Hexagon* pieces. Again, in the upper right is a sketched detail of the wreath finial.

Fig. 7-37 John Ridgway also had to get on the Gothic bandwagon. We call this *Montpelier Gothic* from the Moreland Collection.

Other Early White Ironstone Makers

The Mayers

Messrs. Thomas, John, and Joshua Mayer, according to Jewell, were exceedingly clever potters. He reports that the dinner plates, dishes, etc. of the Mayer Brothers "were characterized by an excellent 'fit' in nesting, lightness of body and neatness of finish." The photographs below seem to strengthen that observation concerning *Mayer's Classic Gothic* shape. Note the details of the mark, the lug handle, the crown finial and the copy of the 1847 registration—all provided by the Dieringers.

Fig. 7-38 A close-up photograph of the beautiful handle details found on *Mayer's Classic Gothic.*

Fig. 7-39 Typical printed markings found on *Mayer's Classic Gothic* pieces.

Fig. 7-40 The incredible crown finial found on pieces of *Mayer's Classic Gothic.*

Fig. 7-41 Here poses T. J. & J. Mayer's incredible contribution to the early Gothic shape. It is remembered as *Mayer's Classic Gothic* and is gathered by the Dieringers.

More Mayer Patterns

BERLIN SWIRL

A *Berlin Swirl* soup tureen by the Mayer Bros. was registered in 1845. Mayer & Elliott, their successors, patented this shape again in 1856. A small plate with the impressed potting year, 1864, was made by the next successor, Liddle, Elliott & Son. This swirl was popular for a lot of years, wasn't it? A sketch of the undertray for the tureen is at the left. An early mark is shown above.

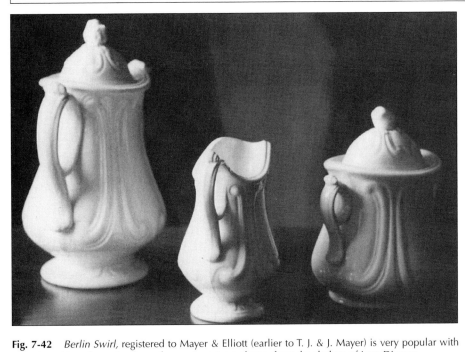

Fig. 7-43 This *Berlin Swirl* vertical toothbrush holder (lacking base plate) belongs to Dan Overmeyer.

Fig. 7-42 *Berlin Swirl,* registered to Mayer & Elliott (earlier to T. J. & J. Mayer) is very popular with collectors. Here the main pieces from a tea set are shown from the shelves of Jane Diemer.

Fig. 7-44 T. J. & J. Mayer formed this early *Curved Gothic* epergne that is not easy to locate. The Blacks shared the picture.
←

Fig. 7-45 The shape of this *Berlin Inverted Diamond* teapot manufactured by T. J. & J. Mayer, was used by several early potters of flow blue and other one-color transfer wares. Photo contributed by Dan Overmeyer.
→

John Wedge Wood
& Other Early Potters

John Wedge Wood (who marked his pieces J. Wedgwood) created at least three unusual fluted shapes in the 1840s. The surround of plates was composed of a series of concave flutes.

Here we also include a few early unknown shapes contributed by collectors.

Below is a partial list of known 1840s manufacturers of white ironstone

J. & S. Alcock Jr.
Samuel Alcock
Edward Challinor
Davenport
James Edwards
*Jacob Furnival & Co.

I. (John) Goodwin
C. & W. K. Harvey
Joseph Heath
*John Maddock
C. J. Mason & Co.
T. J. & J. Mayer
I. (John) Meir
Mellor, Venables & Co.
Minton
Francis Morley
John Ridgway & Co.
Edward Walley
John Wedge Wood

*Since John Maddock (1842-55) Jacob Furnival & Co. (1845-70) and Edward Walley (1845-56)gave no information about dates in their marks, we are unsure which, or if any, of their white ironstone pieces were potted in the 40s.

John Wedge Wood (J. Wedgwood) Patterns

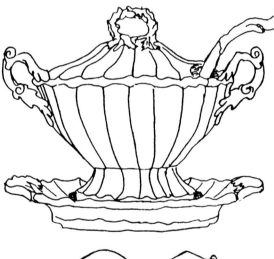

Fig. 7-46 Still working with fluted decorations, J. Wedgwood used full panels, a ring handle, and a neck band on this *Fluted Band* teapot, owned by the Morelands.

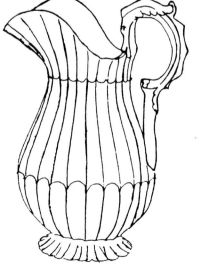

J. Wedgwood's *Coral Shape* used a crabstock finial and "C" handles on the soup tureen (top). A sea horse handle grasps the ewer (bottom) and causes us to use a sea-side nickname.

Fig. 7-47 This *Fluted Band* ewer has a bracket handle (unlike the teapot) but the same full fluted panels and a neck band as the teapot. Collection of Ed Rigoulot and Ted Brockey.

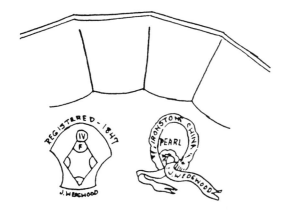

FLUTED PEARL BY JOHN WEDGE WOOD

Thomas Edwards was the first maker to register the *Fluted Pearl* shape, but John Wedge Wood registered this *Fluted Pearl* shape in 1847. The fluted border (left) may have been used with other fluted shapes. Typical markings found on pieces are also shown.

Fig. 7-48 This large *Fluted Pearl* vegetable tureen (top left) has concave fluting inside the bowl with a crabstock bar handle on top.

Fig. 7-49 The *Fluted Pearl* teapot and sugar bowl (top right) boast bracket handles, a wide fluted body, narrow neck, and a leaning six petalled flower as a finial. Pieces belong to Doris and Jim Walker.

Shapes by Other Makers

Handle detail on soup tureen

Fig. 7-50 Francis Morley marked this *Early Swirl* soup tureen with a printed date of May 21, 1845, as well as the usual registration diamond. Information from Anne's Antiques.

This round mark double dates the Frances Morley *Early Swirl* soup tureen shown here to the 1840s. It is an unusual shape.

Fig. 7-52 This leaf-shaped relish dish by T. J. & J. Mayer looks related to *Berlin Swirl* but collectors report another relish for that shape. I wonder?

Fig. 7-51 This reticulated fruit bowl, *Pierced Scroll* marked "John & Samuel Alcock, Jr.," was potted in the 1848-50 period.

Fig. 7-53 Another early 11 1/2" coffee pot photo that includes an "S" handle, broad top trim, broad waist, and graceful spout. Unmarked. Also from the collection of Dan Overmeyer.

Fig. 7-54 Neither the maker's name or the date is legible on this early broad-based teapot with overlapping cover and a "C" handle. Dan Overmeyer owns it.

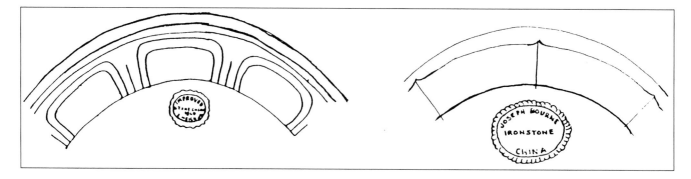

Two early unnamed shapes contributed by collectors. The design on the left was made by C. Meigh & Co.; the one on the right by Joseph Bourne.

A Selection of Early Leaf-Shaped Dishes

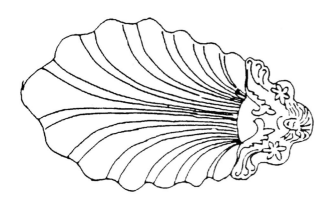

Gothic Cameo. Note the molded "cameo" face on the handle. This shape was made by both J. Wedgwood and Davenport. The example shown carries a J. Wedgwood banner mark.

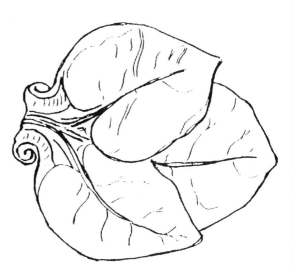

Pond Lily Pad. Three broad leaves compose this dish produced by James Edwards.

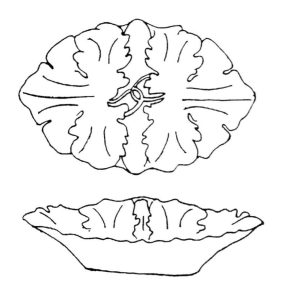

Double Leaf. A pair of huge leaves form this dish made by both James Edwards and Barrow & Co. The example shown carries the mark of "James Edwards - Dalehall," ca. 1848. A top and side view are shown above.

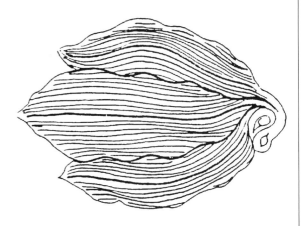

Husk. A group of corn husks form this dish marked "Jas. Edwards & Sons - Dalehall."

The Great Exhibition of 1851, held in London's Hyde Park, had sixty-two exhibitors of china, porcelain, and earthenware. Most displays featured wares that were colorful, beautifully decorated, and lavishly gilded. In a contemporary essay describing the exhibition, R.N. Wornun wrote that "profusion of ornament is the rule."

Jewitt reports that James Edwards received a medal in 1851 "with an additional certificate of merit for beauty of form and excellence of goods exhibited. John Ridgway, a Staffordshire potter, received an award and was praised for the "simplicity of the decoration." The 1851 *Art Journal* felt that the Ridgway exhibit was a refreshing novelty "amidst the jungle of riotous ornamentation."

Today, we find examples of white ironstone potted by T. J. & J. Mayer that includes a backstamp proclaim-ing "1851 Prize Medal." Consequently we have included the word "prize" in some of the nicknames for later Mayer shapes of the 1850's.

Thomas Till & Son exhibited two pattern shapes, one called *Albany* and the other *Virginia*. Godden says that his research reveals that both of the above shapes were available in "White Granite" or "Pearl White Granite", however, no American collector has reported the finding of either shape by Till.

At that same great fair, Charles James Mason exhibited some examples of "White Patent Ironstone, as used in the hotels of the United States of America."

As you can tell, the age of white granite popularity was in full swing on this side of the ocean.▨

Mid-Century Craze For White

By the middle of the nineteenth century, another potting firm from the Staffordshire area concentrated on the American markets, probably shipping more tons of white granite across the Atlantic than had ever before been traded.

The Bootes & Their Patterns

Thomas and Richard Boote, who had purchased the Waterloo Potteries from Thomas Edwards in 1850, may have had contact with the creative Edwards' products and observed the successful marketing of the Mayer Bros., John Ridgway & Co., and other potteries. The Bootes were good businessmen willing to adapt and they began producing enormous sets of white ironstone dishes, hoping to capture the American custom.

Jewitt describes in detail the lavishly decorated jugs, the expert Parian wares, and the groups of figures shaped in ceramic statuary—all expertly done by this company. He lauds some of the very inventive methods the Bootes employed to make unusual effects on the decorative wares. But nowhere does he mention that this company took over the lead in white granite production during the 1850s. These white wares appear not to have been offered to the home markets and to-day English ceramics experts seem to verify this, being unable to locate white granite relics in their country.

Jewitt did discuss the Bootes as being "patentees for a process…by means of one press alone, as many as 100 dozen plates or small dishes could be made in one day."

Let's study the list of patented ceramics and their patentees between the years of 1842 and 1883. The list reveals that T. & R. Boote, working from an earlier location, joined with Walley to patent two shapes in 1845. We have no clue or relic to indicate whether or not these shapes were made of white granite.

Fortunately for collectors, that same list allows us to date the Boote shapes created in the 1850s—most are clearly marked with an impressed date of registry

and most include a shape name. Their *Boote 1851 Octagon* registrations were recorded in July, September and October of that year. It was a beautiful clean-lined shape that must have been produced in quantity, perhaps over a period of years, because collectors locate a diversity of pieces. In 1853 and 1854, the Bootes perfected their famous *Sydenham Shape* which was an immediate success with American customers. Three or four patent dates have been copied from the undersides of pieces, recording changes or improvements of the design. I generalize that these two shapes with their sharp details, graceful potting and gleaming glazes dominated the mid-century North American ceramic markets. Almost immediately, other Staffordshire potters adapted the Sydenham shield (with small variations) to grace their white granite tableware.

Just why the name *Sydenham* was used for this famous shape is not known. We read that Joseph Clementson marked a blue transfer pattern *Sydenham* before white granite became popular. The famous "Crystal Palace" where the Great Exhibition of 1851 was held was moved to Sydenham from the Hyde Park location. It was greatly used for recreation, shows, etc., up to the 1930s when it was destroyed by fire. At any rate, white ironstone collectors love the name Sydenham.

Other Boote shapes made in that decade include *Union Shape, Atlantic Shape, Chinese Shape* and *Garibaldi Shape*. A *Classic Gothic* shape was also made but not dated. The *Grenade Shape* also seems to echo that good potting of the '50s but it was not patented. Though historians make no mention of these unusual Boote productions, collectors need only handle the early Boote pieces to acknowledge that this pottery perfected a body and glaze that were so compatible that their ceramic wares found today are still in a gleaming, uncrazed condition.

Another source adds to our information. Elizabeth Collard in her account of *Nineteenth-Century Pottery and Porcelain in Canada* quotes from the advertisement from

Boote 1851 Octagon

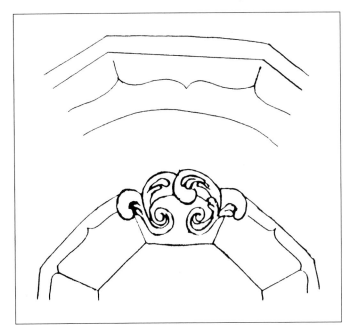

Above note the inward facing ogee lines of this *1851 Octagon* shape as used on plates, both panelled and round. Sometimes the shield turned outward as in the undertray edge beneath the plate surround.

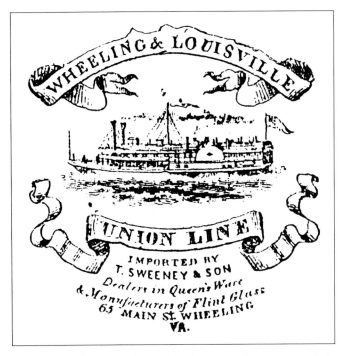

Here is a very elaborate mark found on the bottom of a rectangular *Boote 1851 Octagon* platter from a set ordered for use on steamboats that plied the Ohio River between Wheeling, Virginia and Louisville, Kentucky.

Sydenham Shape

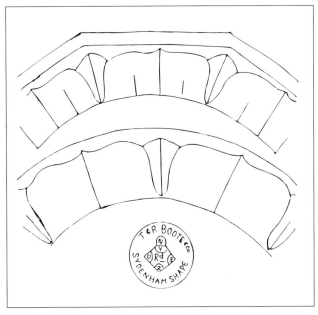

Above are illustrated the two versions of the *Sydenham Shape* plate rim. Above is the decagon-shaped rim with ten shields while the round (less collectible) version below used the motif eight times around the rim.

Here are details of the cover to the rarer oval-shaped tureens above the cover to the tulip-shaped round tureens. At the bottom are the detailed lines of the ladle handle.

Fig. 8-1   Except for a shaving mug, the *Boote 1851 Octagon* toilet set is gathered for its portrait in the Allers' home.

an 1861 trade sale from a Montreal auctioneer: "Boote's White Granite Earthenware, by the *Lady Eyre,* from Liverpool...we have a consignment of 55 crates of the above Celebrated Ware to be sold at auction."

These must have been sets unloaded from that ship—sets we would long to purchase today —all those fabulous shapes of the 50s made by master potters. *Boote 1851 Octagon, Sydenham, Atlantic, Union, Chinese* —were they packed in those 55 crates? Both United States and Canada must have purchased hundreds of those dinner, tea, and toilet sets that traveled in bulk from Liverpool to Quebec, Halifax, Boston, New York, or Philadelphia.

Collard mentions the "celebrated" Boote wares as including popular fancy white stoneware jugs with biblical figures in relief. These graced Canadian homes.

One of the photographs in her book depicts a round *Sydenham Shape* dinner plate with a printed wreath inside the well surrounding the name of a Hamilton Methodist Church. This reminds us that T. & R. Boote probably filled custom orders for hotels, churches, organizations and steamship lines.

The poet James Torrington Spencer, describing a tour of the Staffordshire potteries in the 1860s, inspected the factory of T. & R. Boote in Burslem and talked of their "Granite or Opaque Porcelain, Otherwise Iron-Stone China." Other references by ceramics historians prove that many names for this stoneware were interchanged, even as they were being manufactured.

The Bootes did not join in the production of white ironstone with grain, vintage, floral, or the foliated decorations of the 1860s. We see only *Winding Vine* and *Mocho,* not outstanding designs, but still enhancing uncrazed bodies. We notice half a dozen Boote patents in the 1860s but haven't found those relics in white granite—yet.

Near the end of the '60s, this pottery produced a white *Classic Shape* and a *Senate Shape,* both in plain round shapes, graceful and collectible today.

Writing in the 1870s Jewitt says that "all of these decorative classes of goods have been discontinued by Messrs. Boote, who now confine themselves to the ordinary white granite ware for the American market and the production of glazed and unglazed tiles." None of this related to the early Boote white ironstone. Boote white ironstone wares made during the last quarter of the century were similar to those shapes discussed in a later chapter of this book, "Styles of the Seventies and Eighties."

Later marks of T. & R. Boote usually included the words "Royal Patent Ironstone," "Royal Premium Ironstone" or "Royal Premium Semi-porcelain." The most common were the couchant greyhound or a crowned shield.

The following pages reveal drawings and photographs of *Boote 1851 Octagon, Sydenham Shape,* the *Sydenham* imitators, and a few other potters of the early 1850s. ▨

Notable Pieces of Boote 1851 Octagon

Fig. 8-2 This rare low stew tureen included a ladle but no undertray. Dieringer Collection.

Fig. 8-3 This pedestalled Boote fruit bowl is coveted by collectors. The same sized compote has been found with a rim for a cover. For what purpose could that have been used?

Fig. 8-4 A shell-shaped master server and four individual servers (relish dishes) were registered as parts of *Boote 1851 Octagon* sets.

Fig. 8-5 A desirable pair, the larger a covered hot cake server and the smaller a covered butter dish, pose together.

Fig. 8-6 This popular ring-handled teapot is owned by many collectors but the coffeepot is rarely found. The coffeepot (missing a lid) is from the collection of Ed Rigoulot and Ted Brockey.

Fig. 8-7 This very rare covered beverage server, part of a Boote set, is owned by the Yungingers.

The Sydenham Shape - Choice Examples

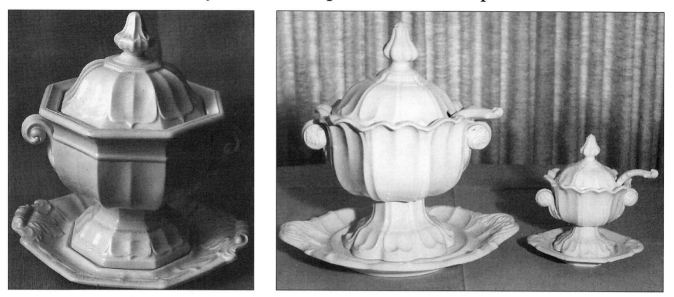

Fig. 8-8 These two photos offer a clear contrast between the *Boote 1851 Octagon* shape and the *Sydenham Shape*. The *Boote 1851 Octagon* tureen in the lefthand photo was made in several sizes, all of which included ladles. The two *Sydenham* tureens on the right highlight the tulip-like lines so popular with collectors. Again, these tureens were made in several sizes and we show a giant version beside a smaller sauce tureen, both from the Black Collection.

Fig. 8-9 This rarer oval shaped *Sydenham* soup tureen comes in several sizes.

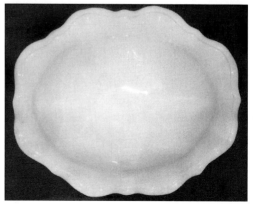

Fig. 8-10a & b This *Sydenham* oval compote is 11 1/2" long, 9" wide and a little over 7" tall. Also shown is the top view. Fortunate owner is Dan Overmeyer.

Fig. 8-11 My favorite *Sydenham* piece, this large oval covered vegetable dish has a leaning artichoke finial with surrounding molded leaves. I saw it in a country inn in the Mohawk Valley of New York State.

Fig. 8-12 The Lautenschlagers garnered these *Sydenham* cup from northeastern U.S. shops: (top) punch cups and three sizes of mugs and (bottom) handleless tea and coffee cups, handled tea and coffee cups, and the precious miniature and saucer. Now, where in the world is the rest of the children's set?

Fig. 8-13 We include in this gallery a tiny jug (less than five inches tall) that is equipped with a six-holed strainer. What do you think could have been its use? The Armbrusters own it.

Fig. 8-14 Dan Overmeyer compares two *Sydenham* beverage pots: the smaller is 9 3/4" in height and the larger one 10 1/4" tall.

Fig. 8-15 This line-up includes *Sydenham* handleless tea and coffee cups to the left, a waste bowl with extra flare at the top, and three handy-sized bowls. All collected by the Lautenschlagers.

Fig. 8-16 Notice the *Sydenham* shield rising up from the base of this sugar bowl and creamer. The ten-sided dinner plates are in great demand; round ones are less expensive.

Fig 8-17 *Sydenham Shape* also included nests of open servers in round, long octagon, and panel-sided shapes. Pieces are hard to find, therefore expensive. Here is a panel-sided example

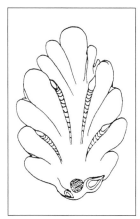

Fig. 8-18 Relish dishes related to the *Sydenham* relish: top left, Boote's *Sydenham* bottom left, *Columbia*; right, *Sydenham* by Clementson.

Boote's *Sydenham* relish dish

Fig. 8-19 This "seen-once" biscuit tray, marked *Sydenham Shape,* is treasured by the Kerrs.

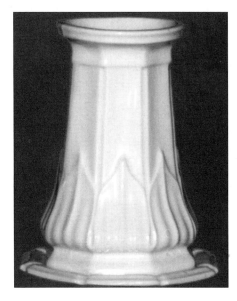

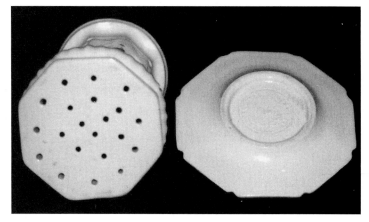

Fig. 8-20 Rare is this upright toothbrush holder — so rare that Jill O'Hara owns the underplate that traveled to Ohio so that Dan Overmeyer could photograph it with its top.

Sydenham Imitators

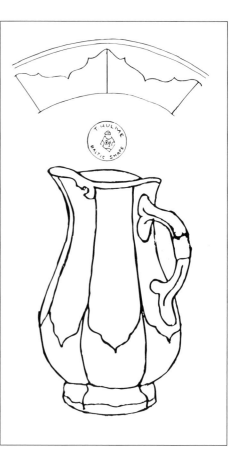

Fig. 8-21 - BALTIC SHAPE - T. Hulme, J. Meir, G. Bowers and G. Wooliscroft marked pieces *Baltic Shape*. J. Meir and Wooliscroft marked the same diamond-shaped registration information on pieces. The rounded jug with hanging shields, seen in the sketch, was also labeled *Baltic Shape*. The three pieces shown in the above photograph are an 11¼" h. ewer, a three-piece soap box with basket-style liner and an octagonal vegetable tureen. The two outer pieces are marked by G. Wooliscroft and the soap box by J. Meir and Son. All have the same registry date so I wonder "Did Wooliscroft and Meir work together?"

Fig. 8-22 The Casavants owned this *Chinese Sydenham* teapot made by Anthony Shaw who placed the Sydenham shields over the panels of a Chinese body.

Fig. 8-23 DALLAS SHAPE - J. Clementson used copper trim on many of his shapes, including this graceful *Dallas* pitcher and handleless cup.

Columbia and Panelled Columbia Shapes

Fig. 8-24 *Columbia Shape* sauce tureen with ladle has a ruffled top edge and includes no panels above the shield.

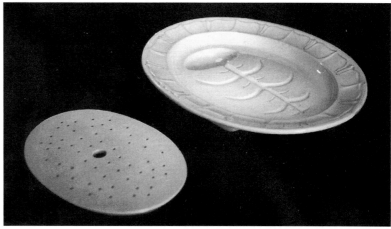

This popular *Columbia Shape* can be distinguished from *President Shape* by the split end in the shield divider (see arrow on plate rim sketch). *Panelled Columbia* has panels above the shield, although often only marked "Columbia." Potters include Livesley and Powell, J. Clementson, E. & C. Challinor, G. Wooliscroft, J. Meir & Son, Elsmore & Forster (marked Foster), W. Adams, and Penman Brown & Co. It was registered by several potteries in 1855. The sketches show details of the Columbia Shape.

Fig. 8-25 A choice J. Clementson well and tree *Columbia* platter includes a perforated liner. Owned by the Horners.

Fig. 8-26 These major pieces of a tea set in *Panelled Columbia* are owned by the Dieringers.

Fig. 8-27 We just had to include this rare *Panelled Columbia* master waste jar (no cover) and a gravy boat.

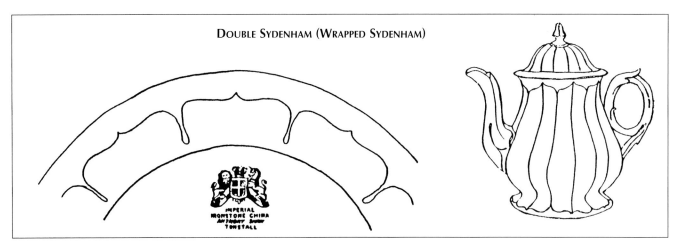

DOUBLE SYDENHAM (WRAPPED SYDENHAM)

I have consolidated *Double Sydenham* and *Wrapped Sydenham* since they are so alike and are made by the same potters: Anthony Shaw, Edward Walley, Holland & Green, W. & E. Corn, John Maddock, Livesley & Powell and T. Goodfellow. Some finials vary but the same shield covers bodies of pieces. One collector reported a *Cora Shape* by John Alcock as being decorated in a like manner.

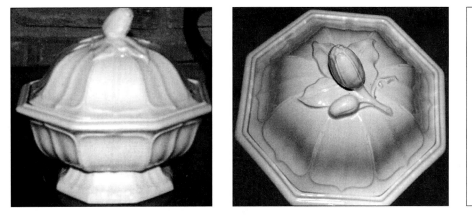

Fig. 8-28 A handsome covered handleless vegetable tureen in the *Double Sydenham* pattern marked by John Maddock. A close-up of the lid is shown on the right. Owned by Eleanor Washburn.

A sketch of a *Double Sydenham* covered vegetable tureen marked by W. & E. Corn.

Fig. 8-29 - GIRARD SHAPE - The pieces of *Girard Shape* by J. Ridgway Bates & Co. (who potted from 1856 to 1858) used the octagon shape and shield in jugs. Note both the Sydenham shield and tulip lines on the beautiful soup tureen above.

MISSISSIPPI SHAPE or MALTESE SHAPE - This same jug has been found marked *Mississippi Shape* by E. Pearson, *Maltese Shape* by E. Corn, and *Baltic Shape* by G. Wooliscroft. Makes it hard for us to generalize, doesn't it?

PERSIA SHAPE - The above border and finial were found on a tureen marked by Edward Corn, *Persia Shape.*

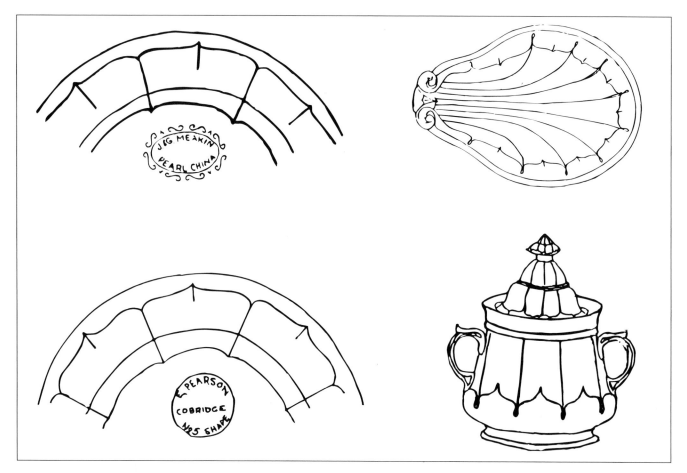

PEARL SYDENHAM - The ribs on *Pearl Sydenham* by J. & G. Meakin are slightly concaved and the shields shoulder each other on the plate surrounds (top left). On the bottom left is a *No. 5 Shape* plate by E. Pearson that has exactly the same design as *Pearl Sydenham.* The relish dish and sugar bowl on the right are examples of Meakin's *Pearl Sydenham* shape which features gleaming surfaces that seldom are crazed.

President Shape

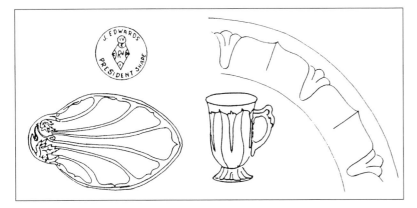

Fig 8-30   Oval, handled fruit compote includes inside rim shields. It's a *President Shape* piece owned by Jack Anspaugh.

We see the Sydenham shield on *President Shape* by John Edwards of Fenton, who registered it in 1855 and 1856. Pitchers are simple and squatty with squared spouts. The tureens are wonderfully potted in both oval and round shapes.

Fig. 8-31   Jack Anspaugh gathered these toilet pieces in *President Shape*. The cover to the master waste jar is not the right cover. The set still looks great!

Fig 8-32   More of Jack's *President* pieces. Notice the two compotes: one oval and one round. Don't ignore the punch bowl with matching cups and the nest of platters.

Fig 8-33   Here an oval covered vegetable tureen and gravy boat in *President Shape* by John Edwards rest on a Dalenberg shelf. Vegetable tureens were also made having three round sizes and three oval sizes. The soup tureens duplicated this practice with large oval ones and a huge round chowder server.

Other Early 1850s Shapes

There were some potters of the early 1850s who did not jump on the Sydenham bandwagon. These shapes are also very collectible.

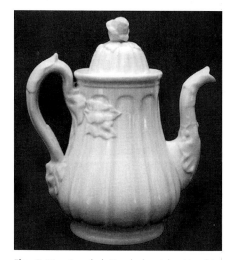

Fig. 8-34 *Arcaded Panels* by John Venables (1853-55) has beautifully molded panels and foliage at the top and terminal of the "C" handle. A tipped, three-dimensional flower forms the finial. Rigoulot and Brockey Collection.

Fig. 8-35 John Alcock potted this *Boxy Decagon* teapot with a familiar split pod finial. There have been reports that this shape was part of a *Paris Shape* set but that has not been verified. Dan Overmeyer owns this great piece.

Fig. 8-36 We are awed by the beauty of this *Fluted Hills* shape from the collection of Francis Hills.

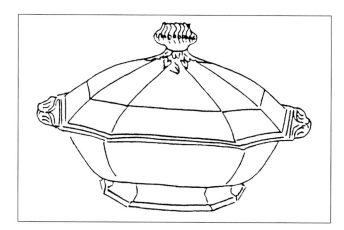

Fig. 8-37 Another 1853 registry is found on this Pankhurst & Co. oval compote, nick-named *Fluted Hops* (upper left) by the owners, Rigoulot and Brockey.

LONG OCTAGON by John Alcock has only been reported once in a creamier body than most white granite pieces made in the 1850s. A sketch of a covered tureen is shown above, right.

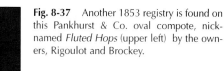

Fig. 8-38 Both of these low covered tureens reveal sixteen facets or panels. The low stew tureen with ladle was formed by Davenport; the nearer one by Francis Morley & Co. These *Many Faceted* pieces are treasured by the Morelands.

←

Fig. 8-39 Two panelled ewers are identified; on the left, a *Many-Panelled Gothic* shape by Samuel Alcock and, on the right, a *Divided Gothic* shape by John Alcock. Both are owned by the Dieringers.

Fig. 8-40 Registered in 1854, these *Montpelier Double Scallop* teapots by John Ridgway & Co. are octagonal with scallops at both top and bottom of bodies. The finials are pine cones. From the Moreland Collection.

Fig. 8-41 T. J. & J. Mayer registered this *Prize Nodding Bud* in September of 1851. Eleanor Washburn unearthed this rare shape in a sugar bowl (above left).

Fig. 8-42 *Adam's Scallop*, potted by William Adams, has an 1853 registration. This vegetable tureen, with cone finial and a long octagon shape, includes a curving horizontal line similar to the decor on *Scalloped Decagon* (above right).

Fig. 8-43 Changed from *Panelled Octagon* to *Panelled Decagon* (I counted wrong) by Elsmore & Forster, these lines were popular with Staffordshire potters. Very similar pitchers were potted by other potters: James Edwards & Son shaped a chubbier, twelve-panelled version that held almost four quarts; E. Challinor & Co. used ten panels on a chunkier version and Michael Tunnicliff of Tunstall made an early version also
➡

Prize Bloom

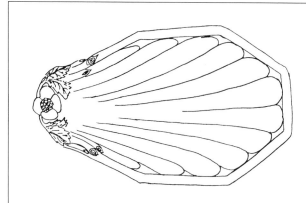

Collectors buy any pieces they locate in *Prize Bloom* registered in 1853 by T. J. & J. Mayer. The body is generally hexagonal with twelve vertical panels overlaying the divisions. The exact potting of the three-dimensional four-petalled flower on all serving pieces (see right) catches the eye of the beholder. A relish is shown on the left

Fig. 8-44   Scarce covered hot beverage server in *Prize Bloom* was discovered by Ray and Priscilla Casavant.

Fig. 8-45   The Dieringers assembled the teapot, covered sugar bowl, and creamer in the *Prize Bloom* shape by T. J. & J. Mayer.

Fig. 8-46   A close-up of the Mayers' treatment on the *Prize Bloom* shape in a covered, handled vegetable tureen. Black Collection.

Fig. 8-47   *Prize Bloom*, potted by T. J. & J. Mayer, is best remembered by the three-dimensional four-petalled flower that decorates all pieces except plates and platters. The bodies of servers are hexagonal with two fluted panels added over each of the six divisions. These three pieces were collected by the Dieringers.

Fig. 8-49

PRIZE PURITAN

Registered by the Mayers in 1851, this shape is recognized by its horizontal decorated band low on the body and its intricate handles on beverage servers. The lovely tureen complete with undertray, on the left, shows the unique crown finial found on covered pieces. This set is in the Lautenschlager Collection. Above is a gravy boat with its high plateau undertray.

Fig. 8-48

SCALLOPED DECAGON

J. Wedge Wood (marked J. Wedgwood) and Davenport shared this shape. The decagon panelled shape was used on cups, chamber sets, beverage pots, plates and pitchers but surprisingly the tureens are oval as seen in the sketch here.

Fig. 8-50 This *Scalloped Decagon* chamber pot belongs to the Dieringers.

Fig. 8-51 This pair of *Scalloped Decagon* jugs, a creamer and a ewer, pose together in the Black home.

Fig. 8-52 The Nobles own this rare foot tub in *Scalloped Decagon.*

Fig. 8-53 Davenport registered this 7 1/2″ *Squat Pot* in 1853. The low oval shape with graceful elevated front rim reminds us of earlier shapes of the 1800s. Collection of Dan Overmeyer.

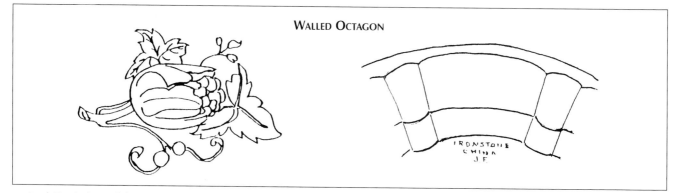

WALLED OCTAGON

Jacob Furnival potted this unique *Walled Octagon* with its octagon shape with a protruding wall. The large pod finial with visible berries draws much attention. The smaller divisions in the plates are ditched (concaved) between the larger divisions. Very collectible.

Fig. 8-54 Note the great pod finial reclining on the top of this *Walled Octagon* vegetable tureen owned by the Washburns.

Fig. 8-55 This handsome pitcher (left) is in Jacob Furnival's very original *Walled Octagon* shape which collectors cherish.

Shapes Named for
Renowned People and Places

Early in the 19th century, when the budding nation of the United States was trying to establish its independence from and acceptance by other nations, the coolness between America and Mother England was felt. Almost certainly, the brisk ceramic trade was affected. However, Englishness was ingrained in the American colonies and no sooner was the War of 1812 finished than Staffordshire wares were again for sale, 'eagerly purchased by dish-hungry Americans.' The clever potters produced blue and white tableware which depicted scenes recalling American heroes and events. Thus, these historical wares helped to ease the friction and also made money for the vigilant English potters.

Maybe the memory of that successful business venture inspired the ceramic manufacturers to use the familiar names of famous people and places to label new white ironstone shapes in the 1850s. In that decade, forty or more shapes were named after well-known heroes or explorers, oceans, bays, lakes, or rivers; a few states; some mythical terms like *Ceres, Hebe,* or *Athens;* the American connotations of *Columbia, Union, President, Prairie,* or *Western;* and also a few familiar terms such as *Gothic* or *Classic.*

Joseph Clementson and His Potting Family

Joseph Clementson had a long history as a leader in the pottery industry in the Staffordshire area. It appears that he knew John Ridgway and at an unusual age (26) apprenticed himself as a printer to the J. & W. Ridgway Co. in the 1820s. He was determined to learn as much about the whole pottery business as he could. From 1832 to 1839, he was a partner with Read, and during the first ten years of registry - after 1842 - he made nine entries—all on Granite Ware with colored transfer patterns. Collectors of ironstone may be interested in the registry in March of 1849 of his very collectible "Classical Antiquities" series. He does not seem to have worked with marketing white granite shapes during those years.

Clementson had visited North America to see what were the needs and tastes of possible American consumers and establish a good rapport with retailers in Canada and the United States. He was a foreigner in business, establishing the system of bills of exchange so that goods and credit could be exchanged reliably. Great Britain was ahead of other countries in this area and we can surmise that the dependable reputation of both Joseph Clementson as a businessman and his son Francis, who continued as a potter's agent in Canada, helped to establish credit.

Like Ridgway, according to Collard, Joseph was a staunch Methodist. During his Canadian visit, "he had an eye out for the Methodist cause as well as for sale of his earthenware. During weekdays he worked to secure orders for the pottery, and on Sundays he 'worked for the Lord', preaching... Many Canadians turned out to hear a man from the Potteries. From his influence, missionary support for the Methodist cause increased in Canada. At the same time, his business connections with the New World thrived.

Joseph worked at his Phoenix Pottery, which displayed that large phoenix bird over its entry. It was enlarged in 1845 and in the mid-fifties, he purchased the old William Ridgway pottery, Bell Works, across the road.

It was during this decade and the next that J. Clementson joined other potteries and produced white granite table and toilet wares in abundance for his

Famous Clementson Shapes

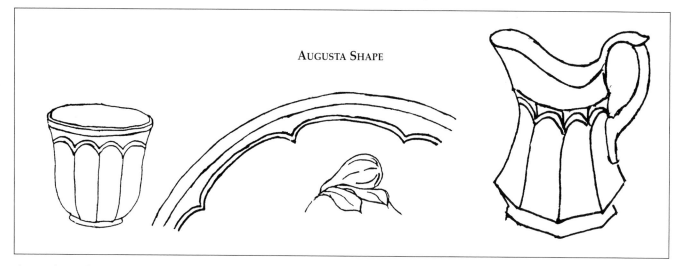

This simple panelled shape is J. Clementson's *Augusta Shape.* Note the fruit finial under the plate rim design.

Lafayette Shape was produced by Joseph Clementson. A border detail is shown here.

◄ J. Clementson registered *Citron Shape.*

Fig. 9-1 Another swirled, stylized style, *Hill Shape,* was produced by J. Clementson and his successor sons. It was often sold with an added copper Teaberry. From the Bedford Collection.

Above are sketches of border details from Clementson's *Hill Shape.*

Fig. 9-2 Joseph Clementson planned this slightly diamond-shaped body on his Nautilus shape. Some pieces were sold with copper lustre bands as on this one found in the Upchurch Collection.

Fig. 9-3 A handled *New York Shape* coffee cup from the Dieringer home.

Fig. 9-4 J. Clementson designed this *New York Shape* family. It is recognized by the crouching split pod finial and ring of thumbprints around the base. From the Dieringer Collection.

Fig. 9-5 Unusually tall at over 11 inches, this *New York Shape* hot chocolate pot was a real find by the Armbrusters.

American markets. Listed here are the Clementson shapes that have been reaped by collectors west of the Atlantic. A number of these were highlighted in Chapter 8.

*Augusta Shape	*Lafayette Shape
Chinese Shape	Nautilus
*Citron	*New York Shape
*Columbia Shape	Panelled Grape
*Dallas Shape	*Prairie Shape
*Hill Shape	*Sydenham

*name marked by potter

In 1865 Joseph handed the Phoenix Works over to his sons, who styled the pottery as Clementson Bros.

Here are shapes found marked by the Clementson Bros.:

Balanced Vine, registered 1867
*Canada, registered 1877
Heavy Square
Plain Uplift

The Clementsons, both father and sons, also used copper lustre on white ironstone bodies. The copper Teaberry treatment with lustre band, a seaweed motif, the better known Tea Leaf sprig, and a touch of flow blue with a red line were all used to enhance that white granite. The Clementson Bros. splashed the bodies of *Heavy Square* with enormous Tea Leaf motifs.

Famous Names by Other Potters

In the 1860s, a few named shapes were recorded on the bottom of white granite dishes but most shape names of that decade were not included in the potters' marks. Whether or not potters attached names to those shapes can only be verified by researchers willing to study the old registration records between 1842 and 1883.

Here are pages of drawings and photographs of the "famous" shapes. Let me introduce you.

Asia Shape, by G. Wooliscroft, may be confused with *New York Shape* although the potting is not as well-done.

Fig.9-6 *Baltimore Shape* coffeepot by Brougham and Mayer, potted in the early 1850s. Owned by the Diemers in Delaware

Chinese Shape

Fig.9-7 *Chinese Shape* was first potted by Anthony Shaw, as shown in the upper right drawing, who registered his shape on April 7, 1856. T. & R. Boote registered their variation on Dec. 8, 1858. The eight flat, vertical panels are slightly concave on the pouring vessels. The Boote version had their spout panels leap upwards gracefully on pitchers. Finials were rosebuds on sugar bowls and teapots while tureens were topped by reclining pods. The pieces in the photograph and lower sketch were fashioned by the Boote firm.

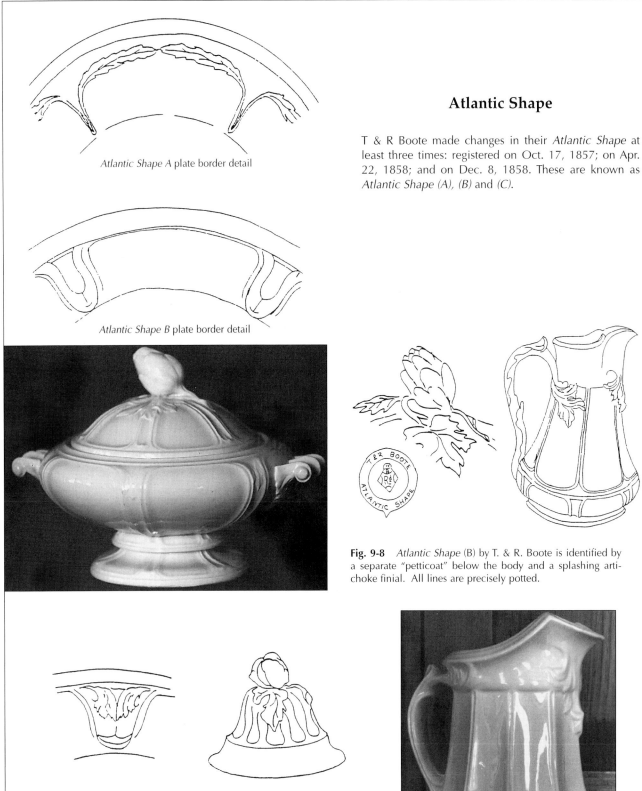

Atlantic Shape A plate border detail

Atlantic Shape B plate border detail

Atlantic Shape

T & R Boote made changes in their *Atlantic Shape* at least three times: registered on Oct. 17, 1857; on Apr. 22, 1858; and on Dec. 8, 1858. These are known as *Atlantic Shape (A), (B)* and *(C)*.

Fig. 9-8 *Atlantic Shape* (B) by T. & R. Boote is identified by a separate "petticoat" below the body and a splashing artichoke finial. All lines are precisely potted.

Fig. 9-9 *Atlantic Shape* (C) by Boote displays large thumbprints around the base of beverage servers (right) and has a bud finial as shown in the sketcch to the left. A detail of the plate border is also shown.

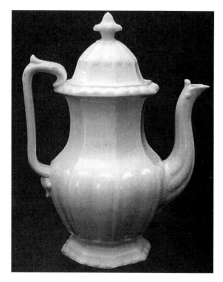

Fig. 9-10 *Classic Shape,* clearly marked by T. & R. Boote in 1868, is so plain, so masterfully potted that any collector would like this large punch bowl, flanked by Wedgwood & Co. *Flora* punch cups. Photo sent by John Black. Another very plain shape is *Erie Shape,* patented before 1868 by Wedgwood & Co. It has been seen on a plain platter with a deep well.

Fig. 9-11 This early shape, marked *Florentine* by C. & W. K. Harvey, was registered July 16, 1850. The body is divided into eight panels, the bottom half of each panel filled with double convex ribs. Teapot is owned by Ed Rigoulot and Ted Brockey.

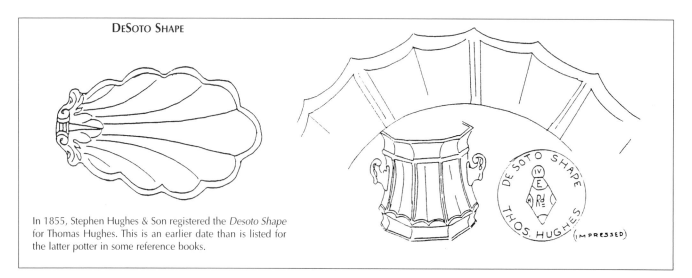

DeSoto Shape

In 1855, Stephen Hughes & Son registered the *Desoto Shape* for Thomas Hughes. This is an earlier date than is listed for the latter potter in some reference books.

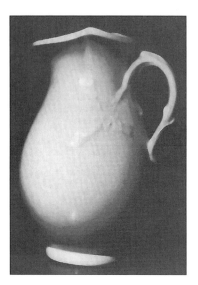

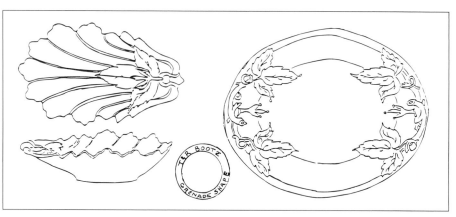

Grenade Shape by T & R Boote is best known by its precisely-molded three-leaved decor.

Fig.9-12 *Garibaldi Shape* ewer (left) registered December 23, 1860, by T. & R. Boote. Courtesy Bill Neuhauser.

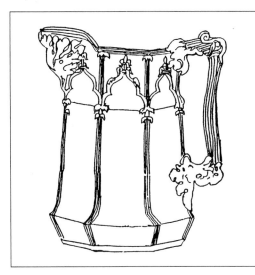

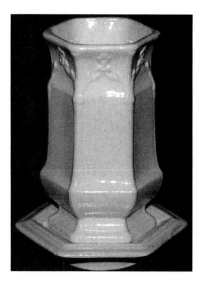

Holland and Green designed *Gothic,* using decor related to Gothic architecture. It doesn't look at all like the early pieces that we label *Gothic.*

Fig. 9-13 The word *Gothic* is stamped on the underplate to this vertical toothbrush holder by Holland and Green. Collection of Dan Overmeyer.

Fig. 9-14 This melon-ribbed teapot, marked *Haveloch Shape* by Holland & Green, used a ring handle and finial, wheat border, and raspberries with foliage.

Sketches of the plate rim and teapot cover for Holland & Green's *Haveloch Shape.*

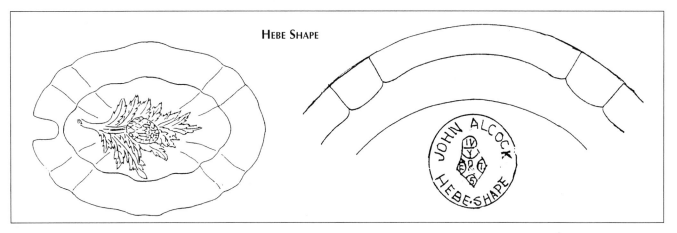

HEBE SHAPE

John Alcock registered this *Hebe Shape* on May 7, 1853. Four other shapes were registered by him on the same day. Who will unearth the shapes for us?

Fig. 9-15 & 9-16 Adams registered his *Huron Shape* in 1858. The dividing sheild & ivy foliage with berries are characteristic. On the left above is a stew tureen, without ladle, which features horizontal ears, a ring finial and tucks fleur-de-lis between the six body divisions. On the right is a hard to find *Huron* creamer.

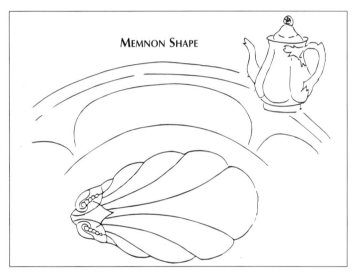

John Meir & Son registered their *Memnon Shape* on Feb. 4, 1857. The teapot bodies are divided into six melon-like divisions each outlined and swooped down into a loop.

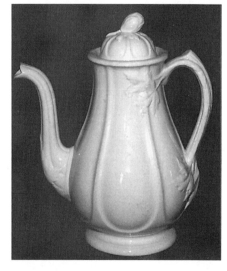

Fig. 9-17 This *Memnon Shape* coffeepot is unusually tall (12¹/₄") and slim, the body being divided by six large loops. Dan Overmeyer sent us this picture and information.

Fig. 9-18 Panelled fluting covers the body of this *Mobile Shape* tureen, marked by G. Bowers. Heath also made this shape. Posed alongside is a *Boote 1851 Octagon* punch cup.

Fig. 9-19 These two rococo-decorated *Napier Shape* pots, one a little taller than the other, were designed by Bridgwood & Son and collected by Dan Overmeyer.

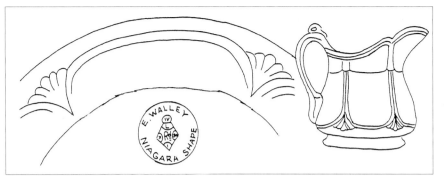

NIAGARA SHAPE, designed by Edward Walley of Cobridge, was registered in 1856. It was made extensively in white granite, and also as a blank for copper lustre trimming, other lustred treatments and some transfer wares. Sketches above show a plate rim and creamer. On the right is a lovely *Niagara* coffeepot owned by Dan Overmeyer. **(Fig. 9-20)**

Fig. 9-21 Very different decorations are found on *Nile Shape:* shell finials and handles, flat twisted rope around edges, and lilies and pads right off the Nile. Geo. L. Ashworth & Bros. registered this shape in 1866, labeling their body as "White Granite Stoneware." Julie Rich and the Morelands own pieces of this unusual shape. Above left is a close-up of the top half of a teapot. A sketch of a sugar bowl is on the right.

Fig. 9-22 Finally, someone sent a snap of *Oriental Shape* by W. E. Corn with a "White Granite" label. Notice the rope around the neck and base and pairs of flowered branches. Thanks to Carol and Frank Fleischman.

Pacific Shape

Figs.9-23 & 9-24 *Pacfic Shape*, potted in 1871 by Elsmore & Forster, was one of the last patterens produced by that company. The sugar bowl has slanting sides widened at the base, an acorn finial, and narrow concaved fluting overall. The pitcher on the right is from the Rigoulet and Brockey Collection.
Note the absence of pedestals on the *Pacfic Shape* punch cups (above). Collection of Suzanne and Rick Nielsen.

Paris Shape

On March 20, 1857 John Alcock patented his *Paris Shape* with its interesting gourd finial. Serving pieces with vertical panels are usually found in gleaming, uncrazed white. Also made by Henry Alcock.

Fig. 9-25 This ring-handled *Paris Shape* gravy boat was potted by Henry Alcock. Owned and photographed by the Dieringers.

Fig. 9-26 This low, large, *Paris Shape* tureen, sold by John Alcock, is called a stew tureen. A matching ladle accompanied most stew tureens but underplates were not made for them.

Fig. 9-27   This *Portland Shape* was superbly potted by Elsmore and Forster. The intricate trumpet-flower finial and curved "C" handles identify this very desirable shape. Copper lustre hoarders long to find this shape with a Morning Glory motif and copper band or a Reverse Teaberr twig. Illustrated are a sugar bowl and tureen cover as well as sketches of a plate border and top view of a tureen cover.

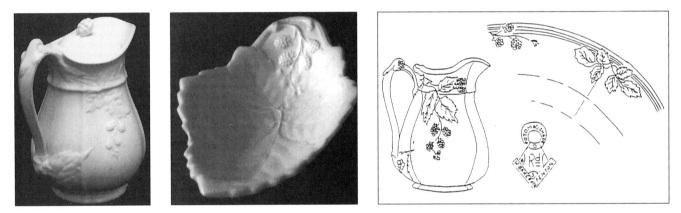

Figs. 9-28 & 9-29   *Potomac Shape* by W. Baker & Co. has been nicknamed "Blackberry" shape. This detailed berry pattern, registered on October 23, 1862, is popular with ironstone collectors. On the far left we show a hot beverage server highlighted by a blackberry finial and blackberry branches on the sides. It is treasured by Sally Scrimgeour. In the center above is a *Potomac Shape* relish dish completely covered with leaves and berries.

Fig. 9-30   *Richelieu Shape,* potted by J. F. Wileman, is a late marked shape. The body is plain and graceful, found here decorated with a Morning Glory motif. Courtesy of Nancy Upchurch.

Fig. 9-31   *St. Louis Shape* by John Edwards of Fenton features an attractive thick flower finial resting on leaves on some pieces while the covered sugar bowl and tureen cover shown above feature a melon-form finial. Plates and bodies are outlined with molded "peanuts" and "circles."

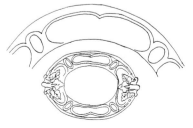

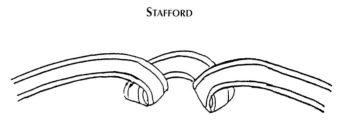

Fig. 9-32 *Stafford*, registered by Samuel Alcock & Co. in 1854, has a crown acorn finial, twined vertical handles, and the same basic body as *Trent Shape* by John Alcock (see below). The tureen on the left with matching ladle and cracker tray is from the collection of Ed and Ted. Above is a detail of the border from a *Stafford* plate. This is sometimes referred as a *Trent* border and may be used to describe trim on other sets. This particular border detail is taken from a *Stafford* shape plate marked by John Alcock but registered to Samuel Alcock.

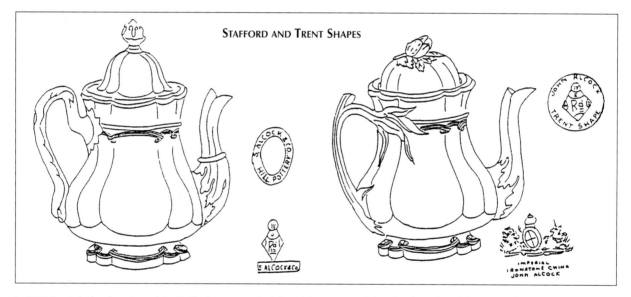

STAFFORD AND TRENT SHAPES

In 1854 Samuel Alcock registered the Stafford teapot on the left and the next year John Alcock produced the teapot shape on the right which was labeled *"Trent Shape."* Notice the nearly matching bodies with different handles and finials.

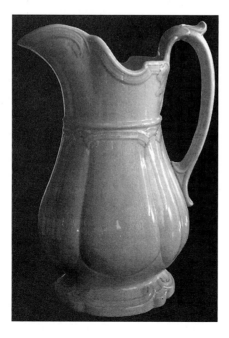

Fig. 9-33 This spectacular cover, in an unidentified patern, was probably from a hot toddy bowl. It features peas, vines and a three-dimensional cauliflower as a finial. Notice the familiar *Trent* border. Was it an Alcock creation? Let us know if you know.

Fig. 9-34 *Trent Shape* ewer by John Alcock is beautifully potted. Notice the double twists in the Trent ribbon. Collection of Ernie and Bev Dieringer.

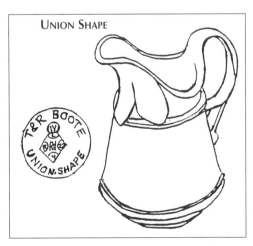

Fig. 9-35 *Sevres Shape* was a graceful creation by John Edwards of Fenton. It is usually found in sparkling white without crazing. The plain bodies boast two finial styles: a nut on teapots and sugar bowls, a cone resting on tureens as shown to the left. The half-flower lug handles on this piece also help identify this shape.

In 1853, John Edwards produced this *Tuscan Shape*. Collectors have found this shape stamped *President Shape*, another pattern offered by John Edwards. Potters err, too.

Fig. 9-36 Because the bodies are so gleaming, the few decorations so clearly modelled, any collector treasures *Union Shape* potted by T. & R. Boote. Jane Diemer located this tea family.

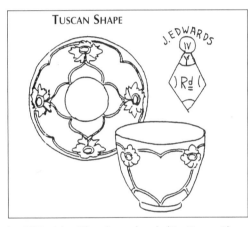

Sketch of the *Union Shape* creamer and mark.

Fig. 9-37 Another *Union Shape* treasure is this tureen with vertical handles branched at the top and a deeply grooved vegetable finial. Collection of Tom and Olga Moreland.

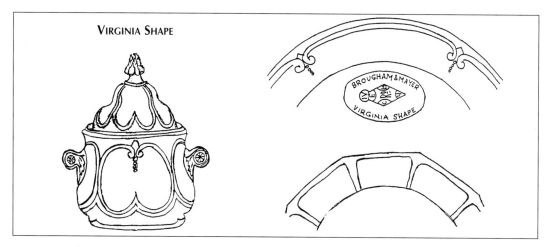

In 1855, Brougham & Mayer created the *Virginia Shape*, using two different borders on flat pieces. The tureens surprisingly show six protruding bubbles on the bodies. Vegetable tureens have no ears. Teapots and sugar bowls are decorated as above with vertical artichoke finials.

Fig. 9-38   The bodies of *Virginia Shape* beverage servers are quartered, each division having top scrolls and double loops at the bottom. This teapot is owned by Laura and Chester Ady.

Fig. 9-39   The "cheeks" on the sides of this *Virginia Shape* tureen look unrelated to the teapot in the same shape, both marked by Brougham and Mayer.

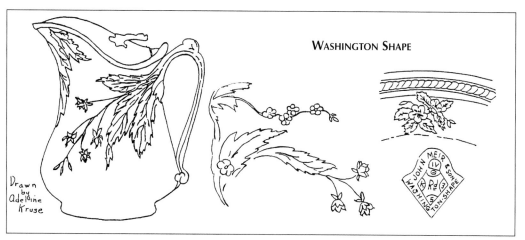

Washington Shape, registered in 1863 by John Meir & Son, was also made by Powell & Bishop with some variations. The edge cable was a Meir touch.

Vertical Panels, Loops, Lobes, and Arches

Many vertical panels, loops, lobes and arches characterized the white granite shapes of the 1850s.

The Alcocks

The Alcock name was prevalent during the white granite years in the Staffordshire area of England. We find white ironstone pieces marked Hill Pottery, S. Alcock, although Samuel Alcock & Co. worked from at least three locations. The discovery of two teapots with *Trent shape* bodies but with different finials and spouts, one marked Samuel Alcock and the other John Alcock, suggests some cooperation between the two potteries. Another *Stafford Shape* dish has been located marked J. Alcock but registered to Samuel Alcock & Co. Samuel worked in Cobridge until 1853 and John began his Cobridge pottery in 1853, working at that location until 1861, a short nine years.

John & George Alcock also worked in Cobridge from 1839-46. They called their body "Oriental Stone." Collectors have identified some reticulated fruit bowls produced by these early white granite makers. They were succeeded by another short-lived firm, John & Samuel Alcock, Jr., who worked from 1848 to 1850.

John Alcock worked in earthenwares, many of his dishes being of white origin. Listed below are some white ironstone shapes produced in this pottery:

Classic Gothic	*Paris Shape
Divided Gothic	Ribbed Berry
*Flora Shape	*Stafford Shape
Gothic Cameo	*Trent Shape
*Hebe Shape	True Scallop
Little Pear	Wheat Harvest
Long Octagon	

John Alcock was succeeded in 1861 by Henry Alcock, who continued to produce his bodies called "White Granite ware," "Parisian Porcelain," or "Royal Warranted Best Ironstone China" through the rest of the century. A toilet set in *Ribbed Berry* by John has also been located, marked Henry Alcock.

Rarely, we find an impressed mark for Richard Alcock of Burslem. He was succeeded by Wilkinson & Hulme who ceased their business in 1885. That's the only clue we have found to date the R. Alcock company.

The J. F. Quandry

Another interesting potter usually marked his wares only J. F. There has been much speculation about who J. F. was. Collectors have been attracted to the pleasing original lines of his sets molded in white granite. Few, if any of his shapes were registered so we could not solve the mystery that way. I've concluded that J.F. refers to Jacob Furnival & Co. based on the following contributions by collectors. One person reports two pieces of *Berry Cluster,* one marked J.F. and the other one displays an impressed FURNIVAL. A second collector from Michigan sent pictures of two *Lily-of-the-Valley with Thumbprints* dinner plates, one marked J.F. and the other Jacob Furnival & Co. I was finally convinced by a Texas couple who sent a photograph taken from the bottom of a teapot. Clearly seen is the familiar J.F. stamp and nearby is the imprint FURNIVAL. I'm a believer now.

Jacob Furnival & Co. worked for twenty-five years from 1845 to 1870. He patented seven shapes during those years but none of them were the shapes listed below that white ironstone fans have identified as having been potted by J.F.

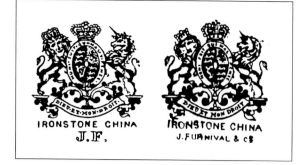

Two early Jacob Furnival marks.

Identified J. Furnival Shapes

Berry Cluster	Loop and Line
Classic Gothic	Panelled Grape
Classic Cameo	Panelled Lily
Fluted Hills	Pomegranate (*Trent*
Gooseberry	edged)
Grand Loop	Quartered Rose
Grape Octagon	Ring O'Hearts
Hidden Motif	Vintage Beauty
J.F.'s Wheat	Walled Octagon
Lily-of-the-Valley	
with Thumbprints	

We find a few pieces by Thomas Furnival & Co. who conducted business in Hanley from 1844 to 1846. Later, sets of white granite were produced by Thomas Furnival & Sons in Cobridge during the last quarter of the 19th century.

However, it is the creativity and excellent potting skills of J. F. that are applauded by serious white ironstone students.

Here follow more drawings and photographs of white granite shapes of the mid-1850s.

ALTERNATE LOOPS - This "Porcelain Opaque" body was made by Bridgwood & Clarke (1857-64)

ARCADED DOUBLE RIBS - This unmarked syrup jug is divided by ten arches with a pair of convex ribs in the bottom of each section.

Fig. 10-1 Framed arches on this Chas. Meigh & Son jug hide a little trumpet flower amid foliage. We call it *Arcaded Trumpet*, a new shape located by Tom Chadwick.

BERRY CLUSTER - Jacob Furnival (sometimes marked J.F. and sometimes FURNIVAL) created this body style. Oval teapots are found in two different bottom-heavy shapes with different handles. The *Berry Cluster* finials enlarges to a huge fruit cluster on a hot toddy bowl.

Fig. 10-2 and Fig. 10-3 Two different styles of Furnival teapots, both use the *Berry Cluster* and same foliage. Which came first or were both potted simultaneously?

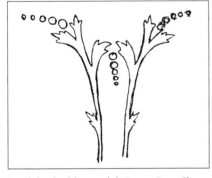

Detail sketch of the panel design on *Berry Cluster.*

Elaborate Six-Panelled Trumpet

Fig. 10-4 Wouldn't we all like to own a hot-toddy bowl in *Berry Cluster* shape by Jacob Furnival? The cover is quartered, topped by huge gooseberries. The ribbed handles are also unique.

Fig. 10-5 Note the concaved areas on the six divisions of this *Elaborate Six-Panelled Trumpet* by J.W. Pankhurst, discovered by Anne's Antiques. It is closely related to the *Six-Panelled Trumpet* shape (see page 88).

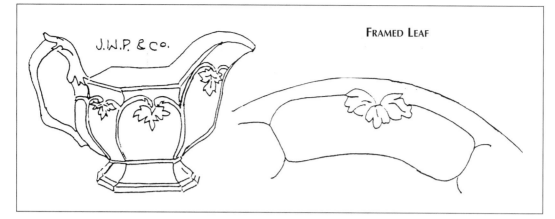

Framed Leaf pieces shaped by J. W. Pankhurst & Co. are eagerly sought by white ironstone assemblers. Most lines are the octagonal ones used so widely in the 1850s. A gravy boat and plate rim are shown in these sketches.

Fig. 10-6 J. W. Pankhurst expertly potted this *Framed Leaf* on each of eight panels and crowned it with a crown acorn finial on this sugar bowl. Owned by the Dieringers.

Fig. 10-7 Notice the split pod finial on this *Framed Leaf* Pankhurst octagonal soup tureen with undertray and ladle. Owned by the Morelands.

Framed Panels

This oval unmarked soap dish resembles the Six-Panelled Trumpet shape. My potter vote would be Pankhurst or perhaps Livesley & Powell. Can you solve this puzzle?

Grand Loop

Fig. 10-8 Collectors are awed by the *Grand Loop* impressed into sides of this teapot by Jacob Furnival. Armbruster Collection.

Fig. 10-9 The Armbrusters discovered this rare vertical toothbrush holder with liner in *Grand Loop* by J. F.

Fig. 10-10 The *Grand Loop* pitcher is by J. F. Courtesy of Anne Miller.

Little Pear (Alcock's)

John Alcock produced this lesser known shape, *Alcock's Little Pear,* which has a little pear finial, of course.

Loop and Dot

Loop and Dot was shaped by E. & C. Challinor after 1862.

Loop and Line

This *Loop and Line,* a not too well-known shape was produced by Jacob Furnival.

Many Panelled Gothic

Fig. 10-11 Anthony Shaw often used this *Many-Panelled Gothic* shape in white granite; he also decorated it with a brown marble transfer, copper lustre band, etc. Earlier in 1853, Venables, Mann & Co. registered this shape with twelve panels, a ring handle and a bud finial (*Twelve Panelled Gothic*). Samuel Alcock also made this shape. This Shaw teapot is in the Diemer Collection.

NIAGARA FAN, registered by Anthony Shaw on April 17, 1856, can be confused with the earlier *Niagara Shape* by E. Walley. Emblazoned with a copper Tea Leaf and band, it is treasured by lustre collectors. The photo **(Fig. 10-12)** of the jug-form pitcher is from Anne Miller.

PANELLED BERRY WITH LEAVES - J. & G. Meakin often used "Pearl China" as a mark on his white granite shapes, among them the *Panelled Berry with Leaves* teapot shown above.

PANELLED SCROLL - This graceful syrup holder with pewter lid is nick-named *Panelled Scroll*. The impressed rectangular mark is illegible. Livesley and Powell?

PANELLED POD - J. & G. Meakin produced *Panelled Pod* with their skill at manufacturing shapes that can be discovered today, uncrazed and unstained in gleaming white.

Pomegranate

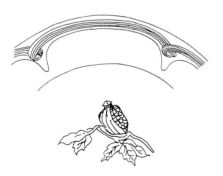

This *Pomegranate* shape by J. F. divides bodies into looping quarters. The finials on tureens are the same as those found on *Chinese* tureens. However, other pieces may be topped by a rosebud. Identify this shape by the Trent-like border, which has single rather than double twists.

Fig. 10-13 This photograph should clear up some confusion. To the left is an Alcock pitcher with double twisted *Trent* border (see Chapter 8). On the right is a J. F. *Pomegranate* chamber pot with the proper single twisted Trent-like border. Wait, look closely, the Alcock one is marked *Stafford Shape*, registered by Samuel Alcock in 1854. Look at page 78. This piece looks like a hybrid between the two *Trent Shapes*. Still confused? Me too.

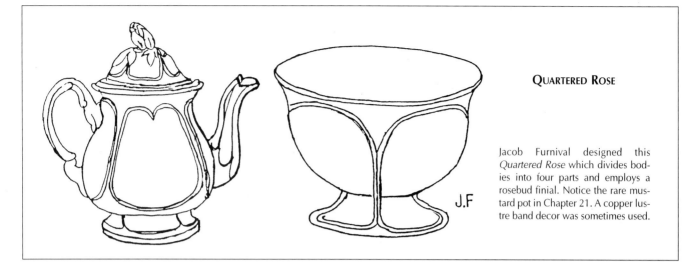

QUARTERED ROSE

Jacob Furnival designed this *Quartered Rose* which divides bodies into four parts and employs a rosebud finial. Notice the rare mustard pot in Chapter 21. A copper lustre band decor was sometimes used.

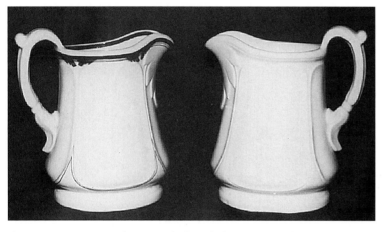

Fig. 10-14 Two *Quartered Rose* jugs, both marked J. F., pose together: the left one has blue trim with a little red line, the right one stands in pristine white. Both are very collectible. Collection of Eleanor Washburn.

Fig. 10-15 The scrolled handles were potted as part of the body on this *Quartered Rose* vegetable tureen potted by Jacob Furnival. Ed Rigoulot and Ted Brockey are the owners.

Fig. 10-16 A Rare *Quartered Rose* covered beverage server with its blue stamp (above) by J. Furnival & Co. is shown in the photograph on the left sent by Dan Overmeyer.

RING O' HEARTS

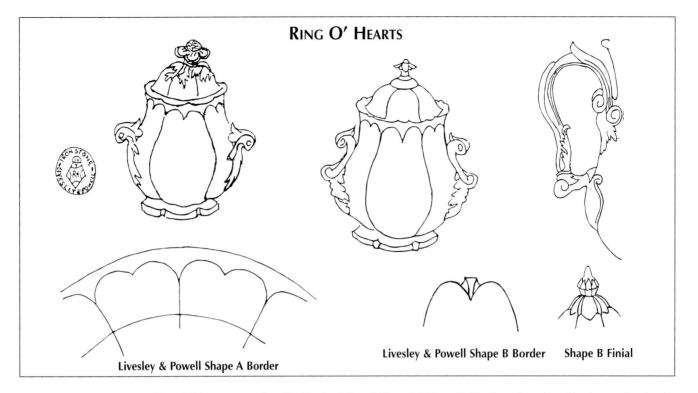

Livesley & Powell Shape A Border

Livesley & Powell Shape B Border   **Shape B Finial**

Top row: Two versions of *Ring O' Hearts* were produced by Livesley & Powell (Shape A & Shape B). The Shape A, registered by them on October 12, 1853, is shown in the sugar bowl on the left. A less embellished version of *Ring O' Hearts* was also produced by Jacob Furnival and is shown in the sugar bowl in the center. Notice the handle and finial differences on the two pieces. To the right is a sketch of the teapot handle used on both versions of this shape produced by Livesley & Powell.

Bottom Row: Shown are the two border variations used by Livesley & Powell. Their plain version is on the left and the version with a tiny motif between the arches, used on some pieces, is shown to its right. At the far right is the acorn finial used on the L. & P. Shape B which replaces the blossom finial found on Shape A.

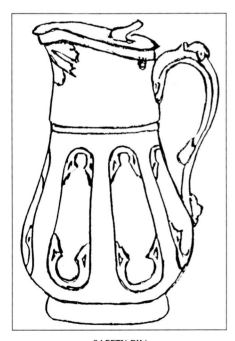

SAFETY PIN

The *Safety Pin* areas on this jug are each welled and decorated with fancy scrollwork. J. & G. Meakin marked the bottom with an impressed circle.

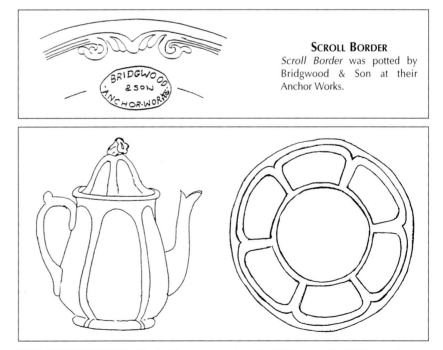

SCROLL BORDER
Scroll Border was potted by Bridgwood & Son at their Anchor Works.

SIX-PANELLED TRUMPET - The Pankhurst teapot above is divided into six slightly-rounded sections, crowned with a leaning trumpet flower. Notice the six framed sections in the plate. J. W. Pankhurst also inserted three deeply concaved areas into the body above. This second shape is called *Elaborate Six-Panelled Trumpet* (see the photo of a teapot on page 83)..

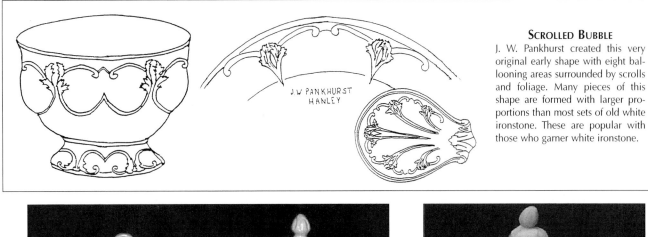

SCROLLED BUBBLE

J. W. Pankhurst created this very original early shape with eight ballooning areas surrounded by scrolls and foliage. Many pieces of this shape are formed with larger proportions than most sets of old white ironstone. These are popular with those who garner white ironstone.

Fig. 10-17 A *Scrolled Bubble* covered tea- and coffeepot gleam in this picture. Notice the ring finial on the smaller 10¼" pot and the acorn finial on the 11½" coffeepot, both by J. W. Pankhurst of Hanley. Both owned by Dan Overmeyer.

Fig. 10-18 In October of 1853, Venables Mann & Co. registered this ring-handled *Twelve Panelled Gothic* teapot with a bud finial. Note the similarity to the *Many Panelled Gothic* shape (p. 85). Information sent by Ed Rigoulot and Ted Brockey.

TULIP

TULIP (nicknamed *Little Scroll)* is a well-known shape made by Elsmore & Forster, registered in 1856. Collectors treasure pieces both round and oval decorated with cobalt blue and copper lustre or trimmed in the same manner with two shades of blue. *Trumpet Flowers* with polychrome touches over purple transfer also were added to this blank.

Fig. 10-19 The top row *Tulip* pieces are oval and the bottom row two are round, all trimmed with medium blue with extra cobalt lines. Sent by Bill Beyer.

Grain and Grape Designs

Elsmore & Forster - "Ceres" & Other Famous Forms

Among ironstone collectors, there are many fans of the Elsmore & Forster firm at the Clayhills Pottery of Tunstall; in fact, some collections are composed only of E. & F. shapes. Historical ceramic accounts such as those by Jewitt, Godden, and Collard reveal few facts about the origin of this company. The very exact detailing, creative designs, and the consistently shining uncrazed condition of E. & F. pieces have been enough to win the acclaim of white granite collectors.

An earlier potter, Thomas Walker, carried on a business at the Lion Works also in Tunstall; he worked from 1845 until 1851, dying about the same time that Elsmore & Forster began their pottery. He had decorated sets of ironstone in a *Simla* transfer pattern and that treatment has been found on pieces marked Elsmore & Forster. On closer observation, we find that E. & F. lifted a floral decoration from the *Simla* border and used it as a central decoration on their purple *Grandmother's Garden* plates. Had Elsmore & Forster worked earlier in Tunstall with Thomas Walker? We wonder.

There is little doubt that the Elsmore & Forster Company is best known for their *Ceres Shape* registered by three numbers on November 2, 1859, one each for the tea, dinner, and toilet sets. The use of grain or hop decorations, especially on tavern jugs, was not a new idea since these two motifs were related to ale or beer drinking. Indeed, on April 26, 1851, Edward Walley registered a jug as *Ceres Shape* which had a wheat decor totally unrelated to the grain designs by E. & F. Before 1859, both John Alcock and Jacob Furnival had already trimmed sets of dishes with heads and blades but it was Elsmore & Forster's wheat shape that was most widely purchased. Their addition of detailed cable, melon ribs, and scallops around wells of plates pleased the American housewives. This pottery offered several variant treatments over the white granite *Ceres* pieces: (1) a copper lustre over the embossed areas, (2) a com-

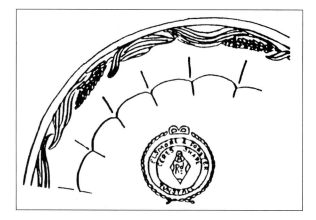

The plate border in *Ceres Shape* by Elmore & Forster. The round mark was sometimes applied to the bottom of pieces.

bination of clear blue with cobalt color over the embossed wheat, or (3) golden kernels with green blades with copper lustred edges. Rarely, collectors have located *Ceres Shape* with a mottled brown Rockingham glazed body (p. 94).

Many other potters soon adapted the pattern with small variations; similar wheat-decorated white ironstone was continuously marketed through the rest of the 19th century. Indeed, a few firms such as Alfred Meakin, S. W. Dean, and A. J. Wilkinson continued using wheat molds into the 20th century. 20th century reproductions have been potted by William Adams & Sons, J. H. Weatherby & Sons, and the American Red Cliff China Co.; all can be identified by differences in color and weight and the clearly marked company names.

Lynne Sussman, in her survey, *The Wheat Pattern*, says that "between 1848 and 1883 twenty grain-inspired raised designs were registered with the (English) Patents Office." Her study reveals at least twenty-three potteries that produced the *Ceres Shape* or slightly changed variations of it. She illustrates fourteen different shapes made by at least forty-two white gran-

This *Arched Forget-Me-Not* shape by Elsmore & Forster was used in white with a copper lustre band, and under a deep purple transfer.

Plain Scallop was a late design from Elsmore & Forster produced around 1870.

ite potters. Most worked in Staffordshire, two in Scotland, and one, the St. Johns Stone Chinaware Company, in Canada. This last firm produced sets of *Wheat and Hops* and also shaped a *Daily Bread* platter with a wheat decoration.

Let's finish the account of the Elsmore & Forster contributions. Probably we will not be able to identify the mold designers but we must acknowledge that they were very talented. Collectors treasure not only *Ceres Shape* pieces, but also the foliated *Morning Glory* and *Laurel Wreath* (sometimes marked *Victory Shape*) sets of white granite. Some dinnerware included an emblazoned copper lustre wreath with other copper touches in *Victory Shape;* rare jugs in this shape include a picture of President Washington within the wreaths on the jugs and pots.

In the mid-1850s, this manufacturer experimented with copper trim on their already popular shapes such as *Gothic, Portland, Panelled Decagon, Tulip, Columbia, Arched Forget-Me-Not,* and the very plain *Fanfare* shape. They are best known by lustre collectors for their copper morning glory motifs, their Tobacco Leaf emblem and a Reverse Teaberry—all centered on white granite. Collectors like finding special treatments on the *Tulip* shape: a clear blue with cobalt blue edging, a flow blue with copper lights, and two shades of purple trim. In the 1860s, E. & F. added copper motifs over their *Plain Scallop* body discussed below.

Also in the late 1860s, these potters used uplift handles and pyriform bodies ringed by a Greek Key in their *Olympic Shape* and tiny fluted coverings over the white granite *Pacific Shape.*

The sugar bowl and creamer are in the plain *Fanfare* shape by Elsmore & Forster. The blank was also used for the Tobacco Leaf motif and copper lustre band.

Just before the close of their works in 1871, this company marketed large open servers, several sizes of compotes and generous individual bowls — all treasured today in a shape nicknamed *One Big and Two Little Ribs.* This style is also found marked by their successors, Thomas Elsmore & Son, and often includes an impressed "PG" for "Parisian Granite."

This firm produced a plain, graceful shape, nicknamed *Plain Scallop,* (called *Crystal* by Tea Leaf collectors) in a lighter weight ironstone body (PG). The spouts and handles are faintly ribbed, finials are acorn-shaped and handles are in uplift lines; the top rim of beverage servers are gracefully scalloped. The simple lines of this and similar plain sets of the 1870s make unique table settings in country homes today.

Ceres Shape by Elsmore & Forster

The most famous shape potted in white granite was probably *Ceres Shape*, named after the Roman goddess of agriculture. This design was created and molded for the Elsmore & Forster Company. Its popularity set the style for wheat-decorated sets manufactured in the 1860s. The husk border with scallops around the edge of the well is shown on page 90. This characteristic decor plus melon ribs on serving pieces was borrowed by many Staffordshire potters.

This *Ceres Shape* by E. & F. included a cable around necks of pouring vessels, around bases including those of punch cups, midway on tureen covers, and around wells on saucers. However, some relish dishes and some tureen covers were made without cables and were both clearly marked Elsmore & Forster, *Ceres Shape*.

Turner & Goddard & Co. also used a cable and only then on the three main pieces of the tea set and on some soup tureens. Collectors like the excellent potting used by this company.

The label, *Ceres Shape* by E. Pearson, is found on the pattern we call *Wheat and Hops*.

Detail on ladle handle

To the right are various sketches of *Ceres Shape* pieces produced by Elsmore & Forster, including the two versions of their relish dish and a detail of the ladle handle. Also shown are the "Ceres Shape" markings used by three makers: Elsmore & Forster, Turner & Goddard & Co. and E. Pearson. Remember, the Pearson "Ceres" is what collectors now call *Wheat and Hops*.

Fig. 11-1 This four piece *Ceres* sauce tureen is an exact mimic of the larger soup tureen. Note the concave ribs inside the ladle. Collection of Dan Overmeyer.

Fig. 11-2 Wheat collectors love to find this *Ceres* covered hot toddy bowl. The ladle is a mid size between the small sauce ladle and the large soup ladle. Collection of Sally Scrimgeour.

**More
Ceres Shapes**

Fig. 11-3 Here the *Ceres* covered sugar bowl poses with the *Ceres* hot cake server. Owners are Dick and Adele Armbruster. ➔

Fig. 11-4 These *Ceres* compotes were made in three sizes. Elsmore & Forster shaped small sauce dishes that are very difficult to locate. Collection of Tom and Olga Moreland. ➔

Fig. 11-5 Three vertical toothbrush holders, left to right: *Wheat* by Goddard & Burgess; *Ceres* by Elsmore & Forster, and *Fuchsia*. Moreland Collection.

Fig. 11-6 Partial *Ceres* toilet set. The toothbrush holder and mug are missing. Probably, a foot bath and waste container were also manufactured. Dream on!

Fig. 11-7 Very , very rare is the covered hot beverage server in *Ceres Shape*. Owners are Dick and Adele Armbruster.

Fig. 11-8 *Ceres* round or oval open servers were made in nests. The diameter sizes of the six bowls in the round sets ranged from about 7 1/2″ to 13 1/2 ″. A sauce dish is also shown.

Fig. 11-9 Another rare *Ceres* piece is this 2⁵/₈″ h. egg cup. Owned by Dan Overmeyer

Fig. 11-10 The Armbrusters located this rare *Ceres* mug with rope around both rim and base. ←

Fig. 11-11 Elsmore & Forster rarely executed their *Ceres Shape* with a Rockingham glaze. Photo provided by Arene Burgess. ➤

Fig. 11-12 Elsmore & Forster sometimes added a flow blue cobalt and a lighter blue color over the wheat heads and leaves on the *Ceres* shape. Here is a decorated covered tureen and undertray. Photo provided by Arnold Kowalsky.

Other "Grain Patterns"

The word "ironstone" often brings to mind that most famous decor of old white china, a wheat design. This fact was driven home most forcibly by Norman Rockwell, the great American illustrator. He chose a scene called "Freedom from Want" for use in one of his Four Freedom Series. It pictures a middle-class American family gathered happily and hungrily around the laden table set with plain ironstone on spotless linen. Grandpa hovers over Grandma as she proudly bears the crispy, brown turkey on the traditional enormous ironstone platter. In the foreground shines a large, covered, blue-white ironstone tureen with melon shaped ribs and borders of heavily embossed white heads and stalks. This well-publicized wheat pattern has grown to symbolize the fruitfulness of our farms.

We begin the series with *Adriatic Shape* potted in 1853 by Barrow & Co. We include it first because of the spectacular wheat sheaf finial, with nearby sickle. We also see this finial, minus the sickle, topping tureens marked James Edwards & Son. We have no clue as to which firm really designed this attractive knop.

On the following pages are drawings and photographs of grain and grape decorated tableware made in the Staffordshire potteries. ❈

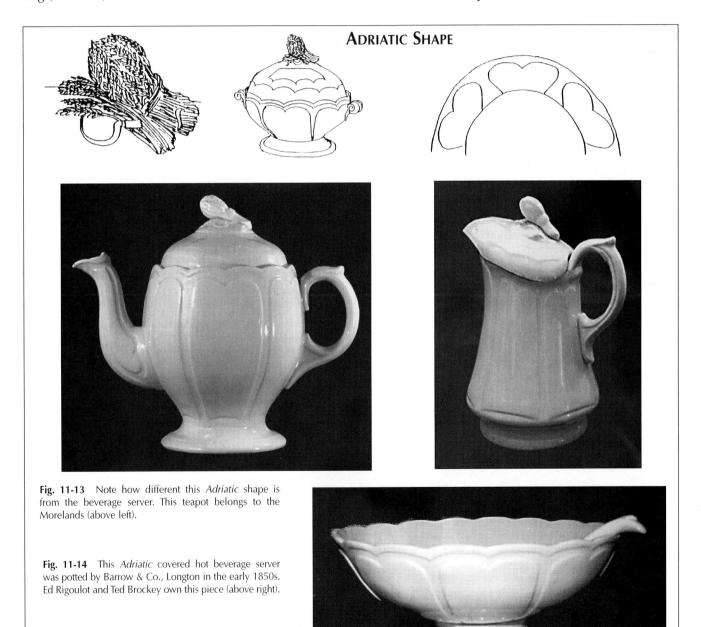

ADRIATIC SHAPE

Fig. 11-13 Note how different this *Adriatic* shape is from the beverage server. This teapot belongs to the Morelands (above left).

Fig. 11-14 This *Adriatic* covered hot beverage server was potted by Barrow & Co., Longton in the early 1850s. Ed Rigoulot and Ted Brockey own this piece (above right).

Fig. 11-15 The diameter of this graceful, large *Adriatic* punch bowl by Barrow is 16". Collection of Tom and Kathy Lautenschlager.

➡

CORN AND OATS

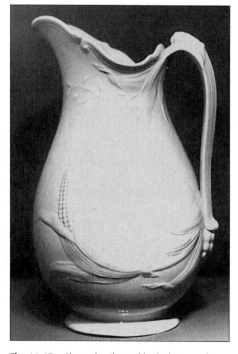

Fig. 11-16 This very collectible *Corn and Oats* shape was made by both Davenport and J. Wedgwood. Tea set owned by Laura and Chester Ady.

Fig. 11-17 Sharp detailing of both the ear of corn and oat heads are impressed on sides of this *Corn and Oats* ewer. Ady Collection.

Fig. 11-18 The ear of corn makes a startling finial on the *Corn and Oats* tureens. Ady Collection.

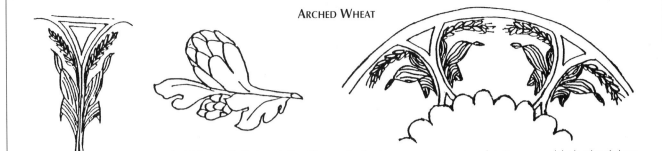

ARCHED WHEAT

Arched Wheat by R. Cochran & Co., Glasgow, Scotland, was an arrangement used six times around the border of plates. The pine cone-type finial rests on a ring of thumbprints on covered servers. It is sometimes found decorated with flow blue under lustre touches.

CANADA

Canada Shape by Clementson Bros. is one of the most desirable white ironstone shapes made during the last quarter of the 19th century. It was registered in 1877.

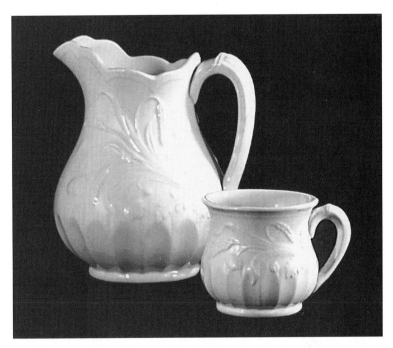

Fig. 11-19   An 1877 registration mark by Clementson Bros. is found under these *Canada* pieces. Notice the pumpkin-shaped bodies on these very collectible treasures. Collection of the Morelands.

Fig. 11-20   Several collectors report that this *Ear of Corn* jug is only marked by an illegible diamond-shaped registry. The Morelands own this one.

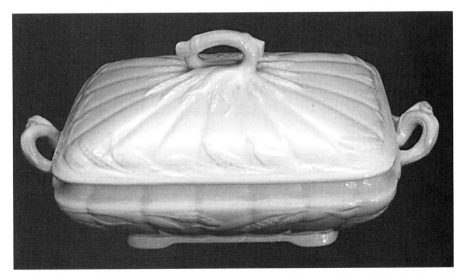

Fig. 11-21   Called *Four-Square Wheat,* this is a square treatment of the usual wheat with ribs. It was made by the Scottish potter, Cochran. From the collection of Sally Scrimgeour.

FOUR-SQUARE WHEAT

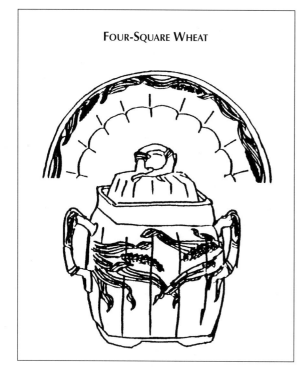

Four-Square Wheat by R. Cochran & Co. was a different wheat treatment on square bodies. It echoed the *Ceres* treatment on flatware. The plates can be identified by a higher middle row of grains in the wheat heads.

PRAIRIE SHAPE

Prairie Shape, registered by J. Clementson in 1861, was also potted by his successors, Clementson Bros. This prairie design used swags on plates instead of the *Ceres*-type husk and scallop borders.

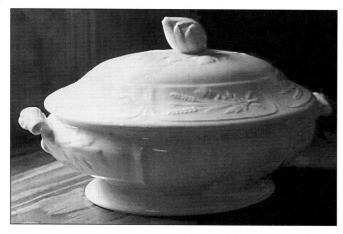

Fig. 11-22 Joseph Clementson registered this *Prairie Shape* tureen in November of 1861.

ROPED WHEAT

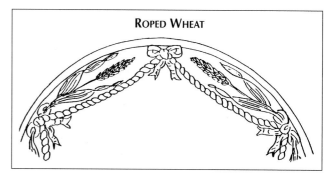

Roped Wheat, registered by Thomas Furnival and Sons of Cobridge in 1878, is a deeply-impressed, busy pattern. It was reported as *The Lorne* by one collector. The handle to the cover of the tureen is a cable and ring decoration with a ring of eighteen thumbprints around it.

PRAIRIE FLOWERS AND WHEAT IN THE MEADOW

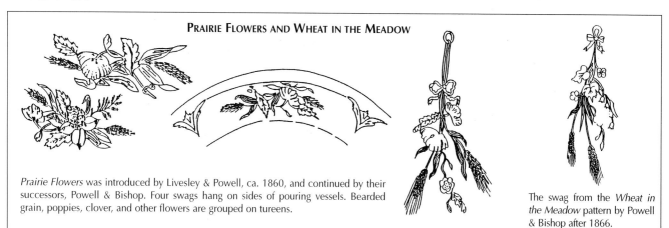

Prairie Flowers was introduced by Livesley & Powell, ca. 1860, and continued by their successors, Powell & Bishop. Four swags hang on sides of pouring vessels. Bearded grain, poppies, clover, and other flowers are grouped on tureens.

The swag from the *Wheat in the Meadow* pattern by Powell & Bishop after 1866.

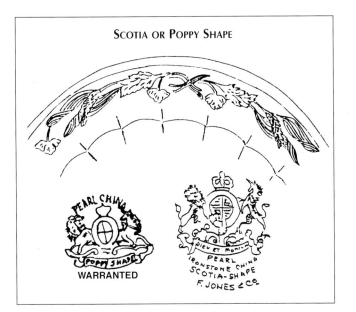

SCOTIA OR POPPY SHAPE

PEARL CHINA
POPPY SHAPE
WARRANTED

DIEU ET MON
PEARL
IRONSTONE CHINA
SCOTIA-SHAPE
F. JONES & Co.

Scotia Shape by Frederick Jones & Co. used a prairie-type border on all pieces. However, instead of using the usual melon ribs, he used concave ribs on all serving and pouring vessels. J. & C. Wileman made this shape too, marking it *Poppy Shape.*

Fig. 11-23 This *Poppy Shape* (Scotia Shape) teapot by Wileman uses concave ribs with wheat and poppy decor. Collection of Jim and Mara Kerr.

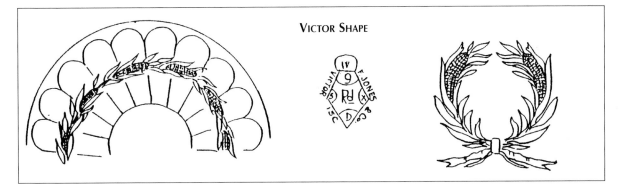

VICTOR SHAPE

Victor Shape was registered by F. Jones & Co. in 1868. A corn wreath decorates the sides of serving pieces. A row of thumbprints is beneath a corn wreath on the edge of plates.

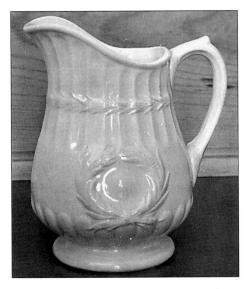

Fig. 11-24 This *Victor Shape* pitcher potted by F. Jones in the late 1860s is often confused with *Laurel Wreath* by Elsmore & Forster. Collectors are John and Jane Yunginger.

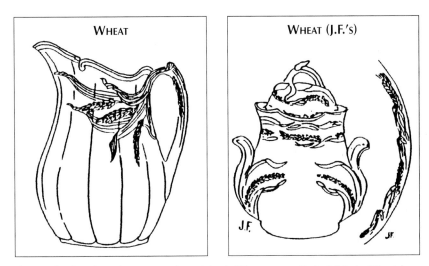

WHEAT

WHEAT (J.F.'S)

J.F.   JF.

The two sketches above show two versions of simple Wheat patterns. To the left is the Wheat shape with weaker mellon ribs than the Ceres Shape. Mellor, Taylor & Co.; David Methven and Sons; Hollinshead & Kirkham; Wilkinson; W. & E. Corn; Henry Meakin; Baker & Co. and others produced this shape. No cable was used. The pitcher shown was marked by Hollinshead & Kirkham, late J. Wedgwood, after 1876. The *J. F.'s Wheat* shown on the right did not use melon ribs or well scallops.

WHEAT AND CLOVER

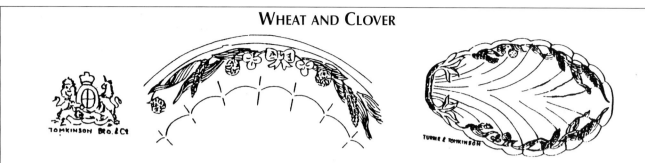

Wheat and Clover, known for its border of wheat, clover leaves with blossoms, and ribbon bows, was made by Tomkinson Bros. & Co., Turner & Tomkinson, Taylor Bros., and Ford, Challinor & Co. This last company often used concave rather than melon ribbing.

Fig. 11-25 These two *Wheat and Clover* pitchers have concave ribs on the left ewer by Ford, Challinor & Co and melon ribs on the right ewer by Turner & Tomkinson. The Morelands own both.

Fig. 11-26 Close up of the detail on a *Wheat and Clover* pitcher & bowl by Turner & Tomkinson.

Fig. 11-27 The above *Wheat and Clover* punch bowl was marked Turner & Tomkinson. Collectors are the Diemers.

Fig. 11-28 This photo of a vertical toothbrush holder with liner was provided by the Diemers! The shape is *Wheat and Clover.*

Fig. 11-29 Seen in the back, a handled, covered hot toddy bowl and, in front, two sizes of punch bowls all in *Wheat* manufactured by Turner, Goddard & Co. Left to right, the diameters are 10 1/2, 9 3/8, and 8 1/2 inches. Moreland Collection.

Fig. 11-30 This *Wheat* tureen has no cable added. Owned by Sally Scrimgeour.

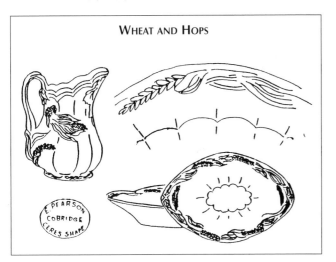

WHEAT AND HOPS

Wheat and Hops was manufactured by J. & G. Meakin, Jacob Furnival, W. Taylor, Robert Cochran & Co., Alfred Meakin, E. Pearson, W. E. Oulsnam & Son, Clementson Bros., and also a North American potter, St. Johns Chinaware Co., in Canada. The design is beautifully molded in three dimensions.

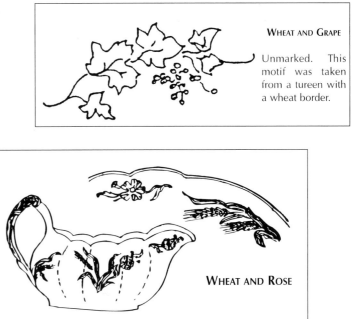

Fig. 11-31 Several potters produced *Wheat and Hops* tureens as part of early sets.

WHEAT AND GRAPE

Unmarked. This motif was taken from a tureen with a wheat border.

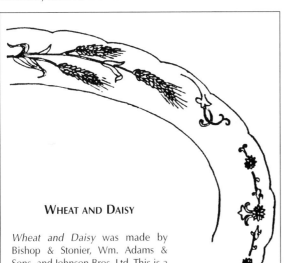

WHEAT AND DAISY

Wheat and Daisy was made by Bishop & Stonier, Wm. Adams & Sons, and Johnson Bros. Ltd. This is a late pattern, thinly potted of ironstone.

WHEAT AND ROSE

Wheat and Rose by Alfred Meakin. This is found on thinly potted materials made in the late 19th and early 20th centuries.

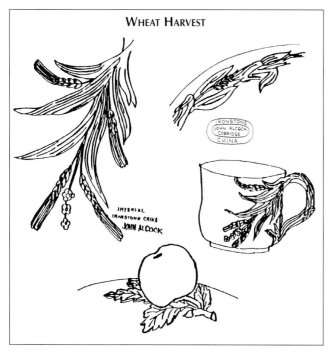

WHEAT HARVEST

Wheat Harvest was introduced before 1861 by John Alcock. The design is very deeply molded. The swag in the left drawing covers the whole side of a pitcher. Apple finial is life-size.

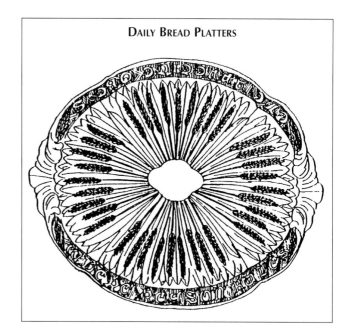

DAILY BREAD PLATTERS

"Where Reason Rules" begins on one side of a bread platter shaped by Davenport. The other side answers "The Appetite Obeys." Most daily bread patters were made by American potters but this is an exception. It has been seen in majolica and on pieces copied by American workers.

Grape Patterns

The graceful leaves of the trailing grapevine and the bountiful clusters it bears have appealed to man through the ages. Ancient civilizations often depicted vine and grape motifs.

These same decorations can be found pressed or etched in molded glass, cast in early silver, painted on antique English porcelains, interwoven in the borders of Staffordshire blues, and included in other early fruit basket china patterns.

The earliest white ironstone vintage design was probably used on one of the *Montpelier* clay bodies by John Ridgway & Co. The grapes and leaves on white ironstone continued until they were later seen on the fabled *Fox and Grapes* after 1891.

Man will continue to use the leaves for food and medicine, the fruit for nourishment, and the dormant vines for making baskets and wreaths. Grapes are an integral part of man's daily life.

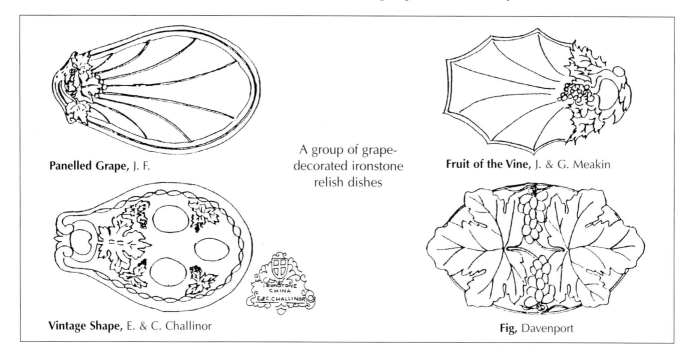

Panelled Grape, J. F.

A group of grape-decorated ironstone relish dishes

Fruit of the Vine, J. & G. Meakin

Vintage Shape, E. & C. Challinor

Fig, Davenport

FOX AND GRAPES

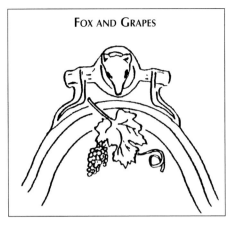

Fox and Grapes, a late pattern, was potted by Thomas Furnival & Sons. A close-up of the handle is shown.

GRAPE CLUSTERS

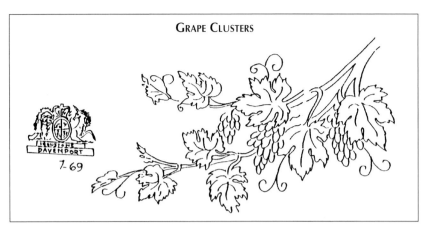

Grape Clusters was a large design manufactured by Davenport.

GRAPE CLUSTER WITH CHAIN

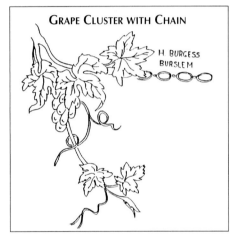

Grape Cluster with Chain, by Henry Burgess, is a detailed pattern located on the sides of a large table jug.

Fig. 11-32 *Grape Cluster with Chain* jug (Henry Burgess) and *Grape Clusters* chamber pot (Davenport) were made around 1870. These are two, closely-related, vintage patterns.

GRAPE OCTAGON

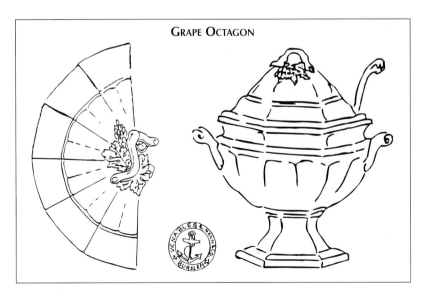

Jugs in *Grape Octagon* shape have been recorded from early in the 1800s, decorated in many styles. In mid-century, it was used as a base for transfer-decorated wares. Different potters varied the foliage and placement of grapes. E. Challinor & Co., J. Clementson, Bougham & Mayer, Livesley & Powell, Edward Corn, Samuel Alcock, Thomas Walker, Hulme & Booth, J. F., Freakley & Farrell, Venables, Mann & Co. and others made this shape.

Fig. 11-33 This is a *Grape Octagon* covered sugar bowl.

Fig. 11-34   This *Grape Octagon* ewer, manufactured by Freakly & Farrall, was a shape used as early as the 1820s. This ewer, of course, was produced in the mid-19th century. Collection of Carol & Frank Fleischman.

Grape Wreath was designed by Bridgwood & Clarke.

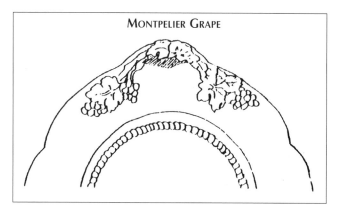

Montpelier Grape was shaped by John Ridgway & Co., circa 1850. The word *Montpelier* referred to the clay body used rather than to a shape name.

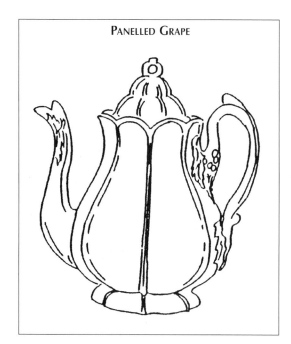

Panelled Grape was fashioned by J. F., Edward Pearson, J. Clementson and Chas. Meigh & Son. Some finials were grape clusters; some, rings.

Fig. 11-35   J. F. (Jacob Furnival) fashioned this graceful *Panelled Grape* tureen. Beside it is a plain mug. Owners are Ernie and Bev Dieringer.

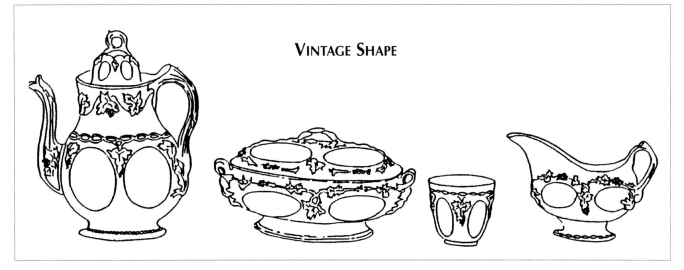

VINTAGE SHAPE

Vintage Shape, named by Adams, was later repeated more extensively by E. & C. Challinor, circa 1865.

Fig. 11-36 These *Vintage Shape* pieces were made by E. & C. Challinor. Adams, in an earlier production, named this shape.

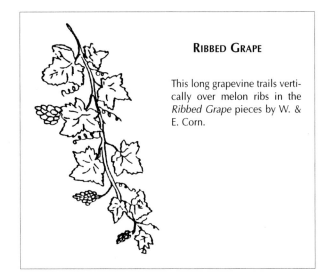

RIBBED GRAPE

This long grapevine trails vertically over melon ribs in the *Ribbed Grape* pieces by W. & E. Corn.

Fig. 11-37 This graceful melon-ribbed syrup server was decorated with grapes, leaves, and vine. It was made by A. Shaw in two sizes, found in plain white and also with copper lustre Tea Leaf. We named it *Vintage Beauty.*

Foliated Shapes

The varied shapes of leaves embossed on white granite were favored by both potters and purchasers in the 1860s. Included most often were foliage from the orchard and leaves from the oak, maple, grape and ivy. Curling branches with leaves echoed the rounded lines of serving vessels, with leaves often nestled beneath handles and spouts. The collector can almost foresee in some of these decorations similarities to the Art Noveau style that was to become popular around the turn of the century. This style encouraged designs to follow the flowing lines of the body to be decorated; certainly leaves and twigs can be adapted to many varied shapes.

One of the well-liked shapes employing foliage is the *Fig* made by both Davenport and J. Wedgwood. One of the puzzles that has concerned white ironstone collectors is the frequency of shapes potted by both of these companies (not seen with marks by other companies), namely: *Scalloped Decagon, Gothic Cameo, Corn and Oats, Sharon Arch, Fig* and *Fig Cousin*. Close examination of the patent registrations reveal that, in 1852, Davenport & Co. had a diamond-shaped mark on the underside of a relish labelled J. Wedgwood; the same Nov. 14, 1856 registration belonging to Davenport & Co. is found on *Fig* pieces sometimes impressed "Davenport" and sometimes marked 'J. Wedgwood;' the same thing is true of a *Sharon Arch* 1861 registration. We conclude that some sharing of shapes was willingly undertaken by these two firms. In 1863, Davenport, Banks & Co. and Edmund T. Wood (successor to John Wedge Wood) both patented the popular design, *Corn and Oats*. At an ironstone convention, two collectors brought graceful curving gravy boats with spouts at one end and an inward-curving handle that ended in an eagle head. One was impressed with the familiar Davenport "peanut" around the anchor and guess who potted the other? John Wedge Wood, of course.

Earlier than these dates, we find *Bordered Classic* white ironstone beauties by Davenport and several fluted shapes by John Wedge Wood in the 1840s. We see no duplication of these shapes so perhaps these two potters did not pool their skills until a later date.

Davenport used a *Fig Cousin* shape with some of the same foliage as that used on *Fig* bodies, adding a copper lustre Tea Leaf motif and band which included some areas of pink lustre. This treatment is widely sought by collectors of copper lustre; especially longed for is the children's miniature set in *Fig Cousin*.

Here follow the lines in drawings and photographs of white ironstone china decorated with leaves. ❈

A drawing of the eagle head gravy boat. Provided by Ernie Dieringer.

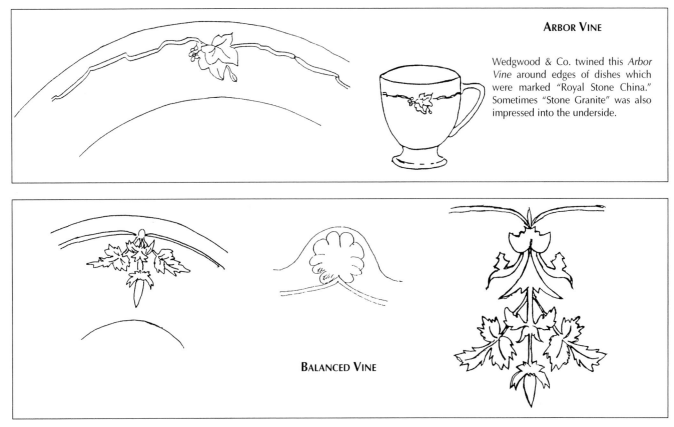

ARBOR VINE

Wedgwood & Co. twined this *Arbor Vine* around edges of dishes which were marked "Royal Stone China." Sometimes "Stone Granite" was also impressed into the underside.

BALANCED VINE

Clementson Bros. registered *Balanced Vine* in 1867. Notice the shell motif under the spouts of jugs (center). The main motif hangs below the neck of vessels. Like many Clementson shapes, it was sometimes trimmed by copper lustre (see Chapter 16).

BLUET

Hope and Carter marked this *Bluet* shape with an illegible late registry between 1868 and 1883. This design is not three-dimensional, simply composed of raised lines.

FINIAL

BORDER OF LEAVES

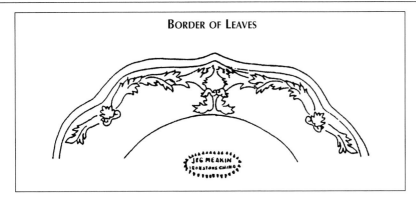

J. & G. Meakin edged this biscuit tray with his *Border of Leaves* design.

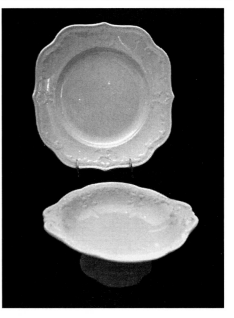

Fig. 12-1 Some collector should gather these squared cookie plates that J. & G. Meakin made in several shapes. This tray and donut stand in *Border of Leaves* is from the Rigoulot-Brockey Collection.

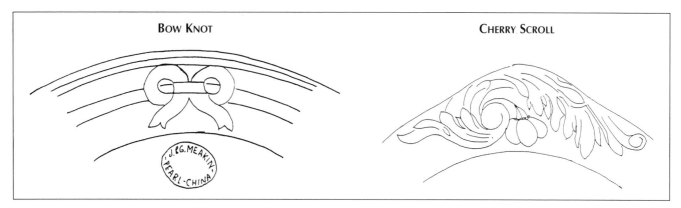

BOW KNOT (left) and **CHERRY SCROLL** (right) - I have only seen plates in these two shapes by J. & G. Meakin. Both *Cherry Scroll* and *Bow Knot* are well potted.

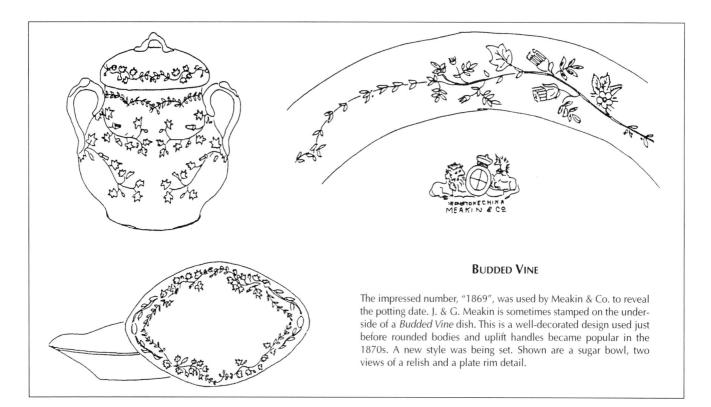

BUDDED VINE

The impressed number, "1869", was used by Meakin & Co. to reveal the potting date. J. & G. Meakin is sometimes stamped on the underside of a *Budded Vine* dish. This is a well-decorated design used just before rounded bodies and uplift handles became popular in the 1870s. A new style was being set. Shown are a sugar bowl, two views of a relish and a plate rim detail.

Fig. 12-2 *Budded Vine* trails foliage over most of this shape by J. & G. Meakin. Notice the rounded lines and uplift handles prevalent on many shapes of the 1870s.

Fig. 12-3 *Cabbage* leaves covered all sides of this shape potted by Mayer & Elliott, registered in 1860. Collection of Julie Rich.

Drape Leaf Shapes

These four patterns are simply called *Draped Leaf.* Letters are added to help in identification. They are not the same letters I have used in former guides.

Draped Leaf (A)

Draped Leaf (A) - James Edwards & Son registered this *A* shape on September 1, 1859.

Draped Leaf (B)

Draped Leaf (B) - "Imperial Ironstone China" was the name for the body of *B* shape by Henry Alcock & Co.

Draped Leaf (C)

Fig. 12-4 This teapot by W. Baker & Co. in *Draped Leaf* (C) is decorated with a copper lustre Morning Glory motif. Dale Abrams Collection.

Draped Leaf (C) - W. Baker & Co. of Fenton called their white granite body "Stone China".

Draped Leaf (D)

Draped Leaf (D) - Little is known about this heavy *D* shape executed in "Porcelain Opaque" by Bridgwood and Clarke.

DRAPED LEAF WITH BERRIES

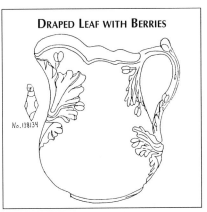

The potter of this design, *Draped Leaf with Berries*, did not include his name; nevertheless, he did register this shape. The numbers are illegible but my guess would be about 1860—perhaps by J. F?

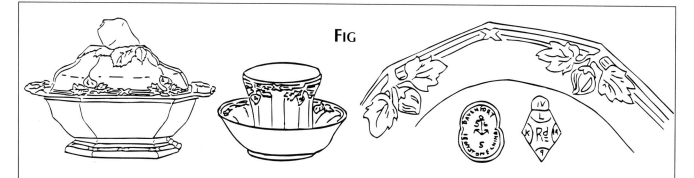

Fig

Collectors treasure pieces of *Fig* manufactured by both Davenport and J. Wedgwood. This shape was registered by Davenport in 1856. The relish dish was composed of a pair of grape clusters with grape leaves as shown on page 102.

Fig. 12-5   Five out of the usual six *Fig* platters nest in this Dieringer collection.

Fig. 12-6   This sided round *Fig* fruit compote was located by the Dieringers.

Fig. 12-7   The *Fig* family pose for their portrait. Teapot, punch cup and tureen are present.

FIG COUSIN

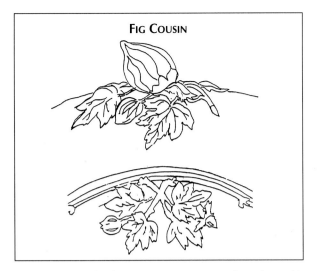

Fig Cousin, made by the same potters as *Fig,* is drawn here. This shape uses some of the same decor as *Fig.* Davenport added copper trim, a Tea Leaf motif and pink lustre to make this decorated shape one of the most collectible Tea Leaf patterns.

Fig. 12-8   *Fig Cousin* uses the same foliage as *Fig* on this table jug.

GOOSEBERRY

This piece of *Gooseberry* was made by J. F. The letters "W. G." on the base may have referred to "white granite."

Fig. 12-9   A pair of *Bordered Gooseberry* jugs by Wedgwood & Co. used this design that was once called "Branch of Three Leaves."

GOURD

James Edwards & Son shaped this *Gourd* tureen about 1855. It is easy to see how this piece may have been shaped from five molds: the finial, the cover, the body, the attached handles, and the pedestal.

HANGING LEAVES

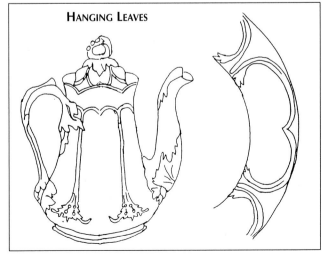

Anthony Shaw used this *Hanging Leaves* shape in white granite in the mid -1850s. It is often found as a blank for a copper lustre Tea Leaf and lustre band decoration (see Chapter 16)

HANGING ARCH

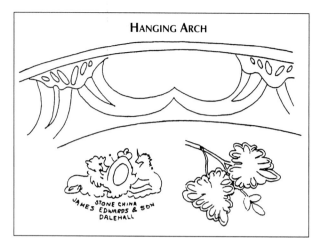

James Edwards & Son manufactured this *Hanging Arch* shape

Fig. 12-10 Swirling lines decorate this *Hanging Arch* tureen made by James Edwards & Son..

HOLLY

Another mid-19th century product, *Holly* shape, was probably potted for several years by John Maddock & Son.

HUSK

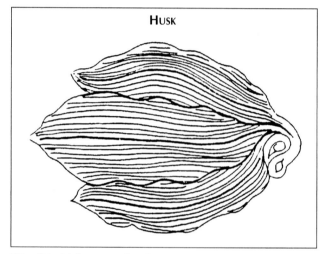

This relish dish by James Edwards & Son is nicknamed *Husk*.

IVY WREATH

John Meir & Son registered this attractive shape on May 2, 1860. How can we secure more pieces of *Ivy Wreath?*

GREAT IVY WITH BERRIES

This early shape, made in heavy, white granite, was marked by John Maddock, who worked from 1842 to 1855. A relish and tureen are shown.

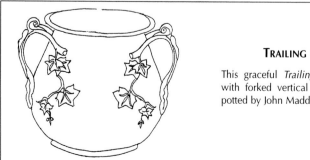

TRAILING IVY

This graceful *Trailing Ivy* pattern with forked vertical handles was potted by John Maddock & Son.

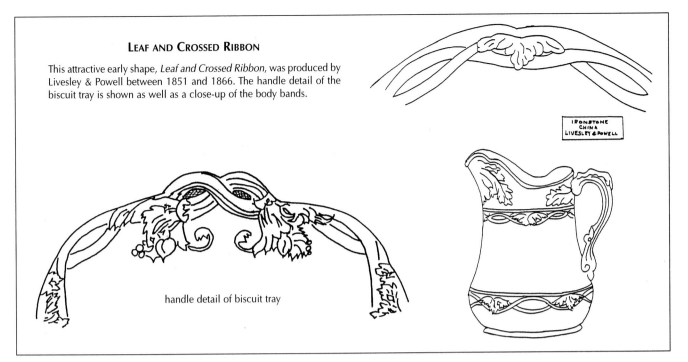

LEAF AND CROSSED RIBBON

This attractive early shape, *Leaf and Crossed Ribbon,* was produced by Livesley & Powell between 1851 and 1866. The handle detail of the biscuit tray is shown as well as a close-up of the body bands.

handle detail of biscuit tray

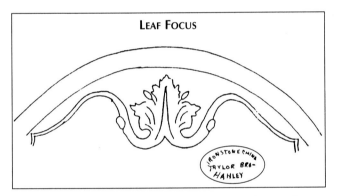

LEAF FOCUS

Leaf Focus was produced by Taylor Bros. A detail of the design is shown.

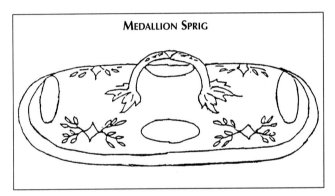

MEDALLION SPRIG

This *Medallion Sprig* shape was manufactured by Powell & Bishop. The decoration is not three-dimensional but is simply outlined. A long cover for a brush box is illustrated.

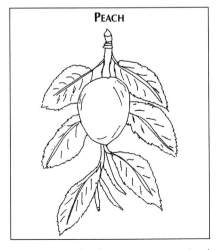

PEACH

A massive, very handsome tureen uses a *Peach* finial and crabstock handles over fruit leaves. It was designed by George Wooliscroft.

Fig. 12-11   PLUM DECAGON J. & G. Meakin shaped a *Plum Decagon* tureen with ten sides topped by a life-sized plum finial (shown). Tureens have open horizontal crabstock handles. The two illustrated are owned by Tom and Olga Moreland

"Oak" Patterns

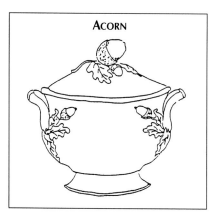

ACORN

"Pearl China" was impressed by J. & G. Meakin on this *Acorn* sauce tureen.

Fig. 12-12   J. & G. Meakin used a three-dimensional *Acorn* decoration on this round compote from the collection of Ed Rigoulot and Ted Brockey.

NUT WITH BUD

John Meir & Son molded this popular shape, *Nut with Bud*, in "Stone China."

Fig. 12-13   I. (John) Meir & Son potted this *Nut with Bud* cov. sugar bowl. Photo sent by the Adys..

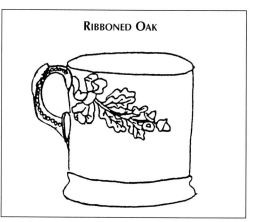

RIBBONED OAK

This *Ribboned Oak* mug was potted by W. & E. Corn. The registry mark is illegible.

TINY OAK AND ACORN

J. W. Pankhurst fashioned this *Tiny Oak and Acorn* tureen which is 12 inches long.

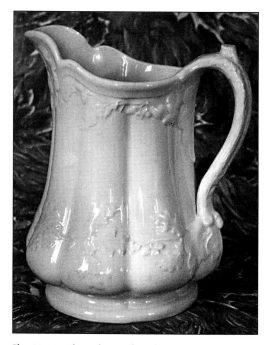

Fig. 12-14   The *White Oak and Acorns* pattern on this table pitcher by Holland & Green is deeply embossed over the melon ribs.

"Pear" Patterns

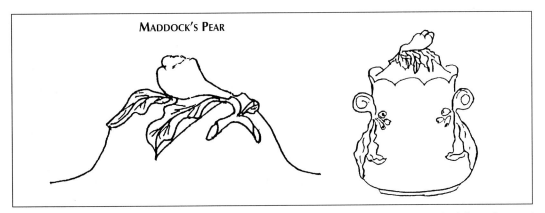

MADDOCK'S PEAR

This *Maddock's Pear* finial and leaves have been located on both a huge waste jar and a foot bath. The body has a sheen and is usually found uncrazed.

Fig. 12-15 Rare foot tub in *Maddock's Pear* has a Florida home with Sally Scrimgeour.

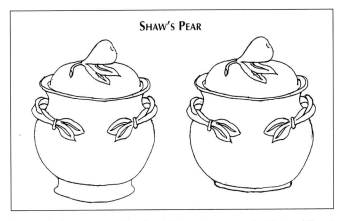

SHAW'S PEAR

This simple shape is topped by *Shaw's Pear* and was potted with two different bases. It was often used as a blank for a copper lustre decor.

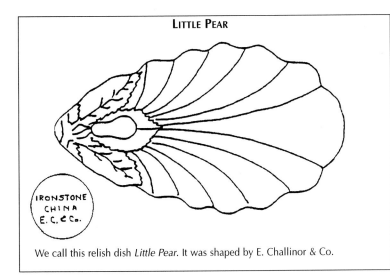

LITTLE PEAR

IRONSTONE CHINA E. C. C Co.

We call this relish dish *Little Pear*. It was shaped by E. Challinor & Co.

HANGING PEAR

This *Hanging Pear* decoration was added to pieces by Liddle, Elliot & Son.

POPPING POD

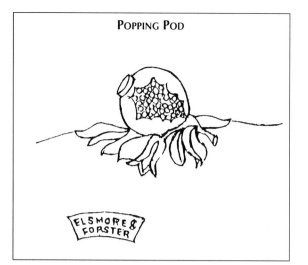

This opening *Pod* was drawn from the cover of a butter dish manufactured by Elsmore & Forster.

SHARON ARCH

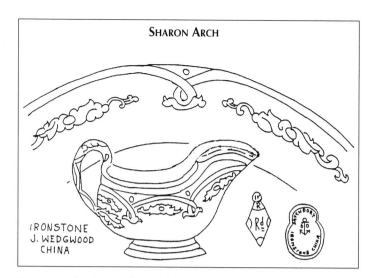

Again we find both J. Wedgwood (John Wedge Wood) and Davenport using the same shape. Pitchers had ring handles. The body itself is heavier than most white granite.

Fig. 12-16 Both J. Wedgwood and Davenport made this *Sharon Arch* shape and both used the same registry mark on some pieces.

STRAWBERRY

This *Strawberry* decor with a berry finial has been seen only on miniature sets potted by Meakin & Co. A design detail is shown.

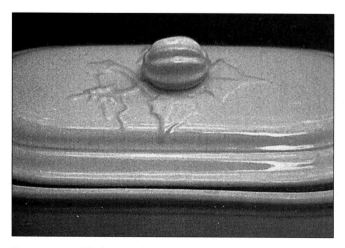

Fig. 12-17 Maddock's *Squash with Vine* horizontal toilet box belongs to Diane Dorman.

STYLIZED BERRY

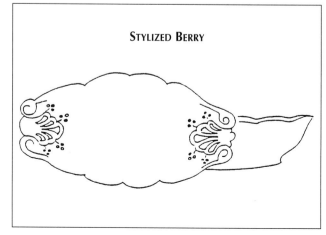

Maddock & Co. manufactured this *Stylized Berry* design in the late 1800s.

Fig. 12-18 Here's the teapot from Texas that told us who J. F. was. This Jacob Furnival piece is owned by the Bedfords. I'm calling this "Texas Furnival."

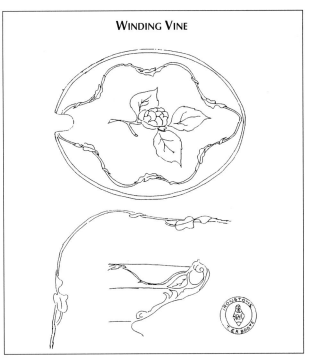

WINDING VINE

T. & R. Boote registered this *Winding Vine* design in 1867. The bodies of servers are rather plain, edged by this well-impressed vine as shown here. A lid and finial are also shown.

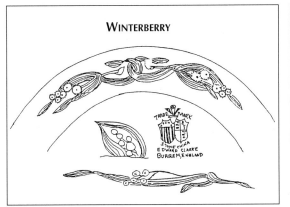

WINTERBERRY

Edward Clarke used this *Winterberry* design after 1865. The long leaves, the berries, and the pointed pod finial are deeply impressed.

Fig. 12-19 The long leaves and pointed pod finial make this *Winterberry* horizontal toothbrush holder by Clarke very attractive.

WREATH OF LEAVES

Fig. 12-20 (Above and right) A mystery potter wrapped pieces with a *Wreath of Leaves* but did not acknowledge himself. Has anyone located a piece with the potter's name?

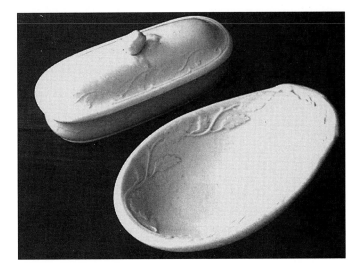

From the Flower Garden

Homemakers have long nurtured flowers near their doors. That same love of flowers is often reflected in designs on walls, pillows, drapes, fabrics and ceramics. The earliest white granite shapes employed sided bodies, vertical lines, panels, and fluting occasionally with a flower finial. During the 1860s, the Staffordshire potters depicted naturalistic flowers from the prairies, meadows, and gardens. These designers sensed that home owners in the United States and Canada might buy earthenware molded with leaves, vines and blooms.

Wedgwood & Co., who marketed several popular floral designs on white granite, acquired the Unicorn Pottery in Tunstall. Their works were large, employing 700 workers in 1862, specializing in wares "for their considerable export trade by designing goods to requirements of foreign companies" according to Hughes.

The names for the bodies of these wares were "Stone China" or "Imperial Ironstone China." Jewitt, in his ceramic history, states that the Unicorn Works were "entirely devoted to production of white granite for the American trade."

Wedgwood & Co. is listed as a potting firm from 1860 on to the present time. They had worked with Podmore, Walker & Co. Godden states that the "& Co." related to Enoch Wedgwood but "it was found advantageous to use the name Wedgwood alone" so from ca. 1860 the firm was restyled "Wedgwood & Co." Floral designs by these potters are especially treasured by collectors.

Registered in February of 1857, the earliest shape marked by this company was *Athens Shape*, labelled P.W & Co. Wedgwood continued to market this collectable set of white granite. Other early Wedgwood patterns are listed here:

Arbor	*Hyacinth
*Athens Shape	*Laurel
Bordered Gooseberry	Plain Round
*Flora	Square-Ridged

*named by the potter

Drawings and photographs of desirable floral shapes are found next in this text. ▧

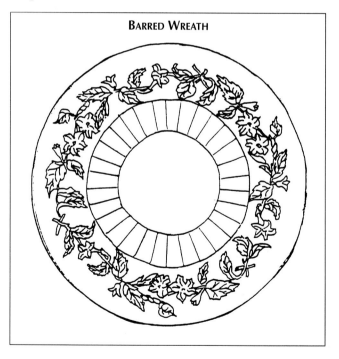

BARRED WREATH

This *Barred Wreath* saucer was made in one of Henry Burgess' more interesting shapes, ca. 1860s.

118

Fig. 13-1 BELLFLOWER - Similar to the *Lily of the Valley* design is a deeply impressed *Bellflower* shape potted by John Edwards in his early potting years at Fenton. This teapot and waste bowl are both treasured by collectors.

DANGLING TULIP

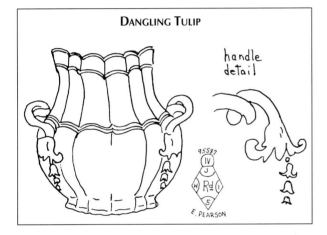

This topless sugar bowl in *Dangling Tulip* was registered by E. Pearson and his firm in 1854.

FLEUR-DE-LIS WITH LEAVES

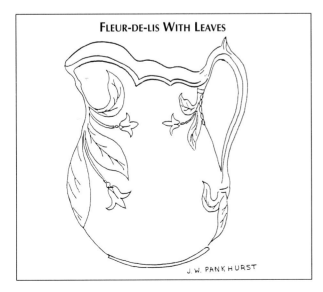

This jug is the only piece yet found in *Fleur-de-lis,* marked by J. W. Pankhurst.

BELL TRACERY

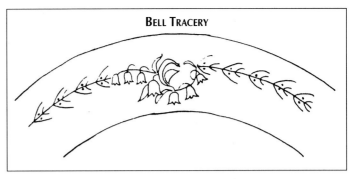

Holland and Green used a *Bell Tracery* outlined decor on lightweight ironstone.

COCHRAN'S RING

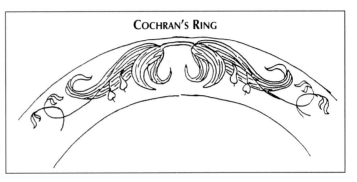

Robert Cochran of Glasgow produced this plate, ringed by blades and blooms. It has been located with flow blue with copper trim, also. We nicknamed it *Cochran's Ring.*

FLORA SHAPE

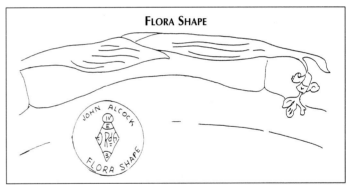

John Alcock registered *Flora Shape* in 1865. Servers are striking with long vertical blades with flowers hanging down over large slightly-covex ribs.

FLORA AND BORDERED GOOSEBERRY

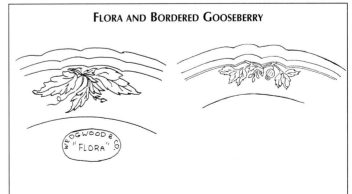

Wedgwood & Co. marked *Flora* (no Shape) on plates with slightly scalloped edges and five motifs displaying flowered foliage (left). The plates are easily confused with *Bordered Gooseberry* plates (right; also see page 111).

Fig. 13-2 Very rare is the round toddy bowl with its clear leaves with flowers under a deep border on the *Flora* design by Wedgwood & Co. Collection of Ed Rigoulot and Ted Brockey.

Fig 13-3 Three very different cream jugs are these: (left) an unnamed pattern by John Maddock; (middle) *Flora Shape* by John Alcock with its flower and leaves hanging down; and (right) an early *Primary Shape* by T. J. & J. Mayer, Moreland Collection.

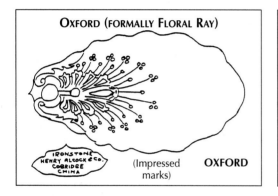

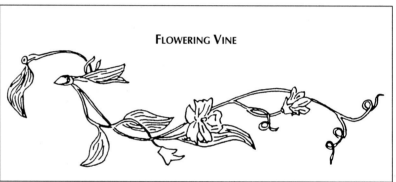

Henry Alcock & Co. (after 1861) designed this *Oxford* relish, the mark was impressed.

This graceful *Flowering Vine* flows over the body of servers. Unmarked.

ARCHED-FORGET-ME NOT

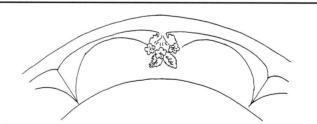

Fig. 13-4 This beautiful low compote was registered (illegible) and marked "Elsmore & Forster." Could it have been an *Arched-Forget-Me Not* tazza? My guess for registry would be an 1864 date. Owned by Irene Burgess. See a sketch of a teapot on page 91. A plate border is also sketched here.

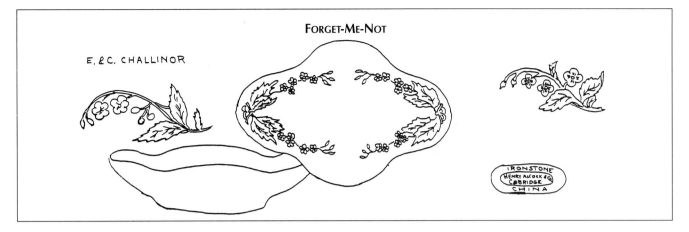

These small *Forget-Me-Not* flowers were used in four groups around plates. Varied treatments were employed by E. & C. Challinor, Henry Alcock, Taylor Bros. and by Wood, Rathbone & Co. This last firm used a trumpet flower finial on their teapot and tureens.

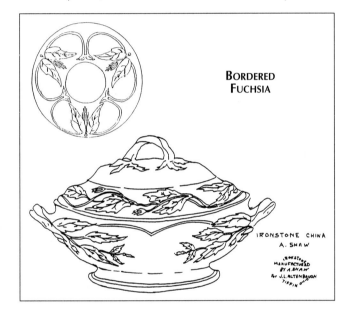

Bordered Fuchsia by Anthony Shaw adds three-dimensional leaves and blooms over Shaw's *Hanging Leaves* pattern. As is true of most of Shaw's designs, this was also a base for the copper lustre Tea Leaf decoration.

Fig. 13-5 This *Bordered Fuchsia* teapot, deeply embossed by Anthony Shaw, is a design overlaying another Shaw shape: *Hanging Leaves*.

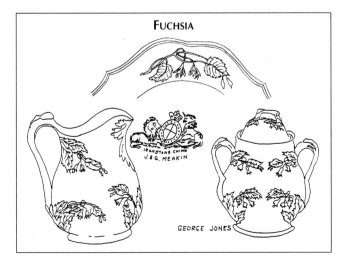

This *Fuchsia* shape was manufactured by both J. & G. Meakin and George Jones. The pieces that are more deeply potted are the most collectible. Some variation occurs. Above to the left is one corner of a squared biscuit tray by Meakin.

Fig. 13-6 Sharp detailing of *Fuchsia* flowers and leaves cover bodies of this shape made by both J. & G. Meakin and George Jones. Meakin fashioned squared biscuit trays in this shape.

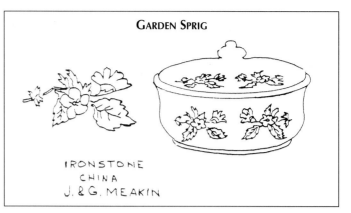

J & G Meakin used this *Garden Sprig* design five times on each plate and over Meakin's usual round shapes.

Fig 13-7 *Garden Sprig* by J. & G. Meakin has lines that were to be used in the plain, round shapes of the 1870s and 1880s.

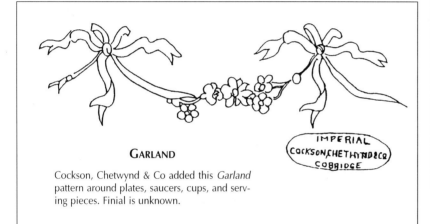

GARLAND

Cockson, Chetwynd & Co added this *Garland* pattern around plates, saucers, cups, and serving pieces. Finial is unknown.

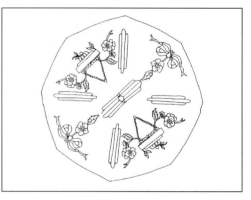

HANGING BASKET - This scace pattern, ca. 1875 was made in toilet and tablesets. A chamber pot lid is shown. Maker unknown.

HIDDEN MOTIF

The tiny motif (shown in the detail) is found around the edge of the lid, inside each scallop of the pot itself, and six times in the border of the plates. Also shown is the round finial. Surprisingly, the large three-dimensional foliage seems totally unrelated to the *Hidden Motif* by J. F.

Fig. 13-8 Jacob Furnival potted this *Hidden Motif*. That motif is so tiny that it doesn't show in the picture but the heavy embossed foliage does. Note the twisted rope handles. From the Moreland Collection.

Hyacinth by Wedgwood & Co was added to their stone granite body. This design is usually deeply impressed on round and oval bodies.

Fig. 13-9   Two *Hyacinth* potters produced this pair: the left pot is by Wedgwood & Co; the right one is by W. & E. Corn of Burslem. From the Moreland Collection.

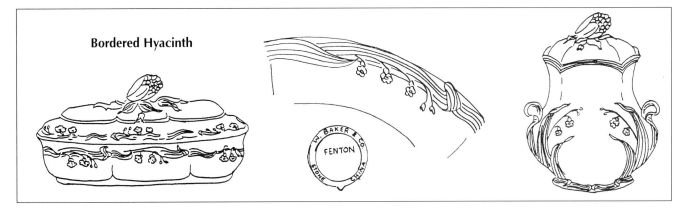

On *Bordered Hyacinth*, the open blossom of the English hyacinth is arranged in borders around plates and edges of serving pieces by W. Baker & Co. There is some confusion about which of the two hyacinth shapes was marked *Lily Shape* by W. & E. Corn.

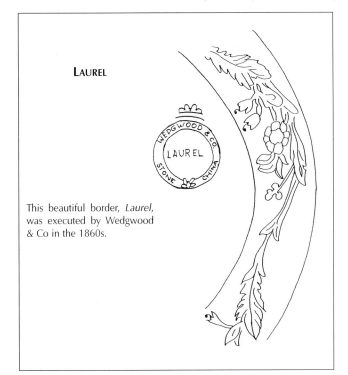

This beautiful border, *Laurel*, was executed by Wedgwood & Co in the 1860s.

Fig 13-10   The *Laurel* decoration twines around the neck and waist of this beautiful teapot made by Wedgwood & Co.

LILY SHAPE

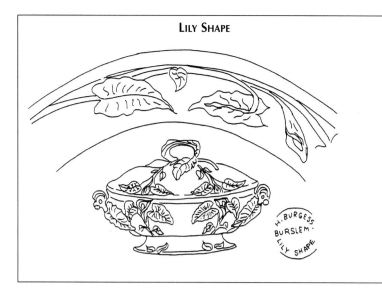

Lily Shape was marked on this excellently decorated body covered with calla lilies by Henry Burgess. E. Corn marked his *Bordered Hyacinth* with the same name.

LILY OF THE VALLEY (EDWARDS)

No. 138585

James Edwards & Son of Dalehall registered this shape on Feb. 27, 1861. *Lily of the Valley* pieces are consistently well-detailed.

PANELLED LILY

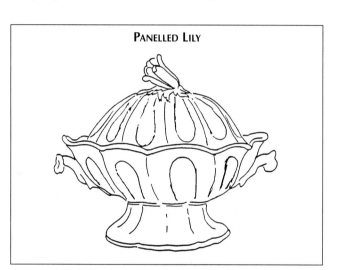

J. F. produced this *Panelled Lily* shape that echoes the tulip lines, introduced on Boote's *Sydenham* tureens. Collectors report the same tureen marked by J. W. Pankhurst of Hanley.

LILY OF THE VALLEY (SHAW'S)

Sometimes confused with the Edwards' shape, Shaw's *Lily of the Valley* can be identified by the round bodies with sprays of lilies on both sides of the stems. Copper Tea Leaf collectors eagerly seek for this shape. Egg cups (large) and bone dishes are found in this style.

Fig. 13-11 A deep relish dish and a sauce tureen (no ladle or liner) were potted by Shaw. His *Lily of the Valley* shape has flowers on both sides of the stem. Unusual pieces in this shape are large egg cups and bone dishes.

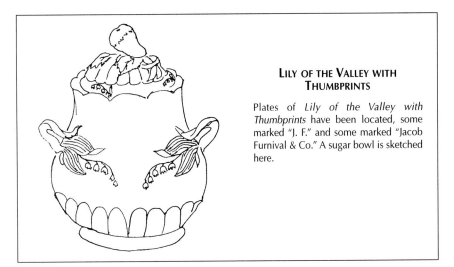

LILY OF THE VALLEY WITH THUMBPRINTS

Plates of *Lily of the Valley with Thumbprints* have been located, some marked "J. F." and some marked "Jacob Furnival & Co." A sugar bowl is sketched here.

Fig. 13-12 The punch cup is a Shaw's *Lily of the Valley* shape.

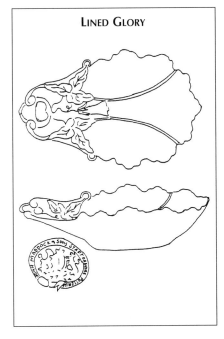

LINED GLORY

MEADOW BOUQUET

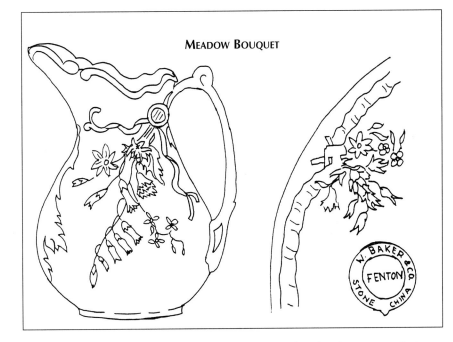

John Maddock & Sons fashioned this *Lined Glory* relish dish.

W. Baker & Co. added the detailed *Meadow Bouquet* design to the sides of pouring vessels. A cone finial rests on top of the covers of serving pieces.

MOCHO

This *Mocho*, marked on this later body shape by T. & R. Boote, sometimes has a bright blue applied pad. Bodies are round or oval with a few little palm-like fronds and flowers.

This deeply-detailed *Morning Glory* shape is the most collectible floral design. Bodies of all servers are covered with the naturalistic vines and flowers. Save your shekels for these works of art by Elsmore & Forster.

Fig. 13-13 *Morning Glory* winds over all surfaces of this vegetable tureen with crabstock handles. Elsmore and Forster created this very collectible shape.

Fig. 13-14 This straight-sided toilet mug is covered with *Morning Glory* vines. The proud owners are the Dieringers

Fig 13-15 Two desirable shapes, *Morning Glory* by Elsmore & Forster and *Ivy Wreath* (see p. 112) by John Meir & Son, pose together. Collection of the Dieringers.

MORNING GLORY WITH THUMBPRINTS

This design, *Morning Glory with Thumbprints & Leaf,* has only been found on this unmarked jug.

MOSS ROSE

Moss Rose is a popular shape by J. & G. Meakin with its detailed rose with leaves, even to the thorny stems. The teapot boasts an unusual forked handle; the plates have twisted cord edges with motifs spaced in the surround.

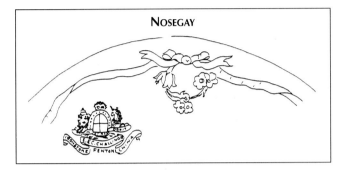

NOSEGAY

SHAW'S SPRAY

This *Nosegay* and ribbon garland edges the plates with five bows with rings of flowers, designed by E. & C. Challinor.

Shaw's Spray has only been found as a tiny motif on plates.

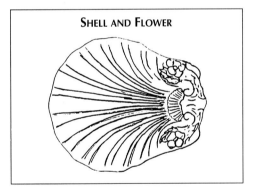

SHELL AND FLOWER

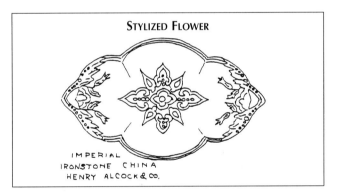

STYLIZED FLOWER

This shell-form relish is unmarked

Another Henry Alcock (after 1861) relish, has open areas in the handles of this *Stylized Flower* shape.

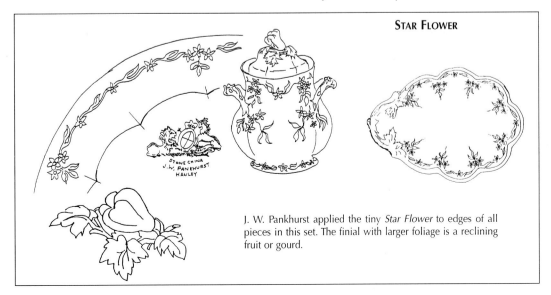

STAR FLOWER

J. W. Pankhurst applied the tiny *Star Flower* to edges of all pieces in this set. The finial with larger foliage is a reclining fruit or gourd.

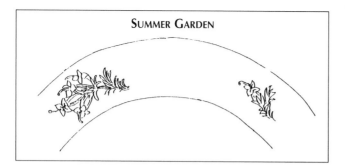

SUMMER GARDEN

George Jones, on his Royal Patent Ironstone, added this *Summer Garden* design with three large and three small sprays on the surround of plates.

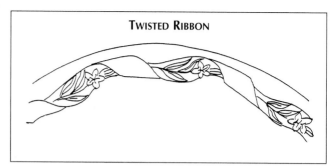

TWISTED RIBBON

James Edwards & Son made this *Twisted Ribbon*, a Romanesque-bordered design, ca. 1860s.

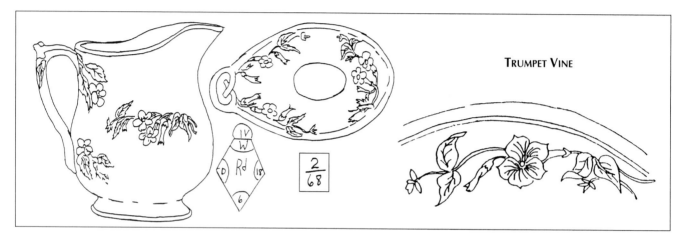

TRUMPET VINE

Liddle, Elliott & Son registered this shape in 1865. The numbers indicate a potting date of Feb, 1868. The potter's name is often omitted.

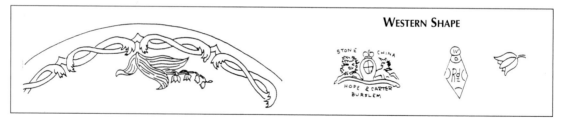

WESTERN SHAPE

Hope & Carter registered the above *Western Shape* in 1862. W. & E. Corn also manufactured similar sets (below left).

Fig. 13-16 The Western Shape by W. & E. Corn includes a chain below the lily-of-the-valley blossoms.

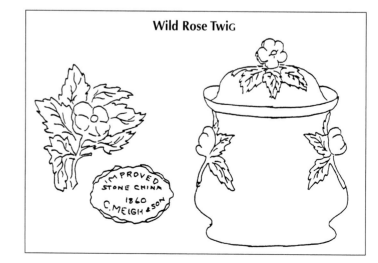

Wild Rose Twig

Wild Rose Twig was made in the pottery of Chas. Meigh & Son after 1860. The same three-dimensional finial had already been used on several shapes by James Edwards.

Classical and Ribbed Themes

As we look over the transfer patterns used before the mid-1800s, we recognize a neo-classic influence, especially on the scenes depicted inside plate wells. Old Greek and Roman ruins of columns, vases, temples, and statues with people standing nearby are often repeated. J. Clementson's Antiquities Series in all-over light blue showed draped figures acting out stories from Homer and some mythography in art.

Some of this influence is found in the white granite shapes in the use of designs in edgings such as Greek and Roman Keys, Romanesque borders, acanthus and fleur-de-lis decorations. The Olympic spirit is caught too in the shapes named by Elsmore & Forster in their *Olympic Shape* and the *Laurel Wreath* shape (Victory Shape) which features the laurel wreaths awarded to victors.

Avid collectors gather the ribbed shapes wherever the old white ironstone pieces can be found. J.W. Pankhurst & Co. (1850-82) was probably the most prolific potter of this kind of decorated granite. The "& Co." was added after 1852 but we cannot be sure that "J. W. Pankhurst" alone was not used for a few years after that date. The *Full Ribbed* shape and the similar *Ribbed Bud* do not have "& Co." on some pieces so perhaps these shapes originated in the early 1850s. Later an attractive shape, *Ribbed Chain* (with the "& Co." added) displayed small ribbing (almost reeding), with chain borders around the necks or waists of bodies.

Jewitt says little about Pankhurst, mentioning that when a Hanley pottery belonging to William Ridgway failed, it was acquired by J.W. Pankhurst & Co. in 1854. The Pankhurst white granite was called "Stone China" made for the American markets. Known shapes created by this company are listed below:

Elaborate Six-Panelled Trumpet
Fleur-de-Lis with Leaf
Framed Leaf
Full Ribbed
Greek Key
Ribbed Bud
Ribbed Chain
Scrolled Bubble
Six-Panelled Trumpet
Star Flower

There are at least three other very collectible ribbed shapes. J. & G. Meakin planned their *Ribbed Raspberry with Bloom* with a body heavily decorated by generous concave ribs at the shoulder of servers and a bottom portion of reeding. The fruit and flowers cling under ring finials, the spout, and near the "C" handles.

Dover Shape, registered in 1862 by W. Adams, entices collectors with narrow concave ribs on plates and cradling narrow convex ribbing around bodies of servers. Jewitt discusses some of Adam's raised patterns, "as, for instance, the *Dover*... being remarkably good, and the forms of the pieces faultless." The reader receives the impression that this may have been the only highly decorated piece of white granite that Jewitt handled. It is possible that most other pieces had long ago left the Isles for American markets. I think Jewitt might have admired the earlier white ironstone dishes had he been able to actually examine them.

Reports have been received about excellent toilet sets in *Ribbed Berry*, potted by John Alcock and his successor after 1861, Henry Alcock. This shape reminds us of the *Full-Ribbed* by Pankhurst. The convex ribbing ends in scallops around the rims of both ewers and basins. The shaving mug photo of this shape (page 135) will only add to your white ironstone addiction.

The drawings and photographs of both classical and ribbed shapes of the 1860s will help you keep scrounging for more and more white.❋

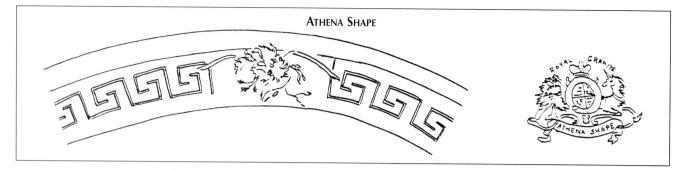

ATHENA SHAPE

I have seen three plates in *Athena Shape*. All were clearly marked *Athena* with an illegible 1865 registry mark, but no potter's name was included.

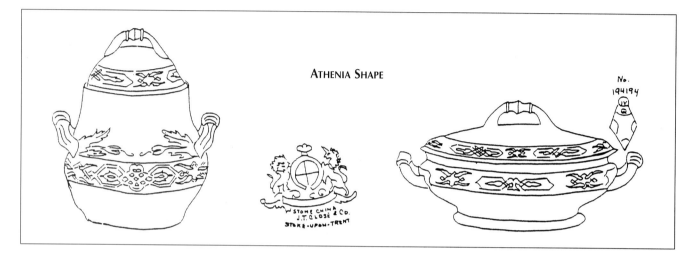

ATHENIA SHAPE

Athenia Shape - Registered in 1866 by J. T. Close & Co., the tureen had uplift handles and a bar finial. The covered sugar bowl was potted by W. Adams & Sons, the predecessor to Close & Co.

Fig. 14-1 These great lion handles and a tipped bud finial grace a hot toddy bowl in *Athens Shape,* registered by Podmore, Walker & Co. also produced by their successors, Wedgwood & Co. All edges are decorated by acanthus leaves. Collection of Francine Horn.

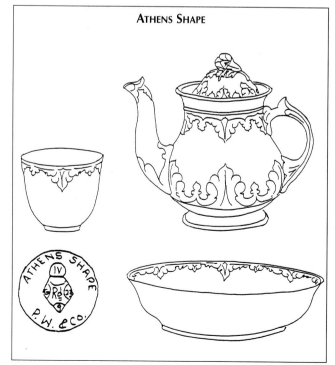

ATHENS SHAPE

Podmore, Walker & Co. registered this *Athens Shape* on Feb. 23, 1857. Stylized acanthus leaves border all dishes in this set. Wedgwood & Co., the name of the successor to the above firm after 1860, continued to manufacture this popular shape during the '60s.

Fig. 14-2 My favorite finial (with exposed stem) tops a *Dover Shape* teapot with a winding vine necklace over a tiny-ribbed body. W. Adams registered this shape in 1862.

W. Adams registered this *Dover Shape* in 1862. The potter used small concave ribs on the plates; he reversed the ribs to convex to wrap tureens and beverage servers. Jewitt mentions this shape. ➤

DOVER SHAPE

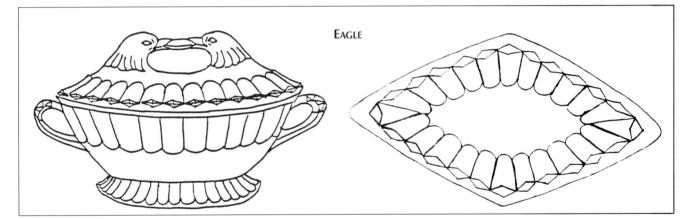

EAGLE

Eagle - Gelson Bros., working from 1867-76, did not produce much white granite. We remember this firm best for their *Eagle* shape, potted just a few years before the first United States Centennial. Notice the unusual diamond-shaped relish drawn here.

Fig. 14-3 The *Eagle* teapot (9 3/4" h.) and *Eagle* coffeepot, an inch taller, were both made by Gelson Bros., Hanley. Notice the difference in the sizes of the diamonds around the neck. The pair of eagle heads as a finial make this shape very desirable to collectors. Owned by Dan Overmeyer.

FULL RIBBED

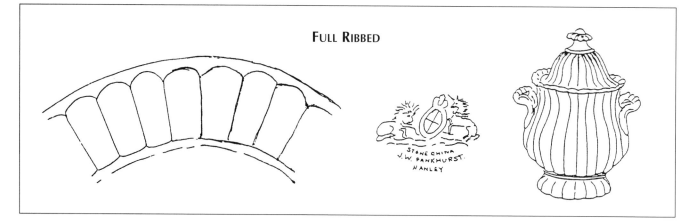

J. W. Pankhurst created this popular *Full Ribbed* shape in the 1860s. The ribs on plates and inside of bowls are concave while ribs on serving vessels are convex. The excellent potting is sought by collectors. The detailed miniature tea set for children is especially treasured.

Fig. 14-4 A *Full Ribbed* teapot by J. W. Pankhurst proudly hovers over two oh-so-rare small egg cups. Ed and Ted sent this photo.

Fig. 14-5 This great *Full Ribbed* ewer and flower-like basin live together in Jane Diemer's collection.

GREEK KEY

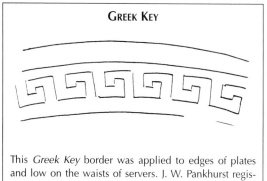

This *Greek Key* border was applied to edges of plates and low on the waists of servers. J. W. Pankhurst registered this shape on Dec. 2, 1863. He employed a pine cone-type finial with a nearby bud and uplift handles on tureens with narrow draping maple leaves below.

LADYFINGER RIBS

Fig. 14-6 Almost all Staffordshire potters of the 1870s and 1880s molded nests of round or square servers with *Ladyfinger Ribs* on the outside surfaces.

LAUREL WREATH OR VICTORY SHAPE

Laurel Wreath was designed by Elsmore & Forster, registered on April 4, 1867. Some pieces are found marked *Victory Shape*. The heavy knot finial is very unusual; a round laurel wreath is embossed on each side of servers. Bands of concave ribs and thumbprints wrap each tureen, drinking vessel, and plate. Avidly collected are two variants; one with copper lustre addition and another with pictures of George Washington within the wreath. All pieces of this shape are very collectible and expensive.

Fig. 14-7

Fig. 14-8 *Laurel Wreath* upright toothbrush holder is lucky to have its underplate with it. From the collection of Jane Diemer.

Fig. 14-7 The three major pieces of a *Laurel Wreath* (sometimes marked *Victory Shape*) tea set by Elsmore & Forster were posed from the collection of Ed Rigoulot and Ted Brockey (above left).

Fig. 14-9 The *Laurel Wreath* tea set pieces with a portrait of our first President inside the victor's wreath. Sent by Mr. & Mrs. John Anderson.

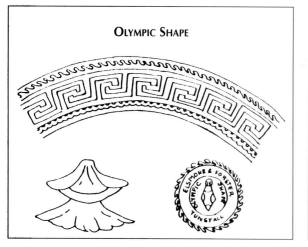

OLYMPIC SHAPE

Olympic Shape was registered in 1864 by Elsmore & Forster. This firm employed a more intricate Greek Key border and a pagoda-type acorn finial. Uplift handles and lines foreshadowed the similar shapes of the 1870s and 1880s.

Fig. 14-10 This *Olympic Shape* tureen by Elsmore & Forster helped to set the style for the plain round shapes of the 1870s and '80s. Note the bottom-heavy body and uplift horizontal handles.

ONE LARGE AND TWO LITTLE RIBS

Fig. 14-11 Around 1870, Elsmore & Forster potted this *One Large and Two Little Ribs* compote and matching individual bowls.

Fig. 14-12 J. & G Meakin and T. & R. Boote also manufactured these useful bowls in *One Large and Two Little Ribs* shape.

Fig. 14-14 The Dieringers own this great *Ribbed Berry* toilet mug by Henry Alcock.

Fig. 14-13 This tiny 5″ h. creamer (*Reeded Grape*) has a registry mark from 1855, patented by Pankhurst and Dimmock. The body is covered with reeding overlaid by grapes and vine. Armbruster Collection.

Fig. 14-15 Convex ribs encircled the bodies of pieces of *Ribbed Berry* by John Alcock, also Henry Alcock. The vine with berry overlays the ribs.

RIBBED BUD

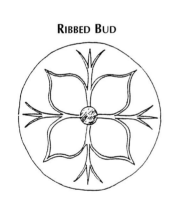

BUTTER DISH LINER

This *Ribbed Bud* shape, also by Pankhurst, is very similar to the *Full Ribbed* design. The serving pieces can be identified by buds with checked decor as finials and the same decoration at handle terminals. The large flower-like basins with matching ewers are very attractive in both shapes.

Fig. 14-16 Three more exceptional *Ribbed Bud* pieces from the Moreland Collection give us access to more great potting. Notice the drawing of the liner to the footed butter dish. Oh, I wish... (above right).

Fig. 14-17 The top view of this *Ribbed Bud* tureen reveals the great potting skills of J. W. Pankhurst. Note the checked areas around the bud finial. The Morelands collect this shape. →

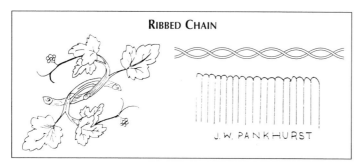

RIBBED CHAIN

J.W. PANKHURST

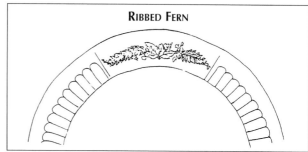

RIBBED FERN

Another ribbed shape, *Ribbed Chain*, was offered by J. W. Pankhurst. Here the ribs are tiny and convex. The chain is sharply detailed, circling necks and borders of covers. The top view of the twined branch finial is shown. A handheld spittoon has been found with this decoration.

Toward the end of the 1880s, A. J. Wilkinson alternated convex ribs with woodsy leaves on this *Ribbed Fern* plate.

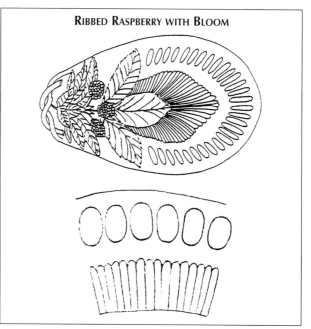

RIBBED RASPBERRY WITH BLOOM

Fig. 14-18 The narrow ribs (reeding) cover nearly all the bodies of these *Ribbed Chain* pieces. The "spit cup" (with holed top missing) is the only one yet discovered in an early shape. Thid gravy boat, punch cup, and hand spittoon are owned by Tom and Olga Moreland.

J. & G. Meakin designed this very detailed embossment that almost covers all surfaces with *Ribbed Raspberry With Bloom*.

Fig. 14-19 Twig handles and finial grace this *Ribbed Chain* tureen by J. W. Pankhurst.

Fig. 14-20 J. & G. Meakin's ribbed contribution, *Ribbed Raspberry with Bloom*, includes berries, flowers and foliage around the ring finials and under spouts. Notice the narrow reeding around bases and the wider concave ribs around necks of servers.

Styles of the Seventies and Eighties

Between 1870 and 1875, the styles of white ironstone dishes seemed to completely change. Certain potteries were adopting more efficient machinery, using mass-production, and selling more tablewares than ever. Jewitt records that many firms gave up other business pursuits and concentrated on the "common white granite" production for foreign markets. Most new molds were of plainer round or squared bodies; many companies added the copper Tea Leaf motif with band to attract American customers.

Many collectors have delighted in gathering the startlingly graceful shapes with plain gleaming surfaces offered by Elsmore & Forster, T. & R. Boote, or J. & G. Meakin in the 1870s. However, other potters offered some uninteresting shapes, poorly potted, that had little to attract buyers except for lower prices. Collard describes how the white ironstone came into low repute. She lauds the early white granite production first, reporting that, "It outsold every other ceramic body because it met every requirement of the country or frontier trade, while at the same time commanding a continuing sale in the cities."

Collard added, "In time, however, the fastidious began to look down on ironstone and all the related wares." A Montreal china merchant spoke of 'White Granite and the commoner goods.' American writers, according to Collard, expressed the hope that public taste everywhere might be elevated by 'expelling' white stonewares 'from all tables.'

Yet, in America, this derogatively labeled 'thresher's china' or 'farmer's china' had a certain rough efficiency that exactly described the quality possessed by white ironstone wares. Certainly, the rural areas of the United States and Canada continued to use these sturdy dishes long after the professional and city dwellers purchased finer porcelains and more colorful earthenwares.

However, during this last quarter century, a few creative designs attract our notice with the animal finials, the rarer all-over embossing by W. & E. Corn, the *Dominion* and *Canada* shapes, and the varied shapes of the company of Anthony Shaw. On the whole, however, the age of creative Staffordshire potting of white granite had lessened by the late 19th century.

J. & G. Meakin

For the "starred" potter of this chapter, I have chosen the firm of James & George Meakin of Tunstall, who succeeded their father in 1852, entering whole-heartedly into the Ironstone China trade. That company continued to conduct a sizable trade in white granite throughout the rest of the century. They built the Eagle Works in Hanley in 1859, employing 245 people, and then enlarged their factory in 1868. Jewitt says that the Meakin's specialty was graniteware in imitation of French China. This company had other works in Cobridge and Burslem but ironstone collectors most often see the Hanley marks. This pottery added the word "England" to their wares before it was required by law in the 1890s.

J. & G. Meakin's earliest shapes were probably *Pearl Sydenham, Panelled Leaves, Panelled Leaves with Berries*, and *Plum Decagon*. We date these tentatively by their similarity to shapes by other potters because the Meakins seldom registered their body shapes. Other Meakin dishes with naturalistic lines gathered by collectors are these:

Acorn	Fuchsia
Border of Leaves	Garden Sprig
Bow Knot	Moss Rose
Budded Vine	Panelled Pod
Chain of Tulips	Ribbed Raspberry with Bloom
Cherry Scroll	Strawberry
Fern with Medallion	Wheat and Hops

Attractive squared cookie plates with rounded corners, all in similar lines, have been found in *Wheat and Hops*, *Fuchsia*, and *Border of Leaves*—all very collectible.

Among the most desirable of Meakin pieces are the gleaming, pyriform jugs in austere, graceful lines that please the eye. Like the Boote potters, the Meakin company had perfected a blend between body and glaze that survived the tests of decades.

Mass-production during the last quarter of the century added these additional Meakin shapes:

Blanket Stitch	Cable and Ring
Block Optic	Miniature Scroll
	Plain Round

Ladyfinger Ribs on a nest of open bowls and cameo-handled sugar boxes have also been found manufactured by this company.

The contributions of other factories of the 1870s and '80s are continued on the following pages.▨

Rounded Shapes of the 1870s & 1880s

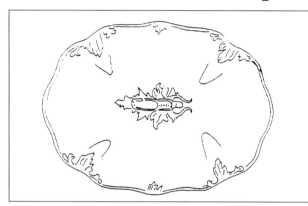

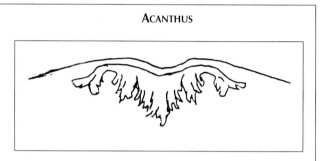

ACANTHUS

Johnson Bros. produced this *Acanthus* shape. The pitchers in the pattern are similar to the *Chelsea* shape.

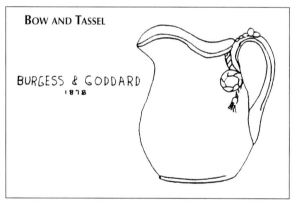

BOW AND TASSEL

BURGESS & GODDARD
1878

The potting year "1878" is stamped on this *Bowl and Tassel* shape by Burgess & Goddard.

BOW KNOT (WILKINSON'S)

The *Bow Knot* decor was added in relief by A. J. Wilkinson late in the 1800s.

BRITANNIA

Registered on Dec. 7, 1878 by Anthony Shaw, this novel shape proclaimed the British Isles with the English rose, the Irish shamrock, and the Scottish thistle. A similar *Britannia* design was also used by Powell & Bishop as shown in Chapter 22.

Fig. 15-1 Alfred Meakin trimmed his *Brocade* pattern with delicate scrolls. This butter dish has the added copper lustre Tea Leaf design. Courtesy of Tom Chadwick

BAR FINIALS ON ROUND OR OVAL TUREENS

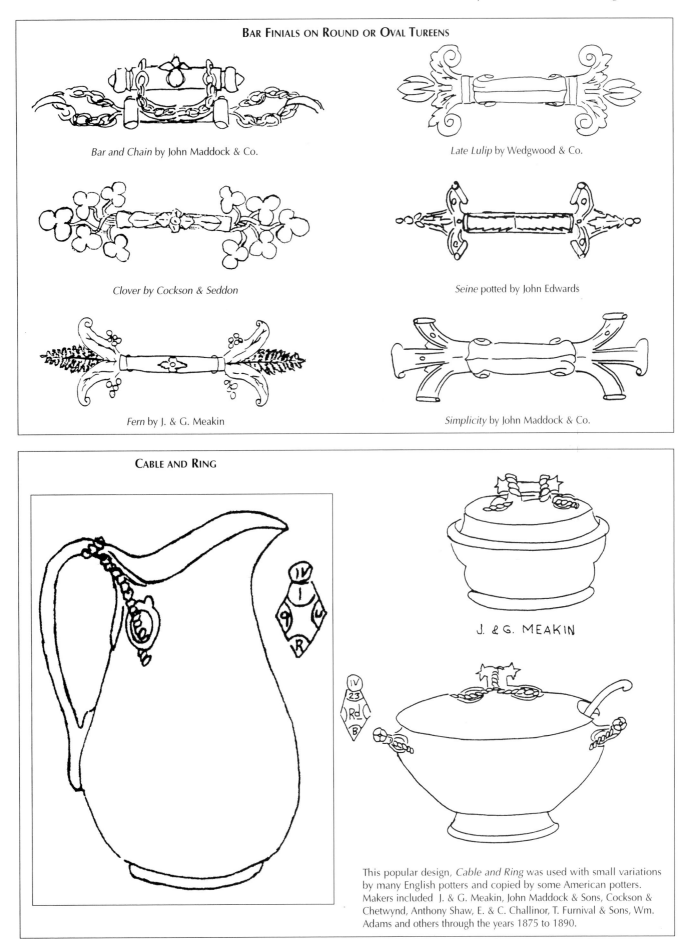

Bar and Chain by John Maddock & Co.

Late Lulip by Wedgwood & Co.

Clover by Cockson & Seddon

Seine potted by John Edwards

Fern by J. & G. Meakin

Simplicity by John Maddock & Co.

CABLE AND RING

J. & G. MEAKIN

This popular design, *Cable and Ring* was used with small variations by many English potters and copied by some American potters. Makers included J. & G. Meakin, John Maddock & Sons, Cockson & Chetwynd, Anthony Shaw, E. & C. Challinor, T. Furnival & Sons, Wm. Adams and others through the years 1875 to 1890.

CANADA

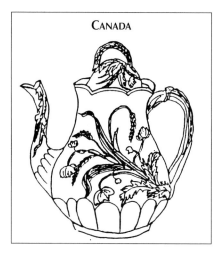

CHAIN OF TULIPS

CHELSEA

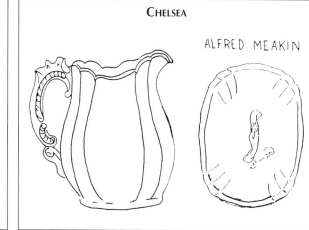

ALFRED MEAKIN

Canada shape has already been included in the Grain chapter. The Clementson Bros. registered this round shape in 1877.

Very graceful plain bodies are touched with this *Chain of Tulips* design by J. & G. Meakin.

Collectors like the lines of Alfred Meakin's *Chelsea*. The Johnson Bros. firm also produced this pattern. It can be found with the copper lustre Tea Leaf motif.

DOMINION

Fig. 15-2 This most interesting shape, *Dominion*, registered by William Baker & Co. in 1877, was probably manufactured for the Canadian markets. However, American collectors would love to find white ironstone with beaver finials and borders of water lilies. Tom and Olga Moreland own this tureen.

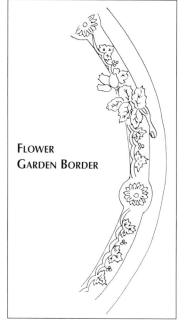

CHRYSANTHEMUM LATE

FLOWER GARDEN BORDER

Fig. 15-3 *Fern,* a typical graceful body by J. & G. Meakin, is always welcomed in a collection of white granite. Courtesy of W. R. Newhauser.

W. H. Grindley potted this *Flower Garden Border* in Tunstall after 1880.

Henry Burgess registered this *Chrysanthemum* shape in 1886. He also emblazoned it with copper Tea Leaf on toilet sets.

FUCHSIA WITH BAND

Mellor, Taylor & Co. named their white granite "Warranted Stone China." This company potted through the 1880s and 1890s.

Fig. 15-4 This plain 19" w. long well and tree platter has an impressed GOTHIC stamped on the bottom next to the name of the firm, Cockson & Chetwynd (1867-1875).

HAWTHORNE'S FERN

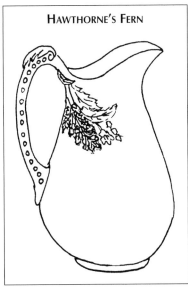

John Hawthorne registered this shape on Mar. 19, 1879.

HEXAGON STRAP

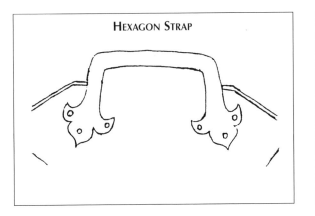

After 1885, Bridgwood & Son shaped this design with bar handles and finials. A handle detail is shown.

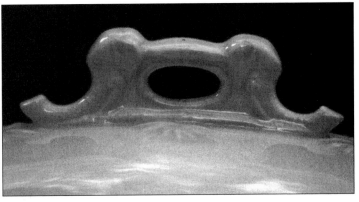

Fig. 15-5 Elephant heads (*Jumbo*) plus an occasional daisy decorate this plain graceful shape marked by Henry Alcock. Collection of Diane Dorman.

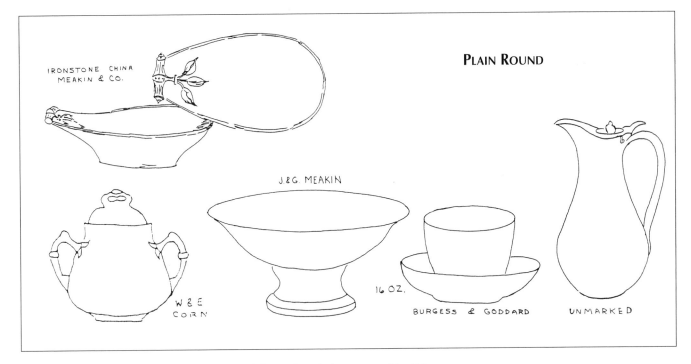

PLAIN ROUND

Here are a few samples of *Plain Round* white granite dishes made in the last quarter of the 19th century.

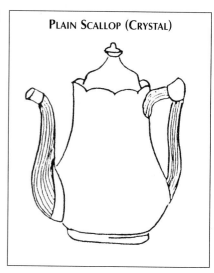

Fig. 15-6   PHARAOH CAMEO - J. & G. Meakin decorated an oval sugar bowl with this *Pharaoh Cameo* as a finial and also as side handles. Other companies used other cameo heads as handles on round or square sugar boxes. A plain cup is shown beside this piece.

Fig. 15-7   This *Plain Berlin* pattern was potted by Liddle, Elliott & Son in the 1860s before the clean, pure lines became popular.

This graceful *Plain Scallop* was one of the last creations by Elsmore & Forster, ca. 1870. Faint lines cover the handles and spouts on this lighter weight ironstone called "Parisian Granite" by that firm. "PG" is often impressed on the underside of small pieces. Tea leaf collectors call this shape "Crystal."

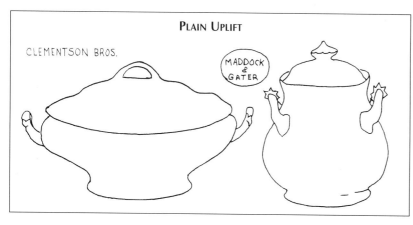

Many varied shapes by many potters of this period employed these *Uplift* handles fastened to plain bodies manufactured from 1870 to 1900.

Fig. 15-8   Small covered vegetable tureen, marked by Alfred Meakin, was made in a late *Plain Uplift* shape. Sent by Eleanor Washburn.

Henry Alcock & Co. designed the *Prunus Blossom* in the Japonism style of the 1880s.

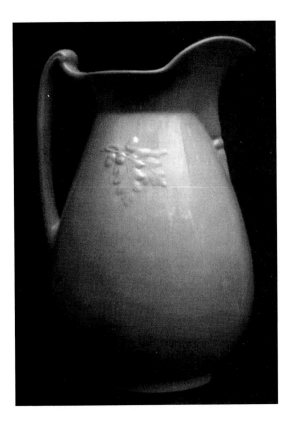

This shape has been nicknamed *Lion's Head* or *Sheepshead* but the John Edwards company impressed a large ROYAL on the bottoms of pieces decorated with the head of the king of the jungle.

Fig. 15-9   Another Newhauser acquisition, this Baker and Chetwynd design (nicknamed *Round Acorn*) would make a great container for autumn flowers.

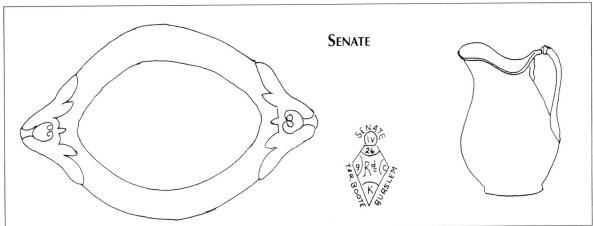

Most of the pieces of Boote's *Senate*, registered in 1870, are very plain, a lighter weight than Boote's earlier plain *Classic Shape*.

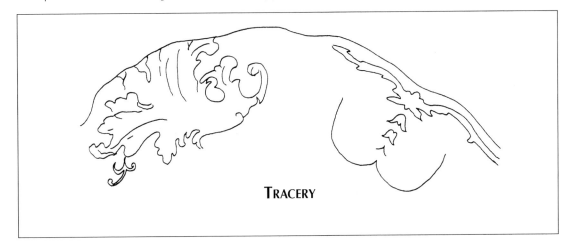

Johnson Bros. used lightweight ironstone with faintly impressed scrolled designs for this *Tracery* shape after 1883.

Squared Shapes of the 1870s & 1880s

Fig. 15-10 BAMBOO - The bamboo-form handles & finials on pieces of this shape give it its name. Many pieces have squared bodies and feature the Tea Leaf lustre motif. *Bamboo* was manufactured in the 1870s by John Edwards, Alfred Meakin and W. H. Grindley.

Fig. 15-11 BASKETWEAVE (SHAW'S) - This late Anthony Shaw contribution was squared near the bases of serving pieces and the *Basketweave* border decorates the edge of plates and lower areas of servers and cups. It is rare and especially desirable with copper lustre Tea Leaf decoration. Photo by Julie Rich. Collection of Roxann Rich.

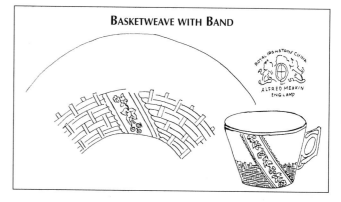

Alfred Meakin potted this pattern in the last decades of the 1800s.

Fig. 15-12 Her is a nice grouping of *Basketweave with Band* collected by Dorothy Riley

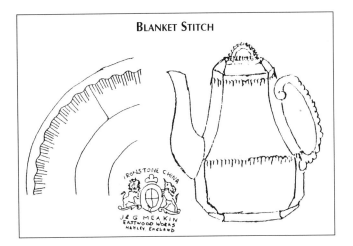

BLANKET STITCH

This popular shape, *Blanket Stitch,* was edged by a sort of blanket stitch and divided by the same border at the low waists of serving pieces. The copper lustre Tea Leaf sometimes highlights pieces.

Fig. 15-13 These two *Block Optic* jugs, potted by J. & G. Meakin, have squared bodies and bracket handles. This pattern also shows up with copper lustre Tea Leaf decoration. Picture sent long ago by William Horner.

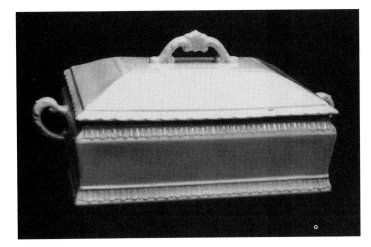

Fig. 15-14 I call this tureen *The Box,* shaped by Bridgwood & Son, and located by Harry Lowe.

Fig. 15-15 Another squared body can be identified by the *Bullet* shaped finial. It was potted by Anthony Shaw, who also decorated this piece with his favorite copper lustre Tea Leaf. Collection of Eleanor Washburn.

CURVED RECTANGLE

This graceful shape has only been seen in a piece marked by Charles Meakin.

FAVORITE

W. H. Grindley used this *Favorite* shape in white granite alone, in white with an added copper lustre Tea Leaf, and as a blank for colored transfer patterns.

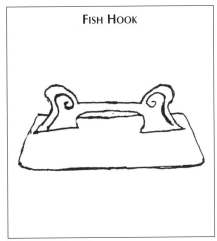

FISH HOOK

This *Fishhook* shape by Alfred Meakin was made in white granite and as a blank for copper lustre Tea Leaf, Moss Rose, and other decorations. The name derives from the "hooks" on the handles and finials. See examples in Chapter 16.

GENTLE SQUARE (ROOSTER)

Gentle Square was potted by T. Furnival & Sons. The bird head handles give it its second name.

Fig. 15-16   This shape, first made by Powell & Bishop and then by their successors, Bishop and Stonier, is called *Golden Scroll* because of the two deeply scrolled corners on each side and the gold lustre that is sometimes used to enhance its body. Harry Lowe Collection.

HEAVY SQUARE

Heavy Square, shaped by Clementson Bros., and decorated by an outsized copper lustre Tea Leaf motif is particularly collectible. Look for photos of pieces in Chapter 16.

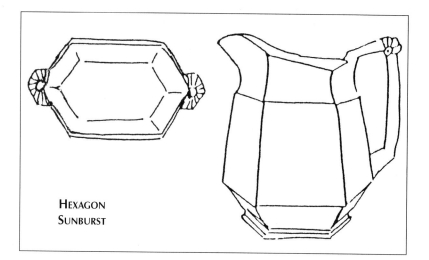

HEXAGON SUNBURST

Hexagon Sunburst is a late shape by Anthony Shaw. The bodies are hexagonal and handles have a rayed decoration. As is true of most of his shapes, Shaw also treated this one with copper lustre.

IONA

Powell, Bishop & Stonier (1878-91) produced *Iona.* It was also sold with a gold lustre sprig motif. This grouping is copied from an early advertisement.

LION'S HEAD

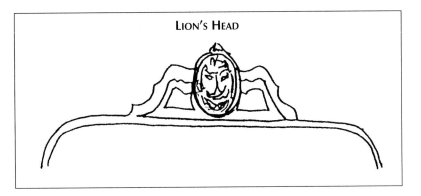

The lion's face inside a medallion trim, an otherwise fairly plain square set called *Lion's Head* made by Mellor, Taylor & Co. Some pieces feature the copper lustre Tea Leaf decor.

PEERLESS

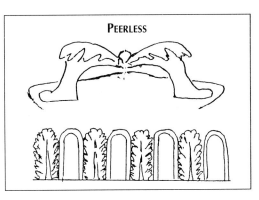

Stamped PEERLESS but nicknamed *Feather,* this shape was produced by the company of John Edwards. This is another shape which can be found with copper lustre Tea Leaf.

Fig. 15-17 This scene displays four pieces of a *Seashore* toilet set by W. E. Corn, registered between 1868 and 1883. The mark is usually illegible.

Fig. 15-18 This detail is taken from the body of a *Seashore* jug. The excellent embossing and molding is unusual on so late a piece of white granite.

SIMPLE SQUARE

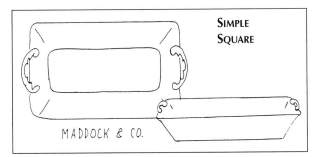

MADDOCK & CO.

Maddock & Co. was one of several companies who produced a *Simple Square* shape. Gold or copper lustre Tea Leaf designs highlight some examples.

SQUARE RIDGED

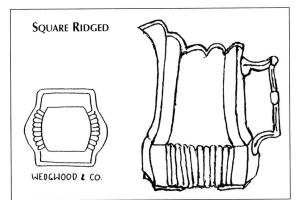

WEDGWOOD & CO.

Fig. 15-19 *Victory* was potted by John Edwards with rectangular serving dishes with rounded corners, topped by bar finials composed of two dolphin heads. Nicknamed: *Dolphin,* but impressed VICTORY by the potter.

Square Ridged was manufactured by Johnson Bros., Wedgwood & Co., H. Alcock Co., W. & E. Corn, Henry Burgess and the firm of Mellor, Taylor & Co. Pieces can be found with a gold or copper lustre Tea Leaf.

Miscellaneous Simple, Late Unnamed Pieces

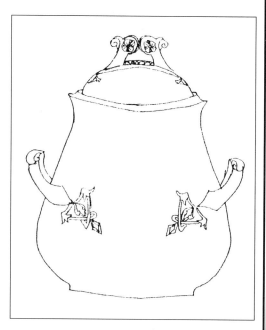

Fig. 15-20   Here's a cheer for the collectors who crave the clean-lined plain shapes as pictured here in a low tazza and a Meakin jardiniere in a staircase corner.

This simple rounded sugar bowl with impressed designs at the handles and finials is a nice example of late pieces produced by T. & R. Boote.

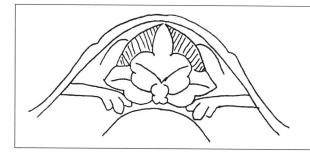

This unnamed pattern with open handles on the ends of an oval platter was made by Elsmore & Forster, c. 1870.

Fig. 15-21   The prolific white granite potters, the Johnson Bros., shaped this square pedestalled compote. Its simplicity makes it beautiful. Courtesy of Harry Lowe.

Fig. 15-22   This pitcher features woodsy ferns and leaves, registered by John Hawthorne in 1879. Collector's now call it *Hawthorne's Fern* (see p.141). Sent by Eleanor Washburn.

Some Common English Pottery
Marks from 1870 to 1900.

White Ironstone with a Copper Touch

Introduction

As we search for the historical roots of white ironstone popularity we find a parallel growth in demand for the same granite bodies with added lustre decoration.

Working in the 1840s, a few Staffordshire potters began to manufacture their ironstone bodies in pure undecorated white with precisely-detailed embossing or molding. The most prominent 1840s potter to do this was James Edwards, quickly joined by the T. J. & J. Mayer, John Wedge Wood, John Ridgway, Edward Walley and others. Before this decade, the ironstone bodies exported for sale in North America had been decorated with colorful designs - pseudo-Oriental, flow blue, floral, scenic, Historical Blue, polychrome or one-color transfers. Now, in the mid-nineteenth century, there suddenly emerged a clamor for all-white stoneware china.

Looking back through the centuries preceding the mid-1800s, we find that ceramics decorated with metallic lustre originated long ago in the Near East. Arabs traveling westward carried the art to 13th century Spain where its manufacture was carried on for years. Gradually the use of these metallic glazes spread to Italy and northern Europe although the only long-term use of the technique seems to have remained with the Spanish and Portuguese.

The copper lustre effect we are discussing was attained by the addition of pigments of gold and/or copper oxide, which would produce a rich ruby red glaze when heated in the kiln. Early in the 19th century, English potters "rediscovered" the use of copper lustre treatments and again began employing them, usually covering the entire surface of relief-molded jugs or the main pieces of tea sets with shining copper. Occasionally, today, we find examples of the same high-relief jug that had been fashioned in two decorative styles during the early 1840s—one is pure white and the other completely covered in a shiny metallic copper glaze.

Remember, it was the decade of the 1840s that introduced all-white granite to the world markets. We can certainly assume that at the Great Exhibition of 1851 in London there was some white ironstone on display. At least one account mentioned "white granite with gilt trim" in a ceramic exhibit. Could it have had a copper gleam? *Perhaps.*

At any rate, we date the North American craze for white ironstone as well-established by the 1850s. Some dated body styles of that decade discovered with added copper lustre include:

1853 January	*Fig Cousin* (Wm. Davenport)	
1853 October	*Ring O' Hearts* (Livesley & Powell - 1851 - 1865)	
1855	*Columbia Shape* (Livesley & Powell)	
1856 April	*Niagara Fan* (Anthony Shaw)	
1856 April (?)	*Hanging Leaves* (Anthony Shaw (1851 - 1900)	
1856 April	*Chinese Shape* (Anthony Shaw)	
1856 November	*Niagara Shape* (Edward Walley - 1845 - 1858)	
1858 December	*New York Shape* (J. Clementson 1839 - 1864)	
1858 December	*Huron Shape* (Wm. Adams)	
1859 November	*Ceres Shape* (Elsmore & Forster - 1853 - 1871)	

Remember that the registry dates above are only a record of when a particular shape was registered and not a verification of when the added lustre was applied. I think we can safely assume, however, that the use of copper lustre trim on white granite was popular in the 1850s. Its use was prevalent for half a century, a long period of time for one ceramic style to be desired by fickle consumers.

Additionally, we cannot leave the subject of copper lustre decorated ironstone without also recalling that some color-decorated ironstone included an occasional copper lustre addition or enhancement. Often, for example, Gaudy Ironstone and Gaudy Welsh feature copper lustre edging or leaves. A few single-color transfers had leaves or flowers similarly decorated. J. Clementson, Jacob Furnival, Elsmore & Forster and Cochran produced sets of white with flow blue edging (sometimes with the addition of a red pinstripe) with copper-brightened touches. Yes, our story of white ironstone must include an occasional copper touch!

The Copper Lustre Story... Tea Leaf and More

by Dale Abrams

Early Lustre Trim

Although the white ironstone is a complete book unto itself, there are numerous branches of the white iron-stone family tree which collectors have found fascinating to explore. One such branch is the family of body styles to which copper lustre decorative motifs have been applied.

Consumer tastes are ever-changing and, eventually, some consumers tired of the types of decorated ironstone wares which had been available to them for over thirty years. By the mid-1800s English potters had decorated white ironstone with many appealing patterns—copies of Oriental patterns, historical blue, flow blue, mulberry and numerous others. By the mid-1840s, however, both undecorated and copper lustre decorated white ironstone were thrust into the forefront of popularity in North America.

As was the case with the body styles themselves, early application of copper lustre (and to a lesser extent gold lustre, also covered in this section) to white ironstone started simply with the addition of lustre stripes

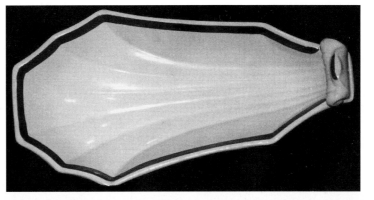

Fig. 16-1 Simple but elegant copper lustre-banded Edward Walley *Gothic* shaped relish, (circa 1845-55).

Fig. 16-2 Lustre-banded *Full Panelled Gothic* coffeepot, creamer, teapot and sugar bowl, unmarked (circa 1845-55). Note the variation in finials. Pieces can be found in several sizes - at least three sizes of pots are known.

or enhancements along the rims, handles and finials of hollowware and flat pieces. Among the early potters to employ the addition of copper lustre enhancement to their wares were Livesley & Powell, Edward Walley and Jacob Furnival. The body styles shown in Figs. 16-1, 16-2, and 16-4, are some of the first on which we discover copper lustre applications.

Once one English potter got into the copper lustre act more were swift to follow. This simple lustre banding featured on the illustrated pieces can be found on many body styles including: *Arched Forget-Me-Not, Augusta Shape, Columbia Shape, Dallas Shape, Grand Loop,* *Grape Octagon, Huron Shape, Lily of the Valley, New York Shape, Niagara Fan, Niagara Shape, Panelled Grape, Pear, Prairie Shape, Quartered Rose, Ring O' Hearts, Washington Shape, Wrapped Sydenham* and others.

Not content with simple banding, potters began to employ lustre applications which were increasingly stylistic and imaginative (Figs. 16-3, 16-5, and 16-6).

Some potters, especially Elsmore & Forster, found that they could use copper lustre to enhance and attract attention to the lovely embossed features of their wares. Some examples of these treatments are illustrated in Figs. 16-7 and 16-8.

Fig. 16-3   These Edward Walley *Wrapped Sydenham* pieces from the 1850s employ a more imaginative "Scallop" decoration, hard to find but collectible.

Fig. 16-4   Unmarked lustre-banded *Cockscomb-Handle* coffeepot (circa 1840s-1850s). This piece can also be found with the Teaberry motif which is especially rare.

Fig. 16-5   Edward Walley's "Spoke" decoration from the 1850s was less popular and few pieces survive today.

Fig. 16-6   Edward Walley experimented with several banding treatments, as can be seen on these two examples of the *Niagara Shape* body style, registered 1856. The lustre application on the leftmost pieces is intended to fully highlight the *Niagara Shape* embossing.

Fig. 16-7 and 16-8 Lustre application highlights the beautiful embossing on the *Ceres Shape* pieces (left), registered 1859, and the *Laurel Wreath (Victory Shape)* items (right) registered 1867, both by Elsmore & Forster. In both cases the body style and lustre motif share the same name (keep in mind, however, that only the body style was registered, not the date that the lustre application was first used). These copper lustre-enhanced pieces are eagerly sought after by collectors.

Tea Leaf Arrives

In the mid-1850s, Anthony Shaw introduced a new decorative motif that was destined to take the consumer market by storm - TEA LEAF! *For almost fifty years, Tea Leaf-decorated ironstone china was a favorite of the American family.* Anthony Shaw's prolific pottery decorated more than 18 body styles with Tea Leaf - far more than any other potter. A variety of Shaw's highly collectible output is illustrated here in Figs 16-9 through 16-17.

Other Tea Leaf Producers

Once Shaw opened the floodgates of Tea Leaf production, other potters followed. A partial list of producers of Tea Leaf ironstone china and other copper lustre decorative motifs include some of the most prestigious English producers of white ironstone and follows:

Tea Leaf of the 1850s & 1860s

Fig. 16-9 *Wrapped Sydenham* (circa 1854). Probably the earliest body style on which we find Tea Leaf. While most Shaw pieces are marked "Burslem" as town of origin, occasionally a "Tunstall" mark can be found, Shaw's pottery site prior to moving to Burslem. This small handleless covered vegetable dish is one of the few pieces so far discovered with the earlier Tunstall mark.

Fig. 16-10 *DeSoto Shape* (registered 1855). Relish dishes like the one pictured are the only items discovered to date in this early Shaw body style.

Fig. 16-11 *Niagara Fan* (registered 1856). With its distinctive finial and traditional Shaw-style Tea Leaf, these early pieces are hard to find and very collectible.

William Adams (& Sons)
Henry Alcock & Co.
Wm. Baker & Co.
Baker, Chetwynd & Co.
S. Bridgwood & Son
Henry Burgess
E. C. Challinor
Joseph Clementson
Clementson Bros
W. & E. Corn
Wm. Davenport & Co.
Edge, Malkin & Co.
John Edwards
Elsmore & Forster
Thomas Elsmore & Son
J. F. (Jacob Furnival & Co.)
Thomas Furnival & Sons
W. H. Grindley & Co.
Thomas Hughes
Johnson Bros.
Livesley & Powell & Co.
John Maddock
Alfred Meakin (Ltd.)
J. & G. Meakin
Mellor, Taylor & Co.
Powell & Bishop (Bishop & Stonier)
Anthony Shaw (& Son)
Edward Walley
Wedgwood (Enoch) & Co.
James F. Wileman
Arthur J. Wilkinson
Wilkinson & Hulme

Fig. 16-12 *Hanging Leaves* (Anthony Shaw, 1860s). The embossing on the milk pitcher and mug shown is typical of the vertical treatment which divides serving pieces into four sections, allowing Tea Leaf motif to be prominently framed on either side.

Add to this list R. Cochran & Co., the one lone Scottish potter to produce copper lustre wares.

A gallery of some of the Tea Leaf ironstone produced by the above potters would make the collector's heart race and includes pieces illustrated in Figs. 16-18 through 16-30.

Fig. 16-13 *Chinese Shape* (registered 1856). Collectors have discovered more pieces to the Shaw *Chinese Shape* set than for any other early dinner and bath service. Covered tureens like the one in this photograph, for example, come in many sizes—including a sauce tureen, punch bowl (oval) complete with posset cups, and a magnificent huge oval soup tureen—all with distinctive *Chinese Shape* ladles. The ironstone is heavy and bright white—a characteristic of early Shaw manufacture.

Fig. 16-14 *Bordered Fuchsia* (Anthony Shaw, 1860s). Not easy to decorate! The heavy embossing allows little room for the Tea Leaf decoration which has to be placed almost at the bottom of the low-waisted serving pieces. Note that this body style is identical to *Hanging Leaves* with the addition of the154 fuchsia leaves and flowers. These are rare pieces, magnificently embossed, and cherished by Tea Leaf collectors.

Fig. 16-15   *Vintage Beauty* (Anthony Shaw, circa 1860s). A magnificent and rare syrup pitcher, diminutive in size and, to date, the only *Vintage Beauty* piece discovered. Syrup pitchers are particularly scarce in Tea Leaf, especially in the early body styles. The only English syrup pitchers known are by Shaw and Davenport.

Fig. 16-16   *Pear* (circa late 1860s). This seldom-seen Shaw body style is distinctive in its pear-shaped finial and squatty pear-shaped body. To date, only tea set pieces have been found - teapot, creamer and sugar. A similarly-shaped child's piece is also known.

Fig. 16-18   Davenport *Fig Cousin* (registered 1853). With its copper lustre Tea Leaf and added pink lustre foliage this is one of the most prized of the Tea Leaf-decorated body styles. At auction you can count on very spirited bidding on *Fig Cousin* items. This vertical toothbrush vase or holder is particularly unusual in that it is shown complete with its small liner underplate.

Fig. 16-17   *Lily of the Valley* (circa 1860s). Collectors **love** this body style and it is very popular and sought after. Consequently it tends to bring strong prices and demand is keen. A wide variety of pieces was made in *Lily of the Valley* and its graceful profile and delicate floral embossing make for a wonderful table setting. The milk jug, high-lipped creamer and posset cup shown in this photo would delight any collector and *Lily of the Valley* children's sets are considered real prizes.

Tea Leaf of the 1870s & 1880s & Beyond

Fig. 16-19 Davenport *Rondeau* (1870s and 1880s). A later arrival than *Fig Cousin*, this body style, still adorned with the very distinctive Davenport Tea Leaf, is not quite as collectible as *Fig Cousin*.

Fig. 16-20 Clementson Bros. *Heavy Square* (registered 1885). Generally found with the Teaberry motif, this *Heavy Square* sugar bowl is the only one discovered to date with a Tea Leaf adornment.

Fig. 16-21 T. Furnival & Sons *Gentle Square* "Rooster" (potted mid-1870s). One of two popular body styles with stylized "animal handles," the pieces in this photo seem to be adorned with rooster-like handles and finials. ➜

Fig. 16-22 John Edwards *Victory* "Dolphin" (mid-1880s). The other of the "animal handled" body styles—this one with a fanciful dolphin-like motif. ←

Fig. 16-23 *Basketweave* (Anthony Shaw, registered 1887). A later square-bodied product, *Basketweave* is distinctive for its intricate interwoven design on the lower portion of the hollowware bodies.

Fig. 16-24 *Cable* Shape (Cable and Ring) (Anthony Shaw, circa 1870s and 1880s). One of the more common of the middle period Tea Leaf-decorated body styles, *Cable* was also potted and decorated with the Tea Leaf motif by Henry Burgess, Thomas Furnival and E. & C. Challinor. This is certainly one of the more popular of the rounded body styles so common in this time frame. A Shaw coffeepot is shown in this photo.

Figs. 16-25 and 16-26 Alfred Meakin's *Bamboo* (1870s-80s) (Left) and *Fishhook* (circa 1880s) (Right) body styles - by far the most common and available. Meakin was perhaps the most prolific producer of Tea Leaf wares and these two body styles form the basis for many collections. Many a collector started the Tea Leaf collecting journey after inheriting a piece of *Fishhook* or *Bamboo* from a favorite family member. So prevalent are these two Tea Leaf body styles that Meakin purists often jokingly insist that "if it isn't Meakin it isn't Tea Leaf."

Fig. 16-27 Unmarked Egg Cups. Tea Leaf collectors always keep a sharp eye out for egg cups—a particularly difficult item to find. Four styles are pictured in this photo including an unusually small egg cup and, on the right, a "Boston" egg cup.

Fig. 16-28 W. H. Grindley & Co. *Favorite shape* (registered 1886). With wonderful rope-like handles and finials, this body style is easy to recognize.

Fig. 16-29 Thomas Elsmore *Plain Round* tea set (1880s). A distinctive Tea Leaf and unusually lightweight body characterize these tea set pieces.

Fig. 16-30 A. J. Wilkinson *Maidenhair Fern* mug (1890s). The dedicate fern leaf adornments around the handles and finials are popular with collectors - especially those who love plants and flowers.

Children's Tea Leaf

In the Tea Leaf collectors' world, children's pieces decorated with Tea Leaf and other copper lustre motifs are especially sought-after. These six photos show several examples of children's ware with their "adult" counterparts.

Fig. 16-32 Unmarked *Crystal Shape* (circa 1870s). Adult and child-size sugar bowls with elegant uplift handles in the Pepper Leaf decorative motif.

Fig. 16-33 Davenport *Fig Cousin* (registered 1853). Hard to find in adult size and an extraordinary rarity in its child-size counterpart.

Fig. 16-35 Powell & Bishop *Simplicity* (circa 1880s). Adult and child-size pots with the Rose motif.

Fig. 16-31 Shaw *Lily of the Valley* (circa 1860s). Three pots—an adult size Tea Leaf coffeepot, a smaller-version child's teapot, and a child's size white ironstone *Lily-of-the-Valley* teapot.

Fig. 16-34 *Grape Octagon* (circa 1840s and 1850s) Livesley & Powell (adult size) with Edward Walley (child size), perhaps the earliest of the child's sets shown in these photos.

Fig. 16-36 Unmarked *Panelled Grape* (circa 1860). Shown in this photo is an adult size and two variations on the children's size - copper banded and copper lustre Chelsea Grape pattern.

Tea Leaf Variants

Tea Leaf was not the only decorative motif to find favor among the English pottery producers and North American consumers in both the United States and Canada. Numerous "variant" decorations were produced, many prior to the production of Tea Leaf. Among the most popular with today's collectors are Morning Glory and Teaberry. The chart on page 163 identifies some of the more common motifs.

Most Tea Leaf collectors eventually add some "variants" to their collections, although there are those whose collections are heavily "variant"-oriented, as well as collectors who are only interested in one or more of the alternate decorative motifs who are not Tea Leaf collectors. It's easy to see why when we look at some of the following photos.

The Teaberry Motif

Fig. 16-37
Potter: J. Clementson
Body Style: *Chinese Shape* (registered 1856)
Decorative Motif: Teaberry—an unusual motif for this body style which is normally found potted by Shaw with a Tea Leaf decoration.

Fig. 16-38
Potter: J. Clementson
Body Style: *New York Shape* (registered 1858)
Decorative Motif: Teaberry

Fig. 16-39
Potter: Unmarked, probably J. F.
Body Style: *Grand Loop*
Decorative Motif: Teaberry

Fig. 16-40
Potter: Clementson
Body Style: *Prairie Shape* (registered 1861)
Decorative Motif: Teaberry

Fig. 16-41
Potter: Elsmore & Forster
Body Style: *Portland Shape* (circa 1850s)
Decorative Motif: Reverse Teaberry—a motif which is distinctive for its copper Lustre Teaberry enhanced with green foliage and berries. A hit with collectors.

Fig. 16-42
Potter: Clementson Bros.
Body Style: *Balanced Vine* (registered 1867)
Decorative Motif: Teaberry

Fig. 16-43
Potter: Clementson Bros.
Body Style: *Heavy Square* (registered 1885)
Decorative Motif: Teaberry—normally found with this large, heavily lustred Teaberry. Very rare when found with the Tea Leaf motif.

Other Floral & Leaf Motifs

Fig. 16-44
Potter: Elsmore & Forster
Body Style: *Portland Shape* (circa 1850s)
Decorative Motif: Morning Glory—collectors are passionate for this variant and many pieces are out there to be discovered in both dinner and bath sets.

Fig. 16-45
Potter: Unmarked (Elsmore & Forster)
Body Style: *Crystal Shape* (circa 1870s)
Decorative Motif: Morning Glory—It is unusual to find the Morning Glory motif on this shape which would more commonly be found decorated with the Pepper Leaf motif.

Fig. 16-46
Potter: Unmarked (Elsmore & Forster)
Body Style: right: *Fanfare* (circa 1860s) and left: *Tulip* (Little Scroll) (registered 1855)
Decorative Motif: Tobacco Leaf—a pair of covered soap dishes, identical motif, but different body styles, both are difficult items to find.

Fig. 16-47
Potter: Edward Walley
Body Style: *Niagara Shape* (registered 1856)
Decorative Motif: Pomegranate

Fig. 16-48
Potter: Powell and Bishop
Body Style: *Washington Shape* (registered 1869)
Decorative Motif: Stylized Pomegranate

Fig. 16-49
Potter: Unmarked (Elsmore & Forster)
Body Style: *Crystal Shape* (circa 1870s)
Decorative Motif: Pepper Leaf

Fig. 16-50
Potter: Unmarked
Body Style: *Panelled Grape* (circa 1860)
Decorative Motif: Botanicals (Note variations of the botanical theme—flowers are found most often and, occasionally, a lucky collector will find a floral version of this motif with a lovely copper lustre butterfly perched on one of the leaves.) Very difficult to find.

Fig. 16-51
Potter: Unmarked
Body Style: *Grape Octagon* (circa 1840s and 1850s)
Decorative Motif: Thistle & Berry—an unusual and hard-to-find motif, usually very heavily lustred with a black or blue underglaze.

Fig. 16-52
Potter: Edward Walley
Body Style: *Niagara Shape* (registered 1856)
Decorative Motif: Pre-Tea Leaf—note the two varying motifs, both of which employ copper lustre leaves connected with green tendrils—a signature style for pre-Tea leaf. The creamer on the left with the smaller more profuse leaf decoration is the more difficult to find—only a small handful of pieces are known.

Geometric Motifs

Fig. 16-53
Potter: Unmarked
Body Style: *Grape Octagon* (circa 1840s and 1850s)
Decorative Motif: Pinwheel

Fig. 16-54
Potter: J. Clementson
Body Style: left: *New York Shape* (registered 1858) and right: *Prairie Shape* (registered 1861)
Decorative Motif: Coral is one of the most difficult of the variant motifs to find. A few dedicated collectors are always on the lookout for pieces to add to their collections. The Coral motif is also found on the *Hill Shape* (Medallion Scroll) body style. Occasionally collectors will refer to this motif as "Snowflake."

Fig. 16-55
Potter: Unmarked
Body Style: *Panelled Grape* (circa 1860)
Decorative Motif: Cinquefoil—two different size coffeepots pictured.

While production of Tea Leaf in England waned towards the end of the 1800s, American potters were eager to enter the Tea Leaf market. Over 25 U.S. potteries produced or decorated many fine examples which today's collectors seek, especially the fine-quality pieces produced by the Mayer Pottery of Beaver Falls, Pennsylvania. Although the 1960s saw a brief resurgence of Tea Leaf production, the Tea Leaf motif failed to capture the heart of American consumers as it had their great-great grandmothers' hearts 100 years earlier. Today, however, even this "contemporary" Tea Leaf is becoming highly collectible.

Dale Abrams of Ohio has done extensive research and has searched for years for white ironstone pieces decorated with copper lustre motifs so that we might add to our knowledge of these wares. He provided the excellent photographs of selections from his collection for this chapter.

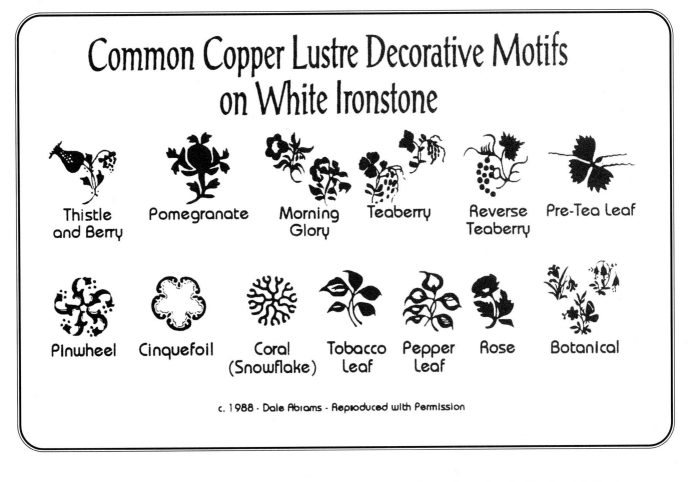

Common Copper Lustre Decorative Motifs on White Ironstone

Thistle and Berry

Pomegranate

Morning Glory

Teaberry

Reverse Teaberry

Pre-Tea Leaf

Pinwheel

Cinquefoil

Coral (Snowflake)

Tobacco Leaf

Pepper Leaf

Rose

Botanical

c. 1988 · Dale Abrams · Reproduced with Permission

Want to learn more about Tea Leaf ironstone china?

Join the Club!

The Tea Leaf Club International, founded in 1980, provides excellent educational material regarding Tea Leaf ironstone china and its variant decorative motifs. Through projects of the Education Committee and through its newsletter, *Tea Leaf Readings,* collectors are presented with a wealth of information not available elsewhere.

Tea Leaf Club membership is approaching 1000 members. The Club sponsors regional meetings across the United States in addition to an annual national convention where knowledgeable speakers present a wide variety of programs of interest to the Tea Leaf collector. Join in the fun and join the Club!

For more information about Tea Leaf, copper lustre decorated white ironstone or Tea Leaf Club membership, contact:

Dale Abrams, 960 Bryden Rd., Columbus, OH 43205.

Suggested Readings for the Tea Leaf Collector

Handbook of Tea Leaf Body Styles, a project of the Educational Committee of the Tea Leaf Club International, by Nancy Upchurch, © 1995. Published by the Tea Leaf Club International.

Grandma's Tea Leaf Ironstone, by Annise Heaivilin, © 1981, currently out of print.

A Look at White Ironstone and *A Second Look at White Ironstone,* by Jean Wetherbee, currently out of print.

American Tea Leaf: Manufacturers, Potters and Decorators, by Julie Rich, © 1992, published by the Tea Leaf Club International.

Body Language: A Glossary of Terms, © 1990, compiled by Nancy Upchurch, published by the Tea Leaf Club International.

Tea Leaf Readings, the official newsletter of the Tea Leaf Club International.

Antique Trader Price Guide to Antiques, October 1987 Issue, special article entitled "Tea Leaf Ironstone" by Jean Wetherbee and Adele Armbruster.

White Ironstone Notes, the official newsletter of the White Ironstone China Association, Inc. An excellent resource to learn more about body styles.

Blueberry Notes, the official newsletter of the Flow Blue International Collectors Club.

American White Ironstone

Throughout history, when man migrated to a new location, one of his first tasks was to shape clay vessels to help sort, store, and cook his food. Later, he molded clay blocks to make shelters.

Crossing the Atlantic in the 1600s, the European colonists followed this familiar pattern, as brick workers and "pott-makers" searched for clay to form bricks, tiles, butter crocks, water coolers, jugs, and bowls. Records indicate that these early potteries were located near Salem, Massachusetts; at New Haven, Connecticut; in Virginia; in New Amsterdam; near South Amboy, New Jersey; and later in Georgia and the Carolinas.

During the following one hundred fifty years, American potters supplied the simple wares for daily living. Fragile, inexpensive redware sufficed at first. Gradually, the body was improved and decorated with simple slip designs. Using wheels, potters threw more durable stoneware into the shapes of crocks and jugs. By 1850, most potters advertised Rockingham and yellowware pieces and, during the same era, the simple sponged wares that are so collectible today helped brighten tables and cupboards. Many of these last wares had been and were still being imported from Mother England.

Meanwhile, British potteries shipped to the New World quantities of china which was sold cheaply to the American homeowners. Native craftsmen did not have the skill to compete nor could they produce at a low cost. A few qualified potters produced fine dishes after the American Revolution, but most companies survived for short periods only.

In the late 1700s, Josiah Wedgwood wrote of the colonies, "They have every material there, equal if not superior to our own for carrying on that manufacture." On the American continent, there were inexhaustible resources for the china maker: endless stores of rich kaolin (the fine, white pipe clay first used by the Cherokees), many other kinds of clay in the Middle West, earths in Alabama, lithomarge in Tennessee, and unknown resources in the ground of the Far West.

By the middle of the nineteenth century, there were major population centers and ready markets were found in every American city and on the farms that dotted the countryside. Finally, then, the native potters began in earnest to produce American-made dishes.

White graniteware was made in most American potteries from about 1870 to 1900. At first, simple patterns and methods were copied from the Staffordshire potters in England. The finer processes, however, were closely guarded secrets passed down generation after generation in England. Much American experimentation was necessary and some Staffordshire workers migrated to work in American potteries.

Jersey City Pottery was founded in 1829. This firm was taken over by Rouse & Turner who, soon after 1850, began to mark whitewares with the English coat of arms in the hopes of capturing some of the market used by the English.

City Pottery of Trenton claimed to be the first company to manufacture white granite in the New Jersey pottery center outside Trenton. This firm received a medal from the New Jersey Agricultural Society for best white graniteware.

The Bennington potters of Vermont were quite aware of the huge imports of all-white ironstone from England in the late 1840s and 1850s. In their United States Pottery Co., J. & E. Norton potted white granitewares from 1850 to 1858.

Norton's well-known "sweetheart" or "presentation" pitchers had a white ironstone base decorated with flowers and gilt. Since so many are initialed or emblazoned with the recipient's name, it seems that each was made to order. This same plain white shape was copied by other American potters in the next decades.

Shortly after Boote registered its popular *Sydenham* pattern, the Nortons used similar lines in gray-white toilet sets that included waste jars and large

Fig 17-1 A rare Bennington *Scroddled Ware* cuspidor in the *Diamond* pattern. Courtesy of Wolf's Auctioneers & Appraisers.

Fig.17-2 A fine Bennington "Flint Enamel" glazed pitcher in the *Alternate Rib* pattern. Courtesy of Wolf's Auctioneers & Appraisers.

footed tubs. Norton also made white ironstone escutcheons, inkwells, keyhole covers, paperweights, and mugs. Their beautiful Parian jugs were covered completely with sculptured designs. A few of these executed in white ironstone are coveted today.

However, these Bennington potters are best known for their single pieces and complete coffee and tea services in flint enamel, Rockingham glazes, and Parian wares.

Vermont potters and others marketed gold-bordered white porcelain dinner sets in the familiar lines of the *Gothic* patterns. Today it is impossible to prove origins, but these sets were probably American in origin, since similar contemporary English china was usually marked.

Collectors who want to identify early Bennington white graniteware should consult the well-illustrated *Bennington Pottery and Porcelain* by Richard Carter Barret.

James Bennett, as early as 1840, settled near East Liverpool, Ohio and began using the nearby clay. A colony of many tiny potteries set up by native potters gathered nearby, many working part-time and employing English methods as much as they were able. However, Bennett was the first early potter of any significance near that site in the Midwest.

By 1850, there were eleven working potteries near East Liverpool; by 1880, East Liverpool alone had twenty-three potteries, firing a total of 67 kilns. Soon after 1850, over 170,000 dozen pieces of ceramic wares were produced annually. By the end of the Civil War, that number had doubled. As elsewhere in the United States, the first priority of native craftsmen was the manufacture of functional, everyday wares. After the war, the migration westward surged again, and the large native market increased. There was a resultant boom in ceramic production.

Fifty percent of American Rockingham and yellowware then produced came from Ohio potteries. The native potters were aware of the American craze for the white graniteware that was so strong in the 1850s; there was a continuing quest to produce similar whitewares. However, the English potting abilities, marketing skills, and years of experience were heavy competition.

Knowles, Taylor, & Knowles drew its first kiln of whiteware in 1872 near East Liverpool, Ohio. This firm made a good grade of ironstone china. By 1886, it was outproducing all other American potteries, employed five hundred men and women, used fifteen tons of clay a day, and turned out a crate of ware every ten minutes.

Some writers have credited John Wyllie, a Staffordshire man who had settled near Pittsburgh, with being the first to make ironstone china west of the Allegheny Mountains. He and his son moved westward to the East Liverpool area where they purchased the two-kiln pottery of Brunt & Hill and equipped it for making whiteware in 1874. Brunt, at another site, claimed 1877 as the date of his first attempt at making ironstone china.

Fig. 17-3 A Rockingham-glazed "Rebecca at the Well" pattern teapot typical of the pieces made at early Ohio potteries.

By 1879, eight East Liverpool potteries were making the stone china. At first, most items were sold either unmarked or marked to make the purchaser think he was buying an English import.

Most of the potteries making whitewares received some of their knowledge from Staffordshire men who had emigrated to America. The J. & E. Mayer Co. of Beaver Falls, Pennsylvania and Thomas Maddock & Sons of Trenton, New Jersey came from well-known pottery families in England.

A relative of the Meakin Staffordshire potters came to work in the East Liverpool potteries. He helped Knowles, Taylor, & Knowles to convert their potworks so that whiteware could be manufactured; he also helped convert at least eight other plants for production of white granite in this pottery area.

It was somewhat difficult to change a potworks so that whiteware, as well as yellowware and Rockingham could be made. The potters had to raise the necessary capital, learn new methods, hire workers with different skills, and sell their products in a market already flooded with good ceramics from Great Britain.

As the Industrial Revolution moved across America, the ceramics workers became alert to new ideas that would speed production and improve their products. In the 1860s, gas-fired potteries were first used. The old charcoal and coal-fired kilns, with their smoke and ash, had often discolored china; the use of new fuel resulted in better dishes. The American potter ceased to use the potter's wheel, and geared machinery helped grind clay to fine powder. Firms had to go farther afield to find the proper clays for the white bodies. A few pieces, such as a crooked bowl or wobbly teapot, remind us of the early struggle of these native craftsmen.

When American potters were struggling to capture a portion of the native china market, they sometimes resorted to marking their wares so that the housewife would think she was buying an import. A few marks look almost exactly like the Royal Arms at first glance. One example of this is a mark stamped by the Glasgow Pottery Co., Trenton, New Jersey. It appears to be the English Arms, except that the pottery monogram replaced the quartered decoration within the shield. The old majestic lion reclines just as proudly as ever, and the fabulous unicorn prances on. Other marks more subtly implied English origins by using an anchor, feather, crown, or garter motifs. Old records reveal that some orders for white American table services were specifically requested to be left unmarked.

By the 1870s, ceramics in America had begun to come of age. Some silversmiths, potters of useful crockery, and molders of glassware had already marketed goods that rivaled similar English products. The most successful chinaware manufacturers in America worked around the potting centers near Trenton, New Jersey and East Liverpool, Ohio. As our country's first

Fig 17-4 A nice example of an early Knowles, Taylor, and Knowles white granite syrup pitcher with hinged metal lid.

centennial approached, a new pride in American-made products increased. The United States government reinforced this feeling by inaugurating high tariffs up to 50 percent on imported ceramic wares. As a result, native potters were challenged to produce china that was acceptable to the American housewife who had long thought good china had to be imported.

In January 1875 at Philadelphia, seventy representatives of the National Association of Potters agreed not to copy patterns from other countries. They also agreed to enter exhibits of native work in the Centennial Exhibition in Philadelphia the following year.

Despite the second resolution, the ceramics exhibit was almost hidden at the exhibition and attracted little attention. Examples of potters' crafts were displayed by the Trenton, Philadelphia, and New York potters, but there were few entries from the Ohio firms. Wares attracting some attention were those of the New York City Pottery, Ott & Brewer, Union Porcelain Works, and Homer Laughlin of East Liverpool. A white graniteware "Daily Bread Platter" was shown by the Trenton Pottery Co.

Miller quotes from *The Potter's Gazette* (December 9, 1876) concerning wares exhibited at the American Centennial Exhibition of 1876 in Philadelphia.

The Dresden Pottery Works, of East Liverpool, Ohio, exhibited ironstone china/table and chamber ware. This ware is shaded with blue, and resembles the well-known Liverpool ironstone.

Miller quotes an excerpt from the January 27, 1877 issue of the same publication:

The Centennial, then, has been of great benefit to the American manufacturers of earthenware..

The demand for plain white goods has been cultivated, and a beautiful pearl-white article is now demanded...

Another Philadelphia Centennial exhibitor that was noticed was the St. Johns Chinaware Co. from St. Johns, Quebec, located about twenty-three miles southeast of Montreal. This was the first pottery in Canada to concentrate on the production of whiteware. It had begun potting in 1874 under the leadership of Farrars, who had migrated from New England. At first they had difficulty finding skilled potters who knew how to work with whitewares. Finally, the company was compelled to employ Staffordshire men for more than half of the work force in that pottery.

The ironstone made by the St. Johns Stone Chinaware Co. was inexpensive, well-made china, some of which was decorated with gilt and flowers. Some all-white dishes marked by this company were in the *Wheat and Hops, Wheat,* and *Scallop* patterns. St. Johns also potted sets shaped in white ironstone and decorated with blue transfer designs in the Staffordshire manner.

Most of the American sets of white ironstone china were plain, with a little design in relief. The English pattern *Cable and Ring* was also made by Greenwood Pottery Co., Cook and Hancock, and American Crockery Co. Wheat motifs, rectangular bodies and round shapes were often used. The potters were struggling with the textures of the clay itself, with the purity of the white color, and the smoothness of the glazes. Collectors can easily gather a group of utilitarian ware of American ironstone including spittoons, invalid feeders, milk pans, mush bowls, "pig" bed warmers, footed tubs, wine coolers, and nests of servers.

In the 1840s and 1850s, Edwin Deakin Peel Pottery, London made a colorful series of bread trenchers. Around the outside rims were the words "Eat Thy Bread with Joy and Thankfulness." The number of wheat heads varied through the years from three in the 1840s to eight in the 1850s. Six ornate feet lifted the servers above table level.

These trays may have been the inspiration for the popular American "Daily Bread" platters. In Chapter 11 on "Grain and Grape Designs," I've included a drawing of an oval bread server marked by Davenport. In this chapter, I include the same drawing, an excellent copy by an American potter.

Rarely we find unusual pieces of American white ironstone, or white granite, as it was often advertised. A few detailed comports were of good design. Of course, all pieces of the Bennington graniteware have become desirable. The most popular collectible has become the "Daily Bread" platters, both marked and unmarked. Almost every firm shaped these oval servers, decorated them with wheat, and varied the wording. Most slogans began with "Give Us This Day" on one border and concluded the quote on the opposite side with "Our Daily Bread." Others admonished "Waste Not - Want Not." Some advised "Where Reason Rules—The Appetite Obeys." I have seen these platters marked with the following labels: T.P. Works (Trenton Pottery Co.); J. M. & Co. (Glasgow Pottery Co.); M. P. & Co.; O. P. & Co. (Onondaga Pottery Co.); John Wyllie & Son; St. Johns, P. Q.; and others.

When American pottery firms had mastered the techniques required to produce acceptable whitewares, they continued to improve as they practiced good ceramics engineering. The heavy white ware made the firms solvent, but the potters still longed to create beautiful porcelain and bone china that could rival the European chinas.

Eberlein and Ramsdell quote that, in 1902, President T. Roosevelt 'determined that the china for the new state dining room must be a home product.' For months a search was made for a pottery equipped to take the executive request. 'There were no American kilns producing china of the quality required.'

It was not until 1918 that the first state dining service was purchased from an American company, planned by an American designer, shaped from American raw materials, fired in American kilns, and decorated by American craftsmen.

But even before this event, Americans had time and again proudly declared, "We made it in America!"

It is my hope that some researcher will have the interest, time, and energy to document American ironstone. That is not to say that the quality of American white ironstone rivals that made in England at that time. As a matter of fact, most American ironstone was decorated and not left plain white. As part of our history, the story of the development of all American products deserves more attention.

I challenge someone to visit the East Liverpool Museum of Ceramics in Ohio, the Bennington Museum in Vermont, and the New Jersey State Museum in Trenton, New Jersey, for there are records available and pieces on display that would tell a wonderful tale. There are facts that have been recorded, and marks that have been researched.

We need a published story of American white ironstone. Collectors are hungry to know the facts. Will someone please gather the facts, photos, marks, and stories of the struggle of native American potters to produce this white ware?

American Bread Platters

Fig. 17-5 Most popular of bread trays is this "Where Reason Rules" piece, unmarked by an American potter, copied from Davenport's earlier platter. The settling (milk) pan and handled bonbon basket were also made in America.

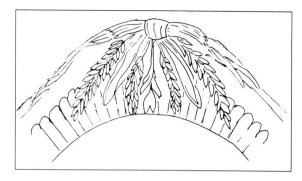

This bread tray, marked and unmarked, was duplicated by many American potters of white granite. Most slogans began with "Give Us This Day" on one side and concluded the quote "Our Daily Bread" on the other side. Note the "Waste Not" answered by "Want Not" on the Wyllie & Son plate shown in the large illustrated ironstone advertisement.

Fig 17-6 A highly collectible American-made *Daily Bread* Platter with usual wheat motif potted by Onondaga Pottery. Collection of James and Doris Walker.

This lower server is a Daily Bread tray by John Moses & Co.

Fig 17-7 Two *Daily Bread* Platters from the same mold. One is decorated with a light navy blue transfer, marked with a blurred arms. The all-white tray was produced by Steubenville Potteries.

A Rare High-Relief American Pitcher

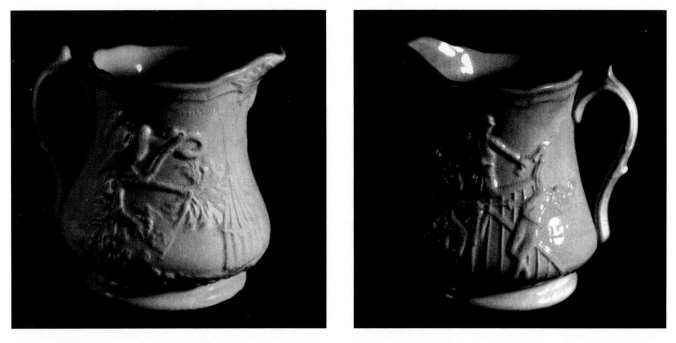

Fig. 17-8 M.A.P. Pottery Company of New Jersey made this high-relief jug with different pictures on either side. Howard and Dorothy Noble own this commemorative piece.

The American potters did few high-relief pieces. A few relish dishes are almost covered by designs. At least one dessert set has been found completely decorated in relief, not executed as well as those made by Staffordshire potters.

The most famous high-relief pitcher shaped in the United States was manufactured by M.A.P.—Millington, Astbury & Paulson, Trenton, New Jersey. It depicts the "Murder of Col. Ellsworth" at Alexandria, Virginia. This assassination scene was depicted by a designer named Poulsen in 1861.

John Jakes retells the story in *The Titans*, page 445:

The Yanks had a martyr now. Some hothead named Colonel Ellsworth had invaded an Alexandria hotel, the Marshall House, to tear down a Confederate banner flying from its roof. In clear weather, the offending flag could be seen in Washington City.

Coming downstairs with the flag, Ellsworth was shotgunned by the hotel owner, who was in turn killed a moment later by one of the colonel's New York Fire Zouves. The colonel's body lay in state in the presidential mansion. The death heightened Northern hatred.

The jug itself is eight inches high with a base diameter of nearly six inches.

One side shows five men: one prone at the left, three standing in the middle around a man at the right being touched by a pointed bayonet. The highest of the three men appears to be flourishing a pistol. The inscription at right labels him "J.W. Jackson the Traitor." Or is it "Johnson"? It is a little blurred and the only two names at the left are also illegible.

On the reverse an eagle is starred with a snake in its beak. To the right is a vertical stack of five guns with a flag on top. The caption on top of that side says "Union and the Constitution."

This decoration on a gracefully shaped jug is anything but beautiful but it does record an event in history that helped to stir feelings that later resulted in our Civil War.

Because of its uniqueness, white ironstone collectors covet this piece.

Ohio Ironstone by John Wyllie & Son

Top: Ohio Ironstone leaf, fish and shell form pickel dishes; Next, Bird bath, mustache cup, bread plate, nest of nappies and nest of tall footed, ribbed salad bowls. Bottom; tier of valenced cake - stands, tall footed compotes, low footed salads, ribbed, ice water pitcher, hall-boy (hotel) pitcher, of footed bowls and butter dish with drainer. All-white Ironstone. (1880s ad for Ohio Ironstone.)

Plain all-white ironstone wares were made in the following named patterns:
Silver, Great Western, Grand, St. Denis, St Louis, Minton, Florence, Normandy, Tulip, Mystic, Stella, Ninevah, Southern.

Mark of John Wyllie & Son on ironstone made by this firm. The mark included combined U.S. and Great Britain seals with a crest of three feathers (Prince of Wales).➡

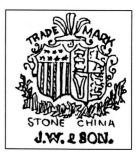

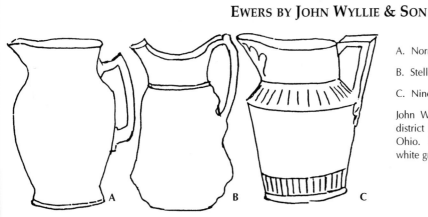

EWERS BY JOHN WYLLIE & SON

A. Normandy

B. Stella

C. Ninevah

John Wyllie was a potter from the Staffordshire pottery district in England. He opened a pottery in East Liverpool, Ohio. He has been credited with the first manufacture of white granite west of the Allegheny Mountains.

Other Pouring Vessels

Fig. 17-9   Sally Scrimgeour, the owner of this 12″ high pewter-covered beverage server, calls it a lemonade server. The spout was made with small holes, decorated sides, and a pewter cover. This is an example of good potting by Knowles,. Taylor & Knowles.

Fig. 17-10   Arrangement of useful pieces by Sally Scrimgeour. Only the 8 3/4″ batter pitcher is marked by Knowles, Taylor & Knowles.

Mark on the small beverage server.

Fig. 17-11   This very different covered creamer-sized jug was shaped by American Crockery Co., Trenton. Julie Rich is the owner.

←

This hotel pitcher nick-named "hall-boy" was made by many American potters in the late 1800s.

Invalid server or pap boat.
Unmarked.

Unmarked church spittoon. Sometimes called a "lady's spittoon".

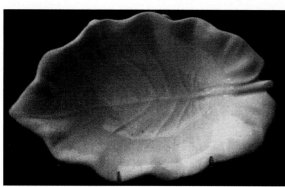

Fig. 17-12   Very different is this unmarked pap boat also from the collection of Dan Overmeyer.

Fig. 17-13   Clumsy, different, and useful are my descriptions
of this unmarked ladies' or church spittoon owned by Dan
Overmeyer. It certainly could be cleaned!

Leaf - Shaped Dishes

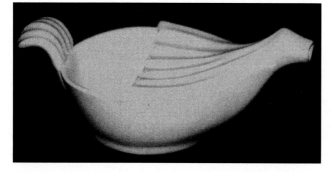

Fig. 17-14   *Veined Leaf* server,
nearly 10 inches long, was shaped
by Onondaga Pottery. John Wyllie
& Son made similar relish and
larger servers. Collection of Ed
Rigoulot and Ted Brockey.

←

John Moses & Co. leaf-molded
dish.➤

Fig. 17-15   The Wheeling Stone China Pottery Co. sold
this low-leaved compote. Collection of Adele and Dick
Armbruster.

Fig. 17-16   This American-made *Leaf* relish was
made by both John Moses & Co. and Wm. Brunt.
Pieces have been found in low plate servers and low
compotes. Both are exact copies of this shape first executed by James Edwards in the 1840s.

American Ironstone Serving Pieces

Fig. 17-17 Most American children's sets were made in simple plain shapes (22 pieces) in white. This blue trimmed set poses in front of Elsmore & Forster's *Tulip* teapot.

Fig. 17-18 John Moses & Co. made a dessert set with all-over relief that included a crossed-vine border, with oak and acorn foliage, and a center wreath. Collection of Dan Overmeyer.

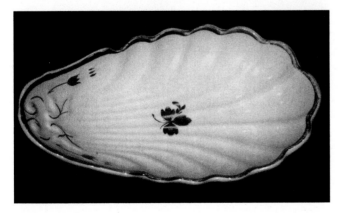

Fig. 17-19 Another American product, this Copper Lustre *Tea Leaf* relish dish was potted by the East End Pottery of East Liverpool, Ohio. Collection of Dale Abrams.

O. P. Co.

This square sugar was shaped by Onondaga Pottery Co. of Syracuse, New York.

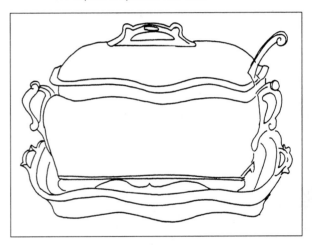

American-made, large rectangular soup tureen, tray, and ladle potted by the Glasgow Pottery Co. of Trenton, New Jersey, founded in 1863 by John Moses.

Fig. 17-20 J. & E. Mayer of Beaver Falls, PA. produced this Tea Leaf coffeepot, cake plate, and egg cup. Collection of Dale Abrams.

Unusual Forms in American Ironstone

Fig. 17-21 This bar bowl, divided through the middle on the inside, boasts double covers of nickel plated metal. The edge of the ironstone bowl is also nickel plated. The fortunate owner of this piece made by John Moses & Co. is Sally Scrimgeour.

Fig. 17-22 Unmarked colander with a bowl width of 7" belongs to Ernie and Bev Dieringer.

Unmarked *Granite Hands.* Also made in England.

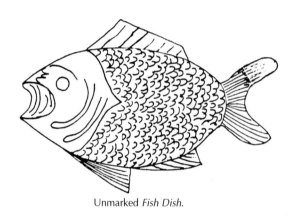

Unmarked *Fish Dish.*

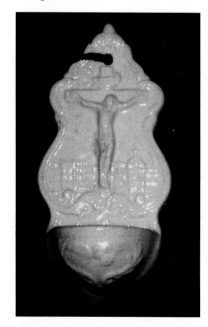

Fig. 17-23 This unmarked holy water dispenser was collected by Dan Overmeyer.

Fig. 17-24 This shaving bowl has a cut-out at neck and a hole that allows convenient hanging. The mark includes a crown with the legible word "Pickman" above. I have been unable to locate information about that potter. Collector is Sally Scrimgeour.

American Potters of White Granite
(Late 1800s)

This list has not been validated by my actual handling of pieces. The names of the potteries have been compiled from lists by other researchers who mention the fact that these native potters produced ironstone. My dates are not necessarily the date when the manufacture of white granite commenced. Some are founding dates for the factories. Marks shown are those I have confirmed appear on white ironstone. This listing is not complete and additional marking information would be appreciated.

Firm and Location	Marks	Date
1 Alpaugh & Magowan Empire Pottery New Jersey	A. & M.	1884
2 American China Co. Toronto, Ohio		1897
*3 American Crockery Co. Trenton, New Jersey	English arms A.C. Co.	1876
4 Anchor Pottery Trenton, New Jersey	Modified English arms with AP monogram in center	1894
5 J. H. Baum Wellsville, Ohio	J.H. Baum	1880 - 1985
6 L.B. Beerbower & Co. Elizabeth, New Jersey	STONE CHINA	1879
7 Beerbower & Griffen Phoenixville Pottery. Phoenixville, Pennsylvania	Arms of state of Pennsylvania and, in circle, initials B & G	1867
8 Edwin Bennett Pottery Co. Baltimore, Maryland (Formerly E. & W. Bennett)	Wreath E.B.	1848- 1936
9 Blunt, Bloor, Martin & Co. Dresden Pottery East Liverpool, Ohio	Dresden China	1875
*10 Wm. Brunt, Jr. & Co. East Liverpool, Ohio	W. B. P. Co.	1865-78
*11 Burford Bros. East Liverpool, Ohio	Royal Arms, scroll, banner, shield & other name marks	White Granite by 1881
*12 Burgess & Campbell International Pottery Co. New Jersey	Circle with rampant lion, Burgess & Campbell	1879
13 Burroughs & Mountford Trenton, New Jersey	B. & M.	1879
14 James Carr N.Y.C. Pottery	J. C. Stone China	1871-1885
15 Carr & Morrison N.Y.C. Pottery New York, N.Y.	J.C. Stone China	1853-1871

*16 Cartwright Bros. East Liverpool, Ohio	Eagle marks, sometimes printed pattern names	White Granite by 1890
*17 Chelsea China Co. New Cumberland, West Virginia	Star, crescent moon, and Chelsea White Granite	1888
*18 City Pottery Co. Trenton, New Jersey	Shield C.P. Co.	1859
*19 Cook & Hancock Crescent Pottery Trenton, New Jersey	Cook & Hancock	1881
20 Coxon & Co. Empire Pottery Trenton, New Jersey	Badge with eagle in center and ribbon beneath with name of firm	1863
*21 Crown Pottery Co. Evansville, Indiana	English Arms with "C.P.C." monogram in center	1891
22 Messrs. Dale & Davis Prospect Hill Pottery Trenton, New Jersey	Royal Arms	1880
23 Eagle Pottery Co. Trenton, New Jersey (Owned by Burroughs & Mountford)		
*24 East End Pottery East Liverpool, Ohio	Royal Arms, crown, sometimes printed pattern names	1894
25 East Liverpool Pottery Co. East Liverpool, Ohio	E.L.P. Co.	1881 White Granite by 1894
26 East Trenton Pottery Co. Trenton, New Jersey	E.T.P. Co. New Jersey Seal also English	White Granite by 1888
27 Empire Pottery Co. Syracuse, New York		1865-1871
28 Etruria Pottery Trenton, New Jersey (Subsequently Ott & Brewer)	Etruria pottery	1863
*29 Fell & Thropp Co. Trenton, New Jersey	English Arms F & T. Co.	Before 1901
*30 Ford City China Co. Ford City, Pennsylvania	Sometimes marked "Turin"	1898-1904
31 Franklin Porcelain Co. Franklin, Ohio	F.P. Co.	1880
32 Globe Pottery Co. East Liverpool, Ohio	Globe Pottery Co.	1881
33 Goodwin & Flentke East Liverpool, Ohio		1878-9
*34 Goodwin Bros. East Liverpool, Ohio	Goodwin Bros.	1876-93

35	Great Western Pottery Co. East Liverpool, Ohio	
36	Griffen, Smith and Company Phoenixville, Pennsylvania (Formerly Beerbower & Griffen)	1878-90
37	Benjamin Harker Jr. & Sons Wedgewood Pottery East Liverpool, Ohio	White Granite after 1877
*38	Harker Pottery Co. East Liverpool, Ohio	Horizontal bow with vertical arrow, H.P. CO.	1879
39	D. F. Haynes & Co. Chesapeake Pottery Baltimore, Maryland	Various marks with initial monogram in the center	1879
40	Wm. A. Homer Boston, Mass.	
41	International Pottery Co. Trenton, New Jersey	1865-75
42	Joseph Jager Peoria Pottery Co. Peoria, Illinois	P.P. Co.	Early 1870s
43	Jersey City Pottery Jersey City, New Jersey (Subsequently Rouse & Turner)	1829
*44	Knowles, Taylor & Knowles East Liverpool, Ohio	K.T. & K	White Granite after 1872
45	Homer Laughlin & Co. East Liverpool, Ohio	HOMER LAUGHLIN	1879
46	Thomas Maddock & Sons Eagle Pottery Trenton, New Jersey	EAGLE POTTERY	1869
47	Maryland Pottery Co. Baltimore, Maryland	Circular eagle, MARYLAND POTTERY CO. (Seal of Maryland after 1883)	1881
*48	Mayer Pottery Co. Beaver Falls, Pennsylvania	Square enclosing a circle with WARRANTED STONE CHINA J. & E. MAYER	1881
*49	McNicol, Burton & Co. East Liverpool, Ohio		1869-1892
*50	D.E. McNichol Pottery Co. East Liverpool, Ohio	Various name marks	1892-1910 (?)
51	Mellor & Co. Cook Pottery Co. Trenton, New Jersey	MELLOR & CO.	ca. 1893
52	Mercer Pottery Co. Trenton, New Jersey	Double Shield MERCER POTTERY CO.	1868

53	Millington & Astbury & Poulson Trenton, New Jersey	M.A.P.	1853 Whiteware after 1861
54	Morley, Goodwin & Flenke		White Granite after 1874
55	Morley & Co. (Later Wellsville Pottery Co.)	M. & Co.	1879–85
*56	John Moses & Co. Glasgow Pottery Co. Trenton, New Jersey	Eagle over shield, J.M. & Co.	1863
57	New England Pottery Co. East Boston, Massachusetts	Seal of state of Massachusetts from 1878 to 1883, N.E.P. Co.; Indian design	1854
58	New Jersey Pottery Co. Trenton, New Jersey		1869
*59	Onondaga Pottery Co. Syracuse, N.Y.	Arms of New York (2 women) O.P. Co.	1871
60	Ott & Brewer Trenton, New Jersey		1867
61	Peoria Pottery Co. Peoria, Illinois	English Arms WARRANTED	1873
*62	Pioneer Pottery Co. Wellsville, Ohio		1885-96
63	Phoenixville Pottery Co. Phoenixville, Pennsylvania (Later Beerbower & Griffen)		1867
*64	Potter's Cooperative Co. East Liverpool, Ohio	Dresden	1876
65	Rhodes & Yates		founded 1858
66	Rouse & Turner Jersey City, New Jersey	R & T	founded before 1850
*67	George Scott & Sons Cincinnati, Ohio		White Granite after 1888
*68	Sebring Pottery Co. East Liverpool, Ohio	(Impressed) crown	1887
69	St. Johns Stone Chinaware Co. St. Johns, Province of Quebec, Canada	English arms St. Johns, P.Q.	1874
70	Speeler & Taylor		
*71	Steubenville Pottery Co. Steubenville, Ohio	S.P. Co. others	ca. 1879
72	Stephens & Tams Greenwood Pottery Trenton, New Jersey	New Jersey Arms with G.P. Greenwood Pottery	1861
73	Taylor & Co. Trenton, New Jersey		1865

74 Taylor, Smith and Taylor, Chester, West Virginia		ca. 1899
75 Taylor, Speeler & Bloor		founded 1856
*76 Tempest, Brockman & Co. Cincinnati, Ohio	B.P. Co.	1867-81
*77 C.C. Thompson & Co. East Liverpool, Ohio	Printed initials over a griffin	ca. 1890
*78 Trenton Pottery Co. Trenton, New Jersey (Various owners)	T.P. CO. CHINA	1852-ca. 1900
79 Union Pottery Co. Trenton, New Jersey		1880
80 United States Pottery Co. Bennington, Vermont		1849
81 Vance Faience Pottery Tiltonville, Ohio (Formerly Avon Faience Pottery Company)		1880
*82 Vodrey & Brothers	Monogram V over B	1879
83 Wallace & Chetwynd East Liverpool, Ohio		White Granite after1881
84 Warwick China Co. Wheeling, West Virginia	Helmet and crossed swords and various other marks	1877
*85 Wheeling Pottery Co. Wheeling, West Virginia	STONE CHINA	1879
*86 Wick China Co. Kittanning, Pennsylvania	Some pieces marked "Aurora" or "Erie"	1889-1913
87 Willets Manufacturing Co. Trenton, New Jersey	W.M. Co.	1879
88 John Wyllie & Sons Great Western Pottery East Liverpool, Ohio	Double shield of English and U.S. seals, J.W. & SON	1874

An asterisk (*) before company name in the list of *American Potters of White Granite* denotes the native potteries which made white ironstone touched with copper lustre.

For further information, consult the little handbook on *American Tea Leaf*, written by Julie Rich and published by the Tea Leaf Club International.

An excellent reference to help research the makers of all kinds of American ironstone: *Lehner's Encyclopedia of U.S. Marks on Pottery, Porcelain & Clay* by Lois Lehner, Collector Books (A division of Schroeder Publishing Co., Inc.) Copyright 1988.

Some Marks Found on American Ironstone

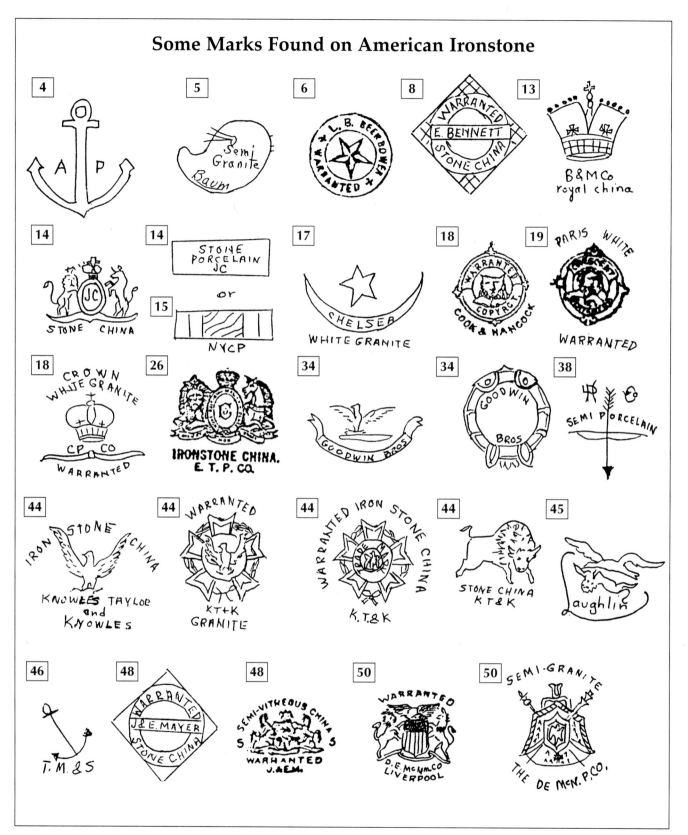

52 WARRANTED IRONSTONE CHINA

52 WARRANTED SUPERIOR IRONSTONE CHINA MERCER POTTERY CO.

53 MAP TRENTON N.J.

56 JM&Co

56 GLASGOW IRON STONE CHINA WARRANTED

56 IRONSTONE CHINA J.M.& Co.

59 CHINA O.P.Co.

59 IRONSTONE CHINA O.P.Co.

62 AURORA CHINA

66 R&T

72 GREENWOOD ART POTTERY

77 C.C.T

82 SEMI-PORCELAIN

84 W G CO

85 THE WHEELING POTTERY CO.

85 WARRANTED THE WHEELING POTTERY CO. MADE IN AMERICA

88 TRADE MARK STONE CHINA J.W. & SON.

Unidentified potter's mark on a spittooon. This inscription is in the circle around the center figures: "The National Home for Disabled Volunteer Soldiers – March 3, 1865"

Utilitarian Pieces

The collectors of white utilitarian pieces really enjoy accumulating their prizes; they are enthusiastic about any item that is different. How about the embossed spittoon which neatly fits into a velvet-lined dovetailed cherry box? Or the handheld spittoon carried so one could spit tobacco juice in church? Or an oval chamber pot with a silencing wall across the middle? Can you see an infant or an invalid drinking from a pap boat long before "bendy" straws were invented?

It is difficult to determine origins of utilitarian pieces. Some of these were made in England or Europe proper and undoubtedly some were shaped in America. Also, we cannot date the decades in which each was made. Nevertheless, we'll continue to gather them as relics from generations past.

Please enjoy these pictures of unusual ceramic creations intended to make everyday life easier. ▓

Bottles & Flasks

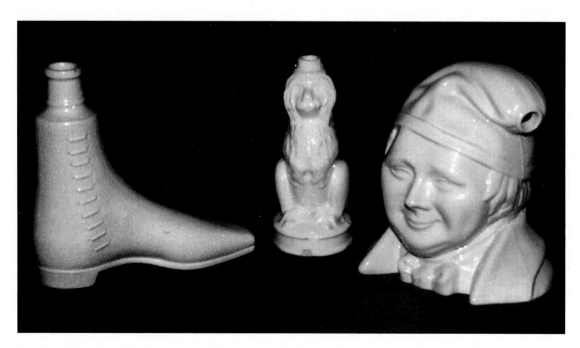

Fig. 18-1   These three flasks (between 6 & 7" h) are quite collectible. Dan Overmeyer wanted you to see them.

Cake Stands

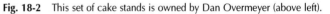

Fig. 18-2 This set of cake stands is owned by Dan Overmeyer (above left).

Fig. 18-3 Handy cake stands are very collectible! This shell-decorated one marked by Davenport is 9 inches in diameter, owned by the Dieringers (above right).

Fig. 18-4 I think potteries, both English and American, made stacks of these footed cake or pastry stands. Potters reported have been J. F., W. V. S. (?), J. M. & Co. (John Moses), J. W. Pankhurst, Anthony Shaw and other makers. The sizes reported range from 6 inches to 15 inches in diameter.
←

Carriers & Holders

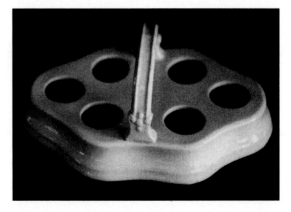

Fig. 18-5 The Dieringers own this handy egg carrier or holder. Unmarked.

Fig. 18-6 J. & G. Meakin often made practical pieces such as this egg holder. A low Boston egg cup rests nearby. Owned by Sally Scrimgeour.

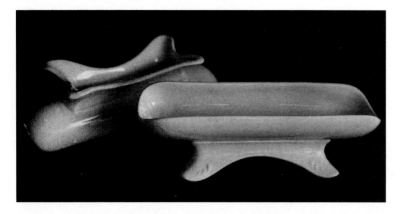

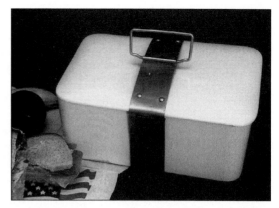

Fig. 18-7   This useful pair of corn ear holders was made by J. & G. Meakin very early in the 20th century. The Dieringers use them.

Fig. 18-8   Very different is this banded white ironstone lunch box. It is marked "C.W.S. & S", "Coracle Brand," Sirram, Birmingham. Sally Scrimgeour discovered this lunch carrier.

Chamber & Bath Accessories

Fig. 18-9   To the left, is an early Gothic spittoon by J. F. and (right) a later one by I. (John) Davis. This pair was posed by Carol & Frank Fleischman.

Fig. 18-10   Very handy little spittoon if you want to chew tobacco in company.

Fig. 18-11   I included this picture to show a late waste pail (with a hole in the cover to receive water) from an Alfred Meakin toilet set. The bails were usually wound by wicker. Moreland Collection. ←

Fig. 18-12   What a handy brush and soap holder for the kitchen or bath! →

Drainers

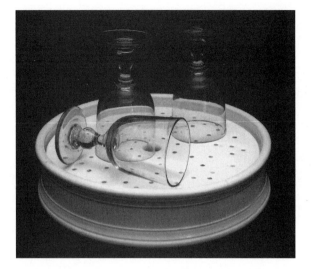

Fig. 18-13 Sally says her favorite ironstone-type piece is this glass dryer made in Belgium, Boch F. La Louriere.

Fig. 18-14 Here is a 7¹/₂″ handled bowl to be used as a colander by the Dieringers.

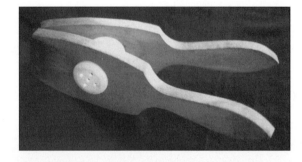

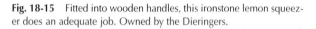

Hand Utensils

Fig. 18-15 Fitted into wooden handles, this ironstone lemon squeezer does an adequate job. Owned by the Dieringers.

Fig. 18-16 Sally also found these ironstone spoons and ladles that she enjoys using.

Fig. 18-17 Add to the list of handy tools this pie bird (top), marked "The Gourmet Pie Cup" Rd. No 369793; the egg separator; and a strainer ladle. Ted and Ed found them.

Hot Water Plates

Fig. 18-18   This covered hot water dish server is unmarked and has a hole in which hot water could be poured to keep food warm.

Fig. 18-18a   Here is the same server with the cover off. It is owned by the Morelands.

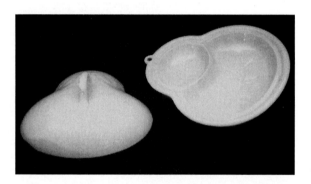

Fig. 18-19   This 12¼″ long covered server has a separate food warmer compartment. It has a crabstock handle and a winding vine decor on the cover. Rigoulot-Brockey Collection.

Fig. 18-20a & b   This is a more common hot plate warmer with a chained ironstone stopper on the side. The elaborate cartouche advertises a hotel and its proprietor. The impressed "Real Ironstone China" suggests that the potter may have been Frances Morley. Armbruster Collection.

Molds

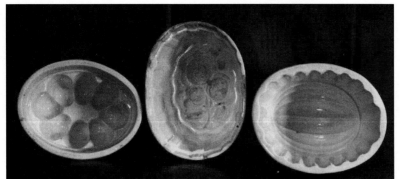

Fig. 18-21 Three unmarked ironstone molds are useful around the kitchen.

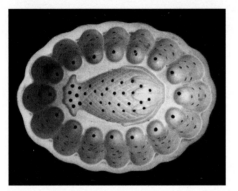

Fig. 18-22 Sally Scrimgeour shows us her great pineapple cheese mold that is 8 1/2″.

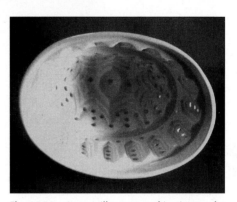

Fig. 18-23 Anne Miller sent us this picture of a fancy cheese mold with draining holes.

Toast Boards & Racks

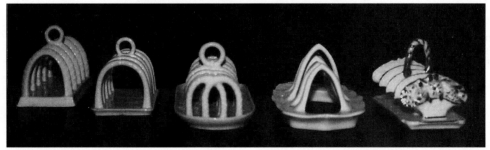

Fig. 18-24 Carol Anderson shared her toast rack collection with us.

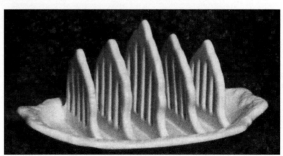

Fig. 18-25 Unmarked toast rack may have adorned a Victorian breakfast table.

Fig. 18-26 Pair of unmarked toast boards, made in an ironstone-type body, have leaves and scrolls in a raised decoration around the hole and in the corners. Owned by Sally Scrimgeour.

For Children Only

Children of the 19th century were often given copies of the same tea sets that their mothers used. Sets were composed of teapot, sugar, creamer, waste bowl, six cups with saucers and six little plates. Most sugar bowls and waste bowls seem larger in proportion than the rest of the set. Potters appear to have been just as careful with the details of potting of the miniature sets as they were in producing the normal-sized ones. The prices of these rare sets are sometimes higher than the adult-sized ones.

The many-pieced dinner sets are very rare. These contain covered tureens with stands and ladles, nests of open servers and platters, stacks of plates but no cups. The occasional emergence of an octagonal server, a tureen, or a gravy boat reminds us that these dinner sets did once exist.

Children's miniature sets have been found in the following shapes:

Balanced Vine
Boote 1851 Octagon
Bordered Gooseberry
Budded Vine
Cable n' Ring
Ceres Shape
Classic Gothic
Columbia Shape
Corn n' Oats
Edwards' Lily of the Valley
Fig
Fig Cousin
Floral Shape (Prairie Flower)
Forget-Me Not
Full Ribbed
Grape Octagon
Ivy Wreath
Lily Shape
Many Panelled Gothic
Montpelier Double Scallop
Moss Rose
New York Shape

Panelled Columbia
Panelled Grape
Plain Round
Plain Scallop (Crystal)
Portland Shape
Prairie Shape
President Shape
Primary Shape (large)
Primary Shape (small)
Sevres Shape
Sharon Arch
Shaw's Lily of the Valley
Shaw's Pear
Six-Panelled Trumpet
Strawberry
Sydenham Shape (cups found)
Twin Leaves
Washington Shape
Wheat and Clover
Wheat and Hops (Ceres)
and others

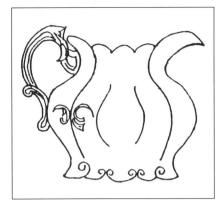

Fig. 19-1 Most American children's set were plain, but this one has swirls and was marked "Kokus Stone China," by Sebring's. These pieces were located by the Armbrusters.

An early embossed American creamer

The few photographs included here show a tureen, an open server, and a gravy boat in miniature size, suggesting that larger dinner sets had been produced. I have only seen a few partial sets. One set by Livesley, Powell & Co. has been seen on a *Fern and Floral* shape (Lechler, p. 203) and this included a soup tureen with ladle and liner, 2 covered sauce tureens with ladles and liners, 2 covered vegetable tureens, 2 gravy boats, 5 platters (various sizes), open compote, 8 dinner plates, 8 soup, 8 salad, and 8 dessert plates. Dinner sets did not usually include cups and saucers. The price range for a set like the one itemized and in good condition would be in the price range of $1,000 to $1,300.

While most American-made children's table wares were 22-piece plain sets, there were a few that displayed some raised designs. The photo (above left) shows one such pattern and to the right I've included a drawing of a different pattern creamer. The same decor is found on the sugar bowl and teapot but the plates, cups with saucers and waste bowl are plain.

The author shares a cup with her little neighbor, Katie.

Fig. 19-2 A miniature *Boote 1851 Octagon* cup with saucer pose with the normal sized pieces. The 22 piece set "for children only" is an exact replica of the larger set (above left).

Fig. 19-3 Wrongly captioned in my "Second Look," this is really the teapot to a children's *Bordered Gooseberry* set. I found more by Wedgwood & Co. (above right).

Fig. 19-4 Both Davenport and J. Wedgwood (John Wood) potted this *Corn and Oats* shape. To the left is a Davenport teapot, echoed by the children's J. Wedgwood teapot to the right. Arranged by the Adys (left).

Fig. 19-5 A family reunion in *Ceres Shape* by Elsmore & Forster includes both adult and children's sizes. Called together by the Dieringers.

Fig. 19-6 A *Full-Ribbed* teapot by J. W. Pankhurst stands guard over miniature pieces made just as meticulously in the same shape.

Fig. 19-7 A *Boote 1851 Octagon* teapot compares its size with pieces of a *Grape Octagon* miniature set in front of a Walker cupboard.

Fig. 19-8 Let's see—there's a *Many Panelled Gothic* creamer and a *Long Octagon* open server. Is the bottom piece a children's soup bowl or a tiny honey dish? (top left)

Fig. 19-9 Parts of a *Primary Shape* mini set by Wooliscroft pose in front of a *Primary Pumpkin* shape blue transfer ewer (top right).

Fig. 19-10 An Edwards' children's *Lily of the Valley* tea set is displayed in front of a later *Chain O' Tulips* teapot by J. & G. Meakin. (left)

Fig. 19-11 Another picture of the *Panelled Grape* miniatures in front of a J. & G. Meakin *Panelled Leaves* jug. The bodies seem related.

Fig. 19-12 *Wheat and Hops* shape by Pearson is marked *Ceres Shape* although it is not the wheat with cable that we usually associate with that name. Ady Collection.

Fig. 19-13 Here's a *Many Panelled Gothic* sugar bowl, a *Shaw's Lily of the Valley* sugar bowl on the top row, and below a *Panelled Columbia* creamer and a rare *Gothic* gravy boat. All miniatures from a Moreland shelf.

Fig. 19-14 This tiny compote stands next to a piece that Dan calls a master salt. Overmeyer Collection.

Fig. 19-15 Anthony Shaw marked this mini cake stand that is 6 3/4 " d. Was it part of a child's set or the smallest of a large set of cake stands? The Dieringers own this piece.

Fig. 19-16 The teapot in *Six-Panelled Trumpet* shape by J. W. Pankhurst is part of a children's miniature tea set. From the collection of Jack Anspaugh.

Fig. 19-17 A great display of miniature pieces from Ted Brockey and Ed Rigoulet are shown: top, (left to right), *Primary Shape* teapot, 4 3/4" h. *Gothic* tureen, *Washington Shape* teapot, and bottom (left to right), *Panelled Columbia* teapot, another *Panelled Columbia* (different potter) teapot and a ring-handled *Montpelier Double Scallop* teapot.

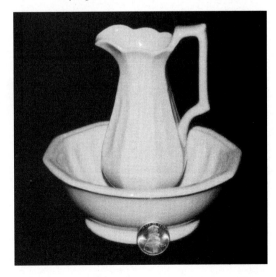

Fig. 19-18 Dan Overmeyer is proud of his doll ewer and basin that has no potter's mark. The set is 4 1/2" h.

Reticulated and High-Relief Treasures

Reticulated Items

Reticulated (pierced) pieces of white ironstone were formed in molds so that a pattern stood out in relief above areas that were to be removed. These sections were then cut out by hand with a penknife leaving an openwork design. This method of decoration was used most often on trays, fruit baskets, or hot chestnut baskets with under trays. Here follow photographs of "holy" dishes garnered by harvesters of white featuring reticulated designs.

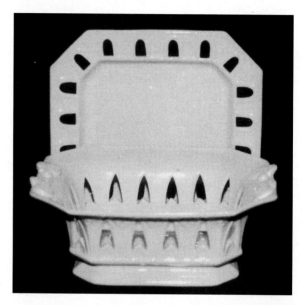

Fig. 20-1 This squared chestnut bowl with tray has lost its handles. We call it *Arcaded Square*. Both belong to Dan Overmeyer.

Fig. 20-2 A white ironstone reticulated fruit or chestnut basket which is marked Alcock, "Imperial Ironstone."

Fig. 20-3   This *Pierced Scroll* set is the same shape as the Alcock bowl. It is from the Overmeyer Collection.

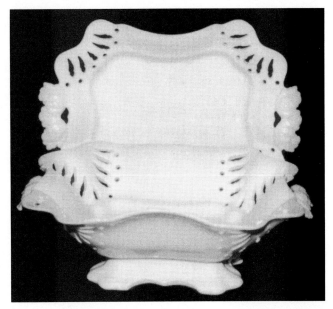

Fig. 20-4   Reticulated chestnut bowl with liner, nicknamed *Lacy Basket,* is unmarked. Located by Dan Overmeyer.

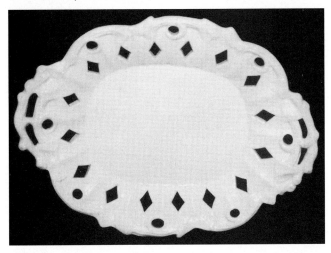

Fig. 20-5   Dan Overmeyer sent this photo of a *Heart and Diamonds* tray. He wanted to find the mated bowl.

Fig. 20-7   This unusual reticulated compote (11 inches in diameter) includes a ring of Sydenham shields around the base. The edge of the bowl also has the shields with cut-outs between them. Rigoulot and Brockey own them and hope someone will say, "I've one just like it marked T. & R. Boote." This one is unmarked.

Fig. 20-6   Here's the bowl Dan Overmeyer needs! This *Heart and Diamonds* chestnut bowl is on display at the Lorning-Greenough House in Jamaica Plain, Massachusetts.

Fig. 20-8   Anthony Shaw potted this 11" high reticulated compote. It is especially sought after by copper lustre collectors who look for a TeaLeaf inside. From the Dieringer Collection.

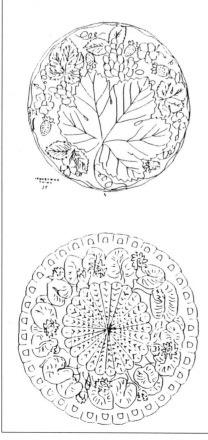

Fig. 20-9   "Ritter House, Cambridge 1850" is labeled on the side of this reticulated centerpiece. "Real Ironstone China" is impressed on the underside, perhaps by Morley. The Dieringers own this prize.

Fig. 20-10   This fruit compote on a square plinth is unmarked.
←

High-Relief Items

Other popular collectibles are the white granite pieces with bodies completely covered with high-relief molding. Some dessert sets included 8" individual plates, different shapes of sandwich or biscuit trays, and footed or pedestalled cake plates. Here are pictures of partial sets of these profusely decorated dishes.

SKETCHES OF HIGH-RELIEF PLATES

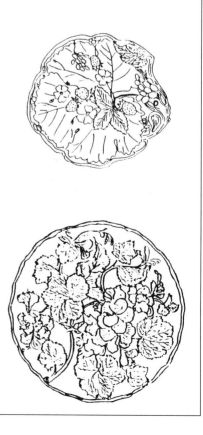

FRUIT GARDEN
Fruit Garden dessert sets were potted by Barrow & Co., Jacob Furnival, and Livesley & Powell. Individual plates, cake stands, a compote, square biscuit trays, and relish dishes were parts of sets. Two types of plates are shown.

LILY PAD
J. W. Pankhurst designed *Lily Pad,* a profusely decorated shape used on plates, a high pedestalled compote, a three-legged cookie plate and probably other pieces.
←

FLOWER BLANKET
Individual dessert plates have been located several times in this *Flower Blanket* executed in gleaming white by Jacob Furnival. ➡

Fig. 20-12 This *Lily Pad* footed doughnut stand was made by J. W. Pankhurst. The stand is very collectible.

Fig. 20-11 Many collectors sent photos of this *Fruit Garden* compote, part of a dessert set. *Fruit Garden* dessert sets were made by Jacob Furnival, Barrow & Co. and Livesley & Powell.

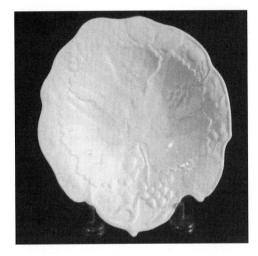

Fig. 20-13 Here's another piece of the *Fruit Garden* set found by the Armbrusters.

Fig. 20-14 This James Edward's *Leaf* compote was made with other matching low relish dishes. All the background is stippled. This shape was copied by several American potteries. Jack Anspaugh Collection.

Fig. 20-15 The decor on this unmarked 11″ dessert tray looks closely related to the *Fruit Garden* shape. Located by the Armbrusters.

Fig. 20-16 This different *Open Flower* compote is owned by Dan Overmeyer.

Jugs and Other Molded Items

Ornate jugs, probably the vessels that most often display high-relief treatment, were potted between 1840 and 1870. Some are breathtakingly beautiful, a very few are close to grotesque in appearance, but all are very collectible. All would be welcomed into a white granite assemblage. I still remember seeing two jugs depicting birds. One was in a shop window and featured swans and water plants with foliage covering the body but I never found the shop open. The other displayed the limbs and leaves of a tree with a nest of hungry baby birds near a large mother robin but that jug was lost in a fire. Therefore, we wonder—will we ever see either jug again? Below are pictures of high relief dishes taken so that you collectors can look and long.※

This most beautiful of high-relief jugs, *Grape with Vine,* is proudly marked by Minton & Co., registered on May 21, 1846.

Fig. 20-17 Cork & Edge's *Babes in the Woods* jugs are available and collectible.

Fig. 20-18 This Victorian *Cherub* jug was made by Barrow & Co. The photo was sent by the Nobles.

Fig. 20-19 This *Large Ivy Trunk* jug has larger relief proportions than most Cork & Edge 'trunk and ivy' jugs. A cartouche on the underside includes an eagle and the words "E Pluribus Unum" over "Pearl White Ironstone" by Cork & Edge. Moreland Collection.

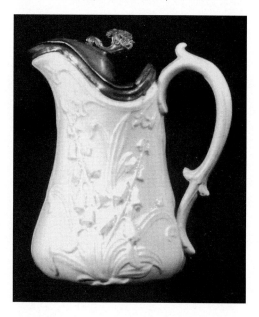

Fig. 20-20 This *Molded Lily of the Valley* syrup pitcher with pewter lid was marked by G. Wooliscroft.

Fig. 20-21 Here's a Cork & Edge family line-up of high-relief table and syrup jugs. Some were found in England. From the Dieringer cabinet.

Fig. 20-22 My *Favorite Grotesque* jug amuses us with its graybeard spout, serpent handles and faces of people and animals amid foliage. I wonder where Dan Overmeyer found it, don't you?

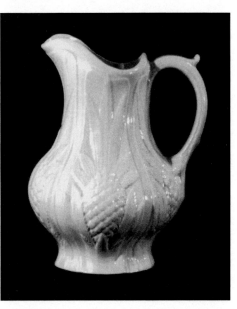

Fig. 20-23 Four *Pineapples* with serrated foliage enfold this jug owned by the Morelands.

Fig. 20-25 The Dieringers found this rare *Trunk with Ivy* mug.

Fig. 20-24 Closely related to the *Babes in the Woods* jug is this *Trunk with Ivy* jug by Cork & Edge.

Fig. 20-26 The smaller of these *Hen on Basket* pieces is about 4½" l. Both belong to the Allers.

Fig. 20-27 This large *Hen on Basket* is intricately detailed. Owned by the Kerrs.

Fig. 20-28 Anne Miller located this unusual *Burgher* tobacco jar with a cap cover and faces on both sides.

Fig. 20-29 This well-designed jug, called *Graybeard with Children,* was unmarked.

Fig. 20-30 This decorative unmarked eagle is creamy white, 13⅝" h. Age is uncertain. Courtesy of the Armbrusters.

The Rare and Wonderful

Cake Stands Through Waste Jars

The focus of this chapter is the photographs themselves. Walk and talk with me as we gaze at this gallery of unique, seldom-seen pieces of white ironstone.

We'll begin with a gallery of dining room accessories, covering everything from cake stands to spoon warmers and we'll finish up showing you chamber and bath accessories in rare ironstone forms.✖

Dining Room Accessories

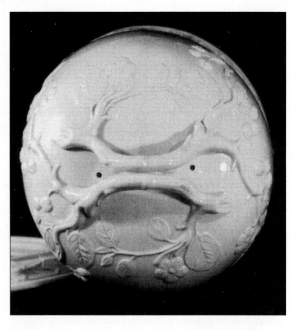

Fig. 21-1a & b   This spectacular cheese bell displays a wandering vine with five-petalled flowers and pods over the bell which rests on a low tray. Nearby is the top view displaying two ventilating holes and crabstock handles. From the Moreland Collection.

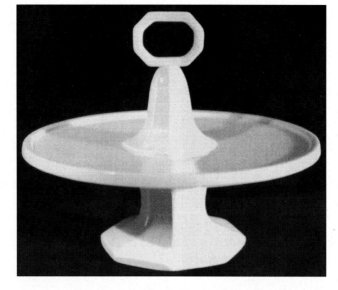

Fig. 21-2 This photo shows a 7"h. candlestick owned by Ed Rigoulot and Ted Brockey,

Fig. 21-3 Rare and wonderful is this handled cake stand with *Gothic* lines, marked "James Edwards, Dale Hall," ca. 1840s. This pedestalled stand was discovered by the Armbrusters.

Fig. 21-4 This 91/4"h. candlestick is marked by Ridgway and was registered in 1846. Dan Overmeyer owns it.

Fig. 21-5 Another cheese bell, a little over 9 inches tall, is covered with woodsy ferns and foliage. This outstanding piece is owned by Dan Overmeyer.

Fig. 21-6 & Fig. 21-7 These low egg cups in *Gothic* shape and *Ceres Shape* are hard to find. Dan Overmeyer owns these two. Can you locate the photo including *Full Ribbed* egg cups?

Fig. 21-8 & Fig. 21-9 Early *Gothic* and *Fluted* shaped compotes are still considered rare and wonderful: (left) ten-sided one by Meir & Son and (right) fluted one by James Edwards. Armbruster Collection.

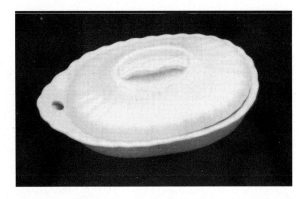

Fig. 21-10 Occasionally, we find tableware handled in decorated white granite. This 9 1/4 knife is marked "GIBBS" on the blade. Moreland Collection.

Fig. 21-11 This choice covered hot dish server is kept warm by pouring hot water under the well and tree base plate. The cover has a scroll border with a ribbed surface. Collection of Rigoulot/Brockey.

A Gallery of Mustards

Fig 21-12 Here is a scarce mustard pot in *Chrysanthemum* shape (also seen with a pewter lid). This belongs to the Morelands.

Fig. 21-13 Thought you'd like to see this unusual pewter-covered graceful little mustard found by Anne Miller.

Fig. 21-14 Wrongly marked in "Second Look," this prize mustard jar is, of course, shaped in *Quartered Rose* by Jacob Furnival.

Fig. 21-15 This *Eagle* covered butter and matching mustard pot were potted by Gelson Bros. in 1869 and bought by Dan Overmeyer in the 20th century.

Fig. 21-16 A great find is this Pedestalled *Gothic* unmarked mustard pot located by Dan Overmeyer.

A Page of Pitchers

Fig 21-17 On the far left is a *Full-Panelled Gothic* jug potted by Edward Walley around 1850. It is rare because this is table size. A similar one was potted by T. & R. Boote in *1851 Octagon*, about 8"h. In group photo to the right is a line-up of syrup jugs with pewter lids: (left to right) - *Pearl Sydenham* by J. & G. Meakin, *Molded Tulip*, Edward's *Lily of the Valley*, and *Molded Lily of the Valley* by Wooliscroft. The Dieringers provided this group shot.

Fig. 21-18 Have you noticed how many different practical pieces were potted by J. & G. Meakin? Here's another, a practical ale pitcher in *Rope with Melon Ribs* owned by Sally Scrimgeour.
←

Fig. 21-19 This Mason-named *Fenton* jug with serpent handle was potted by John Wedge Wood perhaps in the 1840s. Treasured by the Nobles.
→

Fig. 21-20 I'm reminding you that all covered beverage servers are outstanding collectibles! The Casavants spotted this one in *Prize Bloom*.

Fig. 21-21 I included these two covered hot beverage servers to show the difference in size: *New York Shape* (left) and *Ceres Shape*. This *Ceres* piece is a one-of-a kind discovered by the Armbrusters.

Miscellaneous Table Treasures

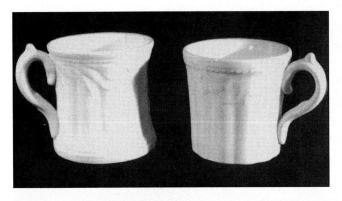

Fig. 21-22   The *Ceres Shape* mug to the left is seldom seen with its cable around both the top and base. The one more usually found is the one to the right.

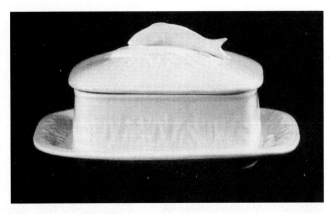

Fig. 21-23   The Morelands can graciously serve their sardines in this very unusual box decorated with three sardines and ocean grasses.

Fig. 21-24 & Fig. 21-25   Here posed are three Victorian spoon warmers. The last two are both marked "Copeland," one registered, both living in the Rigoulot/Brockey cupboard.

Fig. 21-26   Sally Scrimgeour serves her fish on this 11 inch platter, decorated by Jacob Furnival with two fish.

Chamber & Bath Accessories

Fig. 21-29 Here's a repeat photo of the one-of-a-kind Sydenham toothbrush holder owned half by O'Hare and half by Overmeyer.

Fig. 21-27 & Fig. 21-28 These two vertical toothbrush holders (without liners) were probably potted by the same firm, Elsmore and Forster. The one with little feet is, of course, *Ceres Shape*. The other includes no wheat heads in the decor.

Fig. 21-30 What a prize is this *Arched Panel* spittoon with laughing lion handles and a fluted body, marked by Elsmore & Forster. It belongs to the Morelands.

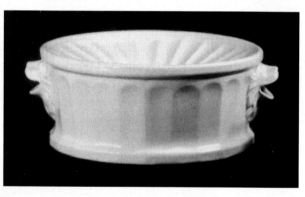

Fig. 21-31 Just as difficult to acquire are early foot baths, part of toilet sets. This *Framed Leaf* bath by J. W. Pankhurst is in the possession of the Dieringers.

Fig. 21-32 I finish this gallery with the recognition that some toilet stools were shaped from white granite. This photo was snapped at an outdoor show in Massachusetts and the piece had a $1,700 price tag. Another report had come in about an elaborate 1895 toilet stool installed in a railroad car later used by Governor Harriman of New York State. All this information was supplied by Ernie Dieringer.

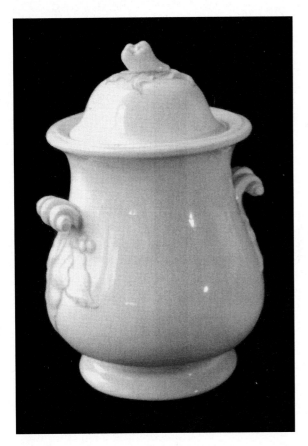

Fig. 21-33 Any early master jar to the toilet set is rare and expensive. Here the Dieringers show their prize in *Maddock's Pear* shape.

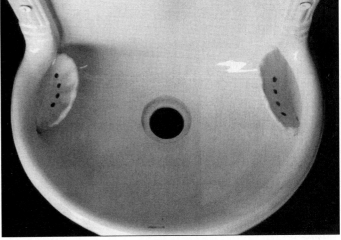

Fig. 21-34a & Fig. 21-34b This remarkable hanging wall sink clings to Sally Scrimgeour's garden wall. It is marked "New Real Sanitas, Fayence, Mfg. in England." Two shells at the side are soap containers.

Still Looking, Still Listening

Do thou, thrice happy England, still prepare
This clay, and build thy fame on earthenware!
—"Isabella"
        by Sir Chas. Williams

Here I close with a potpourri of partial thoughts, surmisings, speculations and many, many questions. These ideas fluctuate regularly and will continue to do so as long as "inquirers want to know."

Let's take time to think about those capable English craftsmen from "The Potteries" located in the Staffordshire region of England. Of course, other centers in England, Scotland, and Ireland produced white granite in the 19th century but the bulk of production took place near present-day Stoke-on-Trent which incorporates the early pottery centres.

What was life like in that area during the 18th and 19th centuries? Jewitt, writing in the 1870s and early 1880s, says that "in this pottery district some fifty thousand persons or more are employed in or dependent on the staple trade of the place, that of china and earthenware manufacturing." He quotes Plot, who wrote as early as 1686 that Burslem, nicknamed the 'mother of the potteries', had 'many different sorts of clay...all within a halfe a mile's distance, the best being found nearest the coale.' It was in this pot-making district that Josiah Wedgwood was born, the Wedgwoods had various works, and where Josiah became the acknowledged leader of the industry during the 18th century. During that era, canals were constructed and the port of Liverpool was nearby—both facts that made bulk transportation easier.

The combined size of the fictile centers was only a little over ten miles long. Homes and potteries were crowded together and we assume that manufacturers and workers mingled with those from nearby potworks. History is rather silent about daily life in those communities but we occasionally hear stories or scan records that raise questions. There must have been a close knit social intercourse that included a grapevine for news, events attended together, intermarriage of families and friendships formed. Was there friendship or intermarriage that might explain why Davenport and John Wedge Wood shared at least a half dozen of the same white granite shapes, even using the same registry information? And how about I. Meir and Wooliscroft? They too shared some of the same registries but were each legally confident to add their own names to the same printed registry letters and numbers. Did they have an agreement to share? We may never know.

Human nature reminds us that living so closely together forces people to cooperate when it is expedient. Also, a few problems arose. Some potters were careful to hire workers that they hoped would not betray their potting secrets. Many competitive potters, often within a year, adopted styles and lines copied from popular productions such as *Sydenham Shape* and *Ceres Shape*. Note examples of the Boote's Sydenham shield adopted quickly by other potters of the 1850s. Records reveal that "Ceres" was a name used interchangeably with the many wheat patterns that mimicked that original creation of Elsmore & Forster. Collard discusses the fact that orders from North American customers listed shapes desired with no reference or concern about which pottery filled the order.

Ceramic history is spiced up by accounts of a few Staffordshire disputes. Ralph Shawe had patented an improvement in potting but watched over his neighbors, threatening them by charging that their changes were infringements on his patent. They tired of this, banded together, and had one person instigate a court action. According to Jewitt, the judge settled the matter with words, "Go home, potters, and make whatever kinds of pots you like." We almost get the feeling that he was settling a family quarrel. Very human were those potters.

In most cases, the heads of those companies were alert to opportunities to produce the attractive, usable dishes that consumers requested. Some potters traveled themselves or sent agents to the New World to see what transatlantic consumers really wanted in the way of table and toilet wares. Pat Halfpenny ventures to say that the purchasers often set the styles; thus, the American retailers often asked for a "Wedgwood or Davenport" shape, not caring if the merchandise was supplied by another company. This practice certainly encouraged flagrant copying of desirable shapes by watchful, competent businessmen. Even though transportation of goods was a lengthy, dangerous and laborious task; even though correspondence took weeks or months, we sense that the master potters must have been ready to copy or renovate shapes that could only have been initiated by some knowledge of what was or wasn't currently selling. Some of this seems to be verified by registry dates on similar shapes. Perhaps, some potters were adroit enough to guess which shapes would become "winners." Again, we can only speculate.

Pat Halfpenny, in her research of old documents, concludes that both wholesalers in England and retailers across the sea were concerned, with the 'state of money.' I quote her words: "Bills of exchange were the most usual methods of payment...Traders used these promissory notes instead of cash whenever they could." She gives an example of a bill of exchange that was not accepted by bankers for 'want of advice.' It bounced! Nevertheless, Britain's "advanced commercial system often forced traders to carry on business with that nation rather than other countries."

Collard, in her Canadian ceramic history, emphasizes that buyers were more interested in the products themselves rather than the producers. She does include advertisements that mention the names of T. & R. Boote and also J. & G. Meakin, both prolific manufacturers of white ironstone, but she states that generally there was not much credit given to the makers themselves. Perhaps, that may reflect the fact that so many excellent potters, such as Challinor, Pankhurst, and J. Furnival did not bother to patent their shapes. It has been left to the avid collectors of the late 20th century to tenaciously pursue the offerings of certain potters. In fact, in those times, each company was probably more interested in selling more earthenware than his neighboring firm that he was in becoming a famous potter. Most were clever hucksters, ever alert to out-advertise, out-create, and out-sell his competitors. There was occasional cooperation in filling orders, sharing modelers, and perhaps improving skills. These workers in clay may have been called "easy-minded" but they were far-sighted enough to improve methods and means so that they could offer goods that would appeal to their customers.

Because the research by Americans must begin with the product rather than the producer, we raise questions. Why were toothbrush holders changed from

horizontal to vertical shapes? Did the closed boxes generate odors? Why did the *Atlantic Shape* evolve into other shapes with the same label? Why did Elsmore & Forster remodel their *Ceres* mug shape? Was it easier or cheaper to mold? Or, do we even know which was the original? Were handled cups in early shapes a result of separate custom orders? Who instigated the changes—the consumers or the manufacturers? Thus, our questions roll on and on. Occasionally, an answer can be found in an old record, but most of the time, collectors can only notice and wonder.

Learning from ceramic history accounts and the bumf of old bills, letters, and advertisements, writers repeat the same surnames again and again in their stories about the potteries. Potters trained their children to use excellent skills, perfected through generations of labor in family potteries. An alert worker could be schooled as an apprentice, as a journeyman, as a young partner, or as a protege of a fully-qualified, experienced potter. Examples of this type of education are recorded by Jewitt in the backgrounds of such leaders as Josiah Wedgwood, James Edwards, Joseph Clementson and others. These persistent men were survivors, financial jugglers, excellent craftsmen, sharp businessmen, and were very reluctant to share their expertise with workers in earth across the Atlantic. And indeed, it is true, that Americans were very slow to perfect skills that enabled them to produce acceptable chinawares. Even then, the most successful American potteries had assistance from able workers who had immigrated mostly from the Staffordshire area.

The story of the decades of ceramic trade carried on between the English potteries (using dangerous journeys across rough seas) and the eastern ports of North America is part of both English and American history. Even when cargoes were unloaded, the tale was not complete. Most ironstone still had to be transported up or down rivers by canoe, flatboat, or steamboat; often across water and over rough trails by freight wagons, pack animals, or clumsy two-wheeled carts; and sometimes through unfriendly Indian territories. Relics are still being located at the bottoms of rivers and lakes. Was it worth it? All to bring eating vessels to wilderness homes?

*　*　*　*　*

We continue to ask questions, to find areas that need closer scrutiny. Collard did excellent research based on old trade records found in Canada and England. Are there comparable records available in the United States? Will someone gather facts to let us know?

Will someone in England come to America to handle the 19th century earthenwares that had never been offered to English home markets? Will some Americans continue to search English records for more clues to the ironstone story? Could two work together—each having only half of the story at hand?

I close with questions still pressing from collectors, with several new unrecorded shapes on my shelf, with photos recently received.✳

* * * * *

Fig. 22-1   Here's an early *Long Octagon* shape by T J. & J. Mayer with the same potter's mark as their *Classic Gothic* shape. Recently a dealer secured a hard grayish white tea set in the same shape in thick porcelain. Could it have been some of the competitive French "porcelaine" that so rattled the mid-century Staffordshire men?

Fig. 22-2   Here is an excellent unmarked fluted mug. Was it one from the 1840s shaped by J. Wedgwood? I just located a creamer, fluted from neck to base, over a rounded body. It was potted by Holland and Green. What shall we call this shape? *Arched Panel?*

Fig. 22-3   Here's an arrangement of great mugs posed by Jane Diemer. Where else could I include them?
top: *Dallas Shape*
middle: *Fig, Ceres Shape*
bottom: *Wheat & Clover, Laurel Wreath, Bow and Tassel*

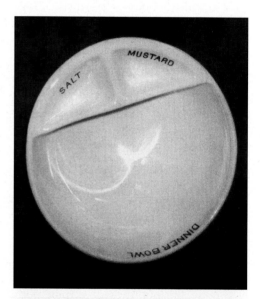

Fig. 22-4a & b   From my mail I extract some photos from the Erdmans in Texas. Is this mark American? They suggest that this is a gruel bowl. But, "salt" and "mustard"?

Fig. 22-5   Another Erdman photo is of a late squared jug with ribbed base and an embossment of ferns on each side. No question here - its a *Ribbed Fern* by A. J. Wilkinson.

Fig. 22-6   Dale Abrams sent this photo of an unmarked copper-banded *Gothic* jug with floral decor under the spout. Ellen Hill includes this same shape in a mulberry jug by J. F. Has anyone seen this in white ironstone? *Floral Gothic*?

Fig. 22-7 & Fig. 22-8   Above are two photographs of American *Daily Bread* platters recently sent by the Armbrusters. The large 12 in. plate to the left looks familiar for it has the same decor as the one in Chapter 17. But, wait- what does it say? "Waste Not" and the answer "Want Not." The second picture to the right, an unmarked round server clearly proclaims "The Staff of Life." One is so detailed, the other, so simple. Both are very collectible.

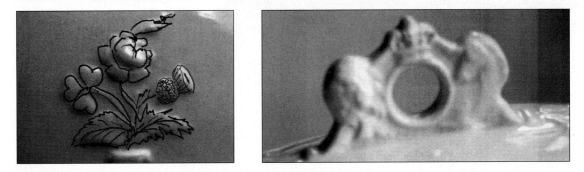

Fig. 22-9a & Fig. 22-9b   Here's recent mail. These photos sent by Jim Kline show the details of Powell and Bishop's *Britannia* shape. Notice that the detail of the English rose, Scottish thistle, and Irish shamrock are not as elaborate as those used by Anthony Shaw. The finial based on the English Royal Arms amuses us.

I could go on and on—but you as collectors must add to the story—which will never be really complete. Happy hunting!

List of Known English Registrations of White Ironstone Shapes

Date	Parcel No.	Patent No.	Potter Name	Place	Shape	No. that day
1843						
Aug. 3	8	9678-80	James Edwards	Burslem	Curved Gothic	3
1844						
April 3	3	17566-72	Thomas Edwards	Burslem	Fluted Panels	7
Sept. 19	4	21700-1	Jn. Ridgway & Co.	Shelton	Primary Hexagon	2
1845						
Jan. 21	6	25199	T. J. & J. Mayer	Longport	Berlin Swirl	1
1846						
May 21	3	35030-1	H. Minton & Co.	Stoke	Grape with Vine (High relief)	2
July 26	1	36167	Ridgway, Son & Co.	Hanley	Candlestick	
1847						
July 16	5	44036-9	James Edwards	Burslem	Pedestalled Gothic Pinchneck Gothic	4
July 27	3	44398	T. J. & J. Mayer	Longport	Mayer's Classic Gothic	1
Sept. 25	5	45992	John Wedge Wood	Tunstall	Fluted Band	1
Oct. 8	4	46265	John Wedge Wood	Tunstall	Fluted Pearl	1
1848						
Mar. 27	8	51185-91	J. & S. Alcock Jr.	Cobridge	Bordered Gothic Alcock's Long Octagon	7
Aug. 23	2	54018	John Wedge Wood	Tunstall	Gothic Cameo	1
Sept. 30	7	54662	John Ridgway & Co.	Shelton	Montpelier Hexagon	1
Dec. 16	3	56631-3	James Edwards	Burslem	Square Rosebud Square Open Flower Square Acorn Finial	3
1850						
July 16	5	70364	C. & W. K. Harvey	Longton	*Florentine	1
Sep. 21	1	72057	Mellor, Venables & Co.	Burslem	Many-Panelled Gothic	1
1851						
Apr. 26	3	78634	E. Walley	Cobridge	*Jug marked "Ceres"	1
July 21	7	79750-3	T. & R. Boote	Burslem	Boote's 1851 Octagon	4
Sept. 2	4	80365	T. J. & J. Mayer	Longport	Prize Puritan	1
Sept. 19	3	80629-30	T. & R. Boote	Burslem	Scallop(1851 Octagon relish)	3
Aug. 29	4	80815-16	James Edwards	Burslem	Twin Leaves Hexagon Flowered Hexagon	2
Oct. 10	6	80913	T. & R. Boote	Burslem	Boote's 1851 Octagon	1
Dec. 2	2	81815	T. J. & J. Mayer	Burslem	Prize Nodding Bud	1
1852						
Oct. 23	4	87219	Davenport & Co.	Longport	Registered to Davenport Marked J. Wedgwood, relish dish	1

This is a chart of English ceramics registrations (between the years of 1842 and 1883) that have been taken from white granite shapes, relics found in America. An asterisk (*) has been placed before shape names impressed or stamped on the actual pieces. Other names have been nicknames used by collectors.

List of Known English Registrations of White Ironstone Shapes (*cont.*)

Date	Parcel No.	Patent No.	Potter Name	Place	Shape	No. that day
1853						
Jan. 14	3	88987	Davenport & Co.	Longport	Fig Cousin	1
Jan. 18	2	89050	Davenport & Co.	Longport	Squat oval teapot	1
Feb. 4	9	89469	J. Pankhurst & J. Dimmock	Hanley	Fluted Hops	1
April 23	2	90876	Wm. Adams & Sons	Stoke	Adam's Scallop	1
May 7	5	91121-4	John Alcock	Cobridge	*Hebe Shape	4
July 18	4	91737	John Edwards	Longton	*Tuscan Shape	1
Sept. 3	2	92340	T. & R. Boote	Burslem	*Sydenham Shape	1
Sept 21	2	92631-2	James Edwards	Burslem	Triple Border	2
Oct. 5	2	92768-70	Venables, Mann & Co.	Burslem	Twelve Panelled Gothic (Closed bud finial) (Ring handled)	3
Oct 12	4	92868-9	Livesley, Powell & Co.	Hanley	Ring O' Hearts	2
Oct. 22	1	93008-9	T. J. & J. Mayer	Longport	Prize Bloom	2
1854						
Mar. 31	1	95469	Holland & Green	Longton	*Gothic Shape	1
Apr. 11	5	95587-8	Pearson, Farrell & Meakin	Shelton	Dangling Tulip (Marked Pearson)	2
June 21	5	96085-6	T. & R. Boote	Burslem	*Sydenham Shape	2
July 18	2	96296	T. & R. Boote	Burslem	*Special Sydenham pieces	1
Sept. 5	3	96773	Samuel Alcock & Co.	Burslem	Stafford Shape (Marked J. Alcock)	1
Oct. 6	4	97141	Davenport & Co.	Longport	Scalloped Decagon	
1855						
Jan. 15	4	99051	Brougham & Mayer	Tunstall	*Virginia Shape	1
Jan. 30	1	99188	John Edwards	Longton	*President Shape	1
Feb 3	4	99231	J. & M. P. Bell	Glasgow	Dolphin-handled jug?	1
Feb 7	2	99310	John Alcock	Cobridge	*Flora Shape	1
Mar. 5	3	99579	Elsmore & Forster	Tunstall	*Columbia	1
Apr. 17	4	99876	Stephen Hughes & Son	Burslem	*DeSoto Shape (Marked T. Hughes)	1
June 7	4	100246-7	John Alcock	Cobridge	*Trent Shape	2
July 24	1	100816	Chas. Meigh & Son	Hanley	Arcaded Trumpet	1
Aug. 27	2	101229-31	Barrow & Co.	Fenton	*Adriatic Shape	3
Oct. 25	3	102325	D. Chetwynd	Cobridge	*Baltic Shape (marked J. Meir)	1
Oct. 29	6	102355	G. W. Reade	Burslem	*Columbia Shape (marked J. Meir)	1
1856						
Jan 5	3	103103	John Edwards	Longton	*President Shape	1
Apr. 7	2	104313-16	Anthony Shaw	Tunstall	Niagara Fan Chinese Shape	4
Apr. 18	3	104393	Ralph Scragg	Hanley	*Mobile Shape (marked G. Bowers)	
Aug. 22	4	105955-9	T. & R. Boote	Burslem	*Union Shape	5
Nov. 14	9	107038	Davenport & Co.	Longport	Fig (some marked Davenport) (some marked J. Wedgwood)	1
Nov. 29	1	107783-5	E. Walley	Cobridge	*Niagara Shape	3
Dec. 18	2	108052	Mayer & Elliott	Longport	Berlin Swirl	1

List of Known English Registrations of White Ironstone Shapes (*cont.*)

Date	Parcel No.	Patent No.	Potter Name	Place	Shape	No. that day
1857						
Feb. 4	5	108854-5	John Meir & Son	Tunstall	*Memnon Shape	2
Feb. 23	9	109180	Podmore, Walker & Co.	Hanley	*Athens Shape	1
Mar. 20	4	109427	John Alcock	Cobridge	*Paris Shape	
Oct. 17	2	111643-4	T. & R. Boote	Burslem	*Atlantic Shape	2
1858						
Apr. 22	5	113565	T. & R. Boote	Burslem	*Atlantic Shape	1
May 31	4	113903	Wm. Adams	Tunstall	*Huron Shape	
Sept. 6	5	115197	James Edward	Longport	Hanging Arch	
Dec. 8	11	117336-8	T. & R. Boote	Burslem	*Atlantic Shape *Chinese Shape	3
Dec. 8	12	117339	J. Clementson	Hanley	*New York Shape	1
1859						
Sept.1	3	121833	James Edwards & Son	Longport	Draped Leaf	
Nov. 2	3	123738-40	Elsmore & Forster	Tunstall	*Ceres Shape (tea set) (dinner set) (toilet set)	3
1860						
Jan. 23	7	125863	Mayer & Elliott	Longport	Cabbage	1
May 2	2	128476	John Meir & Son	Tunstall	*Ivy Wreath	
Oct. 19	4	134555-7	J. Clementson	Shelton	*Hill Shape	3
Oct. 19	5	134558-9	Holland & Green	Longton	White Oak and Acorn	2
Nov. 23	9	136032	T. & R. Boote	Burslem	*Garibaldi Shape	1
1861						
Feb. 27	5	138535	James Edwards & Son	Longport	Edwards' Lily of the Valley	1
Apr. 12	3	139714-5	Davenport & Co.	Longport	Sharon Arch (some marked J. Wedgwood)	2
Nov. 15	3	146352-4	J. Clementson	Hanley	*Prairie Shape	3
1862						
Mar. 13	7	149939	Wm. Adams	Tunstall	*Dover Shape	1
Mar. 22	9	150152	T. & R. Boote	Burslem	Winding Vine	1
July 19	6	153366	J. Clementson	Hanley	*Prairie Shape	1
Sept. 17 or 26	6	154812	Hope & Carter	Burslem	*Western Shape	
Sept. 23	8	156715-7	Wm. Baker & Co.	Fenton	*Potomac Shape	3
1863						
Jan. 12	6	159083	Davenport, Banks & Co.	Etruria	Corn and Oats	1
Jan. 30	3	159573	T. & R. Boote	Burslem	*Prairie Flower or *Floral Shape- (2 names)	1
May 11	3	162261-2	E. Pearson	Cobridge	Peas with Pod	2
Aug. 21	1	165317	J. Clementson	Hanley	*Citron Shape	1
Oct. 31	3	167761-3	Edmund T. Wood (Successor to John Wedge Wood)	Tunstall	Corn and Oats (marked J. Wedgwood)	3
Nov. 3	5	168132	John Meir & Son	Tunstall	*Washington Shape	1
Dec. 2	5	169774	J. W. Pankhurst	Hanley	Greek Key	1

List of Known English Registrations of White Ironstone Shapes (*cont.*)

Date	Parcel No.	Patent No.	Potter Name	Place	Shape	No. that day
1864						
Nov. 10	2	18124-5	Elsmore & Forster	Tunstall	*Olympic Shape Arched Forget-Me-Not (?)	2
1865						
?			?		*Athena Shape	
Sept. 18	6	189782	Liddle, Elliot & Son	Longport	Trumpet Vine	1
1866						
Jan. 3	6	194194	J. T. Close & Co.	Stoke	*Athenia	1
April 14	7	196552-4	Geo. L. Ashworth & Bros.	Hanley	*Nile Shape	3
June 12	1	198135-7	John Edwards	Fenton	*Harve Shape	3
1867						
April 4	9	207201	Elsmore & Forster	Tunstall	*Laurel Wreath *Victory Shape-(2 names)	1
June	11	208819	Clementson Bros.	Hanley	Balanced Vine	1
July 12	5	209530	George Jones	Stoke	Fuchsia?	1
1868						
Jan 7	11	215642	Cockson, Chetwynd & Co.	Cobridge	Plain Uplift	1
Jan 8	5	215674	T. & R. Boote	Burslem	*Classic Shape	1
Sept. 9	5	221312	F. Jones & Co.	Longton	*Victor	1
1869						
Sept. 21	7	233411	Gelson Bros.	Hanley	Eagle	1
Oct. 29	4	235401-2	Powell & Bishop	Hanley	Wheat in the Meadow	2
1870						
Nov. 26	9	248114-6	T. & R. Boote	Burslem	*Senate	3
1871						
Feb. 20	2	250478-9	Elsmore & Forster	Tunstall	*Pacific Shape	2
1877						
Mar. 20	3	308650	Clementson Bros.	Hanley	*Canada	3
Jun. 13	2	310909	Wm. Baker & Co.	Fenton	*Dominion	1
1878						
Apr. 20	2	320606	Thomas Furnival & Son	Cobridge	*The Lorne (Roped Wheat)	1
Dec. 7	2	330485	Anthony Shaw	Burslem	Britannia	1
1879						
Mar. 19	2	333485	John Hawthorne	Cobridge	Hawthorne's Fern	1

Bibliography

Barber, Edwin Atlee. *Marks of American Potters*. Reprint. Southampton, New York: Cracker Barrel Press, 1968.

Barber, Edwin Atlee. *Pottery and Porcelain of the United States*. New York: G. P. Putnam's Sons, 1893.

Barret, Richard Carter. *Bennington Pottery and Porcelain*. New York: Crown Publishers, Inc. 1958.

Burton, William, F. CS. *A History of English Earthenware and Stoneware*. London: Cassell & Co. Ltd, 1904.

Chaffers, William. *Marks and Monograms on Pottery and Porcelain*. London: Bickers & Son, 1876.

Church, Arthur H. *English Earthenware Made During the 17th and 18th Century*. Revised Edition. London: Wyman and Sons, 1904.

Cole, Ann Kilborn. *How to Collect the New Antiques*. New York: David McKay Co., Inc., 1966.

Collard, Elizabeth. *Nineteenth Century Pottery and Porcelain in Canada*. Montreal: McGill University Press, 1967.

Cushion, J. P. and Honey, W. B. *Handbook of Pottery and Porcelain Marks*. Fourth Edition. London: Faber & Faber. Copyright 1980.

Drepperd, Carl. *The Primer of American Antiques*. Garden City, New York: Doubleday & Co., Inc. 1944.

Earle, Alice Morse. *China Collecting in America*. New York: Empire State Book Co., 1924.

Eberlein and Ramsdell. *The Practical Book of Chinaware*. Philadelphia and New York: J. B. Lippincott Co., 1925.

Gaston, Mary Frank. *Collector's Encyclopedia of Knowles, Taylor & Knowles China Identification & Values*. Paducah, Kentucky: Collector Books, 1996.

Godden, Geoffrey. *Antique Glass and China*. New York: Castle Books, 1966

Godden, Geoffrey A. F. R. S. A. *Encyclopaedia of British Pottery and Porcelain Marks*. New York: Crown Publishers, Inc. 1964.

_____. *Godden's Guide to Mason's China and the Ironstone Wares*. Church Street, Woodbridge, Suffolk, England: Baron Publishing, 1980.

Graham II, John Meredith and Wedgwood, Hensleigh Cecil. *Wedgwood*. New York: The Tudor Publishing Co., 1948.

Hayden, Arthur. *Chats on English China*. London: T. Fisher Unwin Ltd., 1904.

Heaivilin, Annise Doring. *Grandma's Tea Leaf Ironstone*. Des Moines: Wallace-Homestead Book Co., 1981.

Hill, Ellen R. *Mulberry Ironstone*. Self-published. Madison, New Jersey, Copyright 1993, also revisions.

Hudgeons, Thomas E., III. *Price Guide to Pottery and Porcelain*, 3rd Ed. Orlando, Florida: House of Collectibles.

Hughes, Bernard and Therle. *Encyclopedia of English Ceramics*. London: Lutterworth Press, 1956.

Jewitt, Llewellynn. *The Ceramic Art of Great Britain*. Originally published in 1883. England, Poole: New Orchard Editions, Ltd. Copyright 1985

Kamm, Minnie Watson. *Old China*. Grosse Pointe, Michigan: Kamm Publications, 1951.

Ketchum, Wm. Jr. *The Pottery and Porcelain Collector's Handbook*. New York: Funk & Wagnall's. 1971.

Klamkin, Marian. *American Patriotic and Political China*. New York: Charles Scribners & Sons, 1973.

Lechler, Doris Anderson. *English Toy China*. Marietta, Ohio: Antique Publications 1989

Lehner, Lois. *Encyclopedia of U.S. Marks on Pottery, Porcelain, and Clay*. Collector Books, Paducah, Kentucky., 1988.

Lewis, Griselda. *A Collector's History of English Pottery*. New York: The Viking Press, 1969.

Mankowitz, Wolf and Haggar, Reginald. *Concise Encyclopedia of English Pottery and Porcelain*. New York: Hawthorn Books, Inc. 1957.

McClinton, Katharine Morrison. *A Handbook of Popular Antiques*. Reprint. New York: Random House, 1965. Distr. by Crown Pub., Inc.

____. *Antiques, Past and Present*. New York: Clarkson N. Pottery, Inc., 1971.

Miller, George L. "Classification and Economic Scaling of 19th Century Ceramics" U.S.: Reprinted from Historical Archaeology, Vol. 14. 1980

Moore, N. Hudson. *The Old China Book*. New York: Tudor Publishing Co., 1903.

Nelson, Glenn. *Ceramics*. New York: Holt, Rinehart, and Winston, Inc., 1971.

Ramsay, John. *American Potters and Potteries*, New York: Tudor Publishing Co., 1947.

Raycraft, Donald R. *Early American Folk & Country Antiques*. Vermont, Japan: Charles E. Tuttle Co., Inc. 1971.

Reynolds, Ernest. *Collecting Victorian Porcelain*. New York: Frederick A. Praeger, 1966.

Sandon, Henry. *British Pottery and Porcelain for Pleasure and Investment*. New York: Arco Publishing Co., Inc. 1969.

Spargo, John. *Early American Pottery and China*. Reprint. New York: Garden City Pub. Co., Inc. 1948.

Sussman, Lynne. *The Wheat Pattern: An Illustrated Survey*. Canada. Minister of Supply and Services Canada. Copyright 1985.

Thorn, C. Jordan. *Handbook of Old Pottery and Porcelain Marks*. New York: Tudor Publishing Co., 1947.

Upchurch, Nancy J. *Handbook of Tea Leaf Body Styles*. US: Tea Leaf Club International. Copyright 1995.

Watkins, Lura Woodside. *New England Potters and Their Wares*. Boston: Archon Books, 1968 reprint.

Wetherbee, Jean. *A Second Look at White Ironstone*. Des Moines: Wallace-Homestead Book Co., 1985.

Williams, Petra. *Flow Blue China - An Aid to Identification*. U.S.A. Jefferson, Kentucky: Fountain Head East Copyright 1971, 1981.

Magazines and Unpublished Materials

"American Ceramic and the Philadelphia Exhibition." *Antiques*, July 1976, pp. 146-158.

Collard, Elizabeth. "The St. Johns Stone Chinaware Company." *Antiques*, October 1976, pp. 800-805

Halfpenny, Pat. "Joseph Clementson: A Potter 'Remarkable for Energy of Character'. *Northern Ceramic Society Journal*, Vol. 4, 1984 (p. 194) of Doc.1 and (p.197) Doc.4.

Kowalsky, Arnold & Dorothy. Unpublished notes: "A Study in Blue" and "The Clementson Family - A Look into Successful Marketing"

Meissen-Helter, Pauline. "What is Ironstone?" Unpublished.

Rainwater, Dorothy T. "Spoon Warmers.," *Spinning Wheel*, October 1977, p. 35.

Index of Shapes

Asterisk (*) denotes name provided by potter.

Potter's Index

Potters discussed or illustrated in this book are listed here.
U.S. potters are not included (see Chapter 17).

Price Guide

A guide to photographed pieces appearing in this book.

Fig. 19-3	Miniature teapot (with cover)	.75
Fig. 19-4	Adult teapot	.275
	Child's teapot	.195
Fig. 19-5	Children's complete set in *Ceres* (22 pcs)	.1,000-1,150
Fig. 19-6	Complete set with handled cups	.900-1,100
Fig. 19-7	Miniature teapot	.195
	Set (22 pcs.)	.600-810
Fig. 19-8	Creamer	.65
	Open server	.45
	Honey dish	.10-20
Fig. 19-9	Miniature children's set:	
	Average size	.310-400
	Larger (child's) size	.310-400
Fig 19-10	Large teapot	.120
	Miniature set (22 pcs.)	.650-725
Fig. 19-11	Adult table jug	.110
	Children's set (English)	.650-725
	Children's set (American)	.275-335
Fig. 19-12	Pearson *Ceres* set (lacks 1 cup & saucer)	.450-510
Fig. 19-13	Sugar (TL)	.78
	Sugar (TR)	.95
	Creamer (BL)	.72
	Gravy boat (BR)	.58
Fig. 19-14	Master salt	.NMP
	Tiny compote	.110-145
Fig. 19-15	Small cake stand	.150-175
Fig. 19-16	Child's teapot	.115
Figl 19-17	Teapot (TL)	.95
	Tureen (TM)	.110
	Teapot (TR)	.120
	Teapot (BL)	.110
	Teapot (BM)	.110
	Teapot (BR)	.135
Fig. 19-18	Bowl with pitcher	.NMP

Chapter 20

Fig. 20-1	Chestnut bowl with tray (as is)	.224
Fig. 20-2	Fruit bowl	.225
Fig. 20-3	Fruit bowl and tray	.285-325
Fig. 20-4	Bowl with tray	.310-335
Fig. 20-5	Underplate tray	.110-140
Fig. 20-6	Basket	.210-235
Fig. 20-7	Compote	.NMP
Fig. 20-8	White compote	.285
	Tea Leaf compote	.450-600
Fig. 20-9	Centerpiece	.225-310
Fig. 20-10	High compote	.225-255
Fig. 20-11	Garden compote	.155-185
Fig. 20-12	Footed stand	.235-275
Fig. 20-13	Server	.145-165
Fig. 20-14	Low compote	.88
	Relish (same design)	.48
Fig. 20-15	Handled tray	.135-160
Fig. 20-16	Medium compote	.190-235
Fig. 20-17	High-relief jug	.135-155
Fig. 20-18	Cherub jug	.225-245
Fig. 20-19	Tree Trunk jug	.138-160
Fig. 20-20	Syrup jug	.220-240
Fig. 20-21	Line of jugs (range)	.180-250
Fig. 20-22	Grotesque jug	.NMP
Fig. 20-23	Pineapple jug	.210-280
Fig. 20-24	Trunk with ivy	.175-225
Fig. 20-25	Trunk mug	.210-260
Fig. 20-26	Small hen	.75-95
	Larger hen	.150-175
Fig. 20-27	Large hen on bsket	.175-210
Fig. 20-28	Tobacco jar	.95-125
Fig. 20-29	Relief jug	.190-225
Fig. 20-30	Large eagle	.NMP

Chapter 21

Fig. 21-1	Large cheese bell	.890
Fig. 21-2	Candlestick	.NMP
Fig. 21-3	Handled cake stand	.335-440
Fig. 21-4	Candlestick	.NMP
Fig. 21-5	Cheese bell	.650-775
Fig. 21-6	Egg cup	.NMP
Fig. 21-7	Egg cup	.NMP
Fig. 21-8, 9	Large compote	.260-310
	Fluted compote	.245-285
Fig. 21-10	Knife	.NMP
Fig. 21-11	Covered server	.155-225
Fig. 21-12	Mustard pot	.150-170
Fig. 21-13	Plain mustard (pewter **lid**)	.125-175
Fig. 21-14	Mustard jar	.165-210
Fig. 21-15	Butter dish	.235
	Mustard pot	.125
Fig. 21-16	Mustard pot	.175-220
Fig. 21-17	Pewter-lidded table jug	.350
	Syrup jugs (L to R)	
	1-	.225
	2-	.210
	3-	.235
	4-	.240
Fig. 21-18	Ale pitcher	.250
Fig. 21-19	Fenton jug	.140
Fig. 21-20	Hot beverage server	.450-510
Fig. 21-21	Hot beverage server (L)	.335-400
	Hot beverage server (R)	.NMP
Fig. 21-22	Mug (L)	.155
	Mug (R)	.70
Fig. 21-23	Sardine box	.110-160
Figs 21-24, 25	Range	.225-325
Fig. 21-26	Fish platter	.155-175
Fig. 21-27	Ceres (no base)	.210
	Ceres (with base)	.NMP
Fig. 21-28	(Without grain)	.95-120
Fig. 21-29	Vertical brush holder	.NMP
Fig. 21-30	Fluted spittoon	.250-325
Fig. 21-31	Foot bath	.950-1,075
Fig. 21-32	Toilet stool	.NMP
Fig. 21-33	Master waste jar	.550-650
Fig. 21-34	Wall sink	.NMP

Chapter 22

Fig. 22-1	Teapot (drawing)	.210
Fig. 22-2	Fluted mug	.85
Fig. 22-3	Baltic	.60-75
	Fig	.95-125
	Ceres	.70
	Wheat and Clover	.65
	Laurel Wreath	.75
	Bow and Tassel	.45
Fig. 22-4	Gruel bowl	.45-65
Fig. 22-5	Square ewer	.75-95
Fig. 22-6	Table jug (copper **banded or white**)	.145
Fig. 22-7	Round wheat tray	.140-160
Fig. 22-8	Round bread tray	.140-160
Fig. 22-9	Britannia tureen	.68-75

All prices are based on the item **being in "mint"** condition

*NMP - *No Market Price;* these **items represent such** rarities that it is not currently possible to **establish fair market** values for these pieces.

About the Author

Jean Wetherbee was born in Canajoharie (an Indian name meaning "the pot that washes itself") in the scenic Mohawk Valley of New York State. She and her husband Bernard reared four children on the six-generation family farm in that historic area. They declared, "A farm is the best place on earth to raise a family." Her love of the earth, her joy in growing things, and her bond with the past are woven into her writings.

Her interest in white ironstone evolved from a few family pieces, her own collecting, and her curiosity about how and why this earthenware came to America.

Earlier facts were compiled in *A Handbook on White Ironstone* (1974), *A Look at White Ironstone* (1980), and *A Second Look at White Ironstone* (1985). This guide is a continuation of those investigations.

Presently, Wetherbee still looks for, sells, and studies white ironstone—habits hard to break. She also volunteers in a New Hampshire rehabilitation center, teaching GED courses to young people who need high school equivalency credit. "There's always something interesting to do somewhere."